Routledge Revivals

Employment Policies in Developing Countries

First published in 1974, *Employment Policies in Developing Countries* is an attempt to take stock of experience that has been acquired in a number of developing countries in matters relating to employment promotion. It begins with a discussion of the nature of the employment objective, its role in the development process and with some attempt to quantify the dimensions of the problem. In Part Two employment promotion measures are examined in relation to each of the major economic sectors, while Part Three is concerned with vocational training, migration, and demographic policies. Finally, some suggestions are made as to how developing countries might define employment goals and formulate programmes for their attainment. This book is a must read for scholars and researchers of economics, labour economics and public policy.

Employment Policies in Developing Countries

A Comparative Analysis

J. Mouly and E. Costa

Routledge
Taylor & Francis Group

First published in 1974
by George Allen & Unwin

This edition first published in 2022 by Routledge
4 Park Square, Milton Park, Abingdon, Oxon, OX14 4RN

and by Routledge
605 Third Avenue, New York, NY 10017

Routledge is an imprint of the Taylor & Francis Group, an informa business

© International Labour Organization 1974

Publisher's Note
The publisher has gone to great lengths to ensure the quality of this reprint but points out that some imperfections in the original copies may be apparent.

Disclaimer
The publisher has made every effort to trace copyright holders and welcomes correspondence from those they have been unable to contact.

A Library of Congress record exists under LCCN: unk82008888

ISBN: 978-1-032-32199-8 (hbk)
ISBN: 978-1-003-31335-9 (ebk)
ISBN: 978-1-032-32200-1 (pbk)

Book DOI 10.4324/9781003313359

Employment Policies in Developing Countries

A Comparative Analysis

by

J. MOULY and E. COSTA

Edited by P. LAMARTINE YATES
for the International Labour Office

Published on behalf of the
International Labour Office, Geneva

LONDON GEORGE ALLEN & UNWIN LTD
Ruskin House Museum Street

ISBN 0 04 330245 9

Printed in Great Britain
in 10 point Times Roman type
by Alden & Mowbray Ltd.
at the Alden Press, Oxford

Contents

7

CONTENTS

NOTE

The countries and territories mentioned in this book are designated by the names by which they were known at the time of preparation of the manuscript. In some cases changes have occurred in the meantime.

Preface

Until very recently, economists and policy-makers in developed and developing countries alike have been content to look mainly to economic growth to solve the problems of poverty and unemployment. It is certain that, at least in the countries of the developing world, these problems will not be solved without rapid economic growth. But it is equally certain that economic growth is not enough.

Over the decade of the 1960s national incomes in most developing countries did in fact grow, by historical standards, exceptionally quickly – much more quickly than they did in the now industrially advanced countries at a comparable stage of their development. But, in the first place, it has been estimated that developing countries spend between 30 and 70 per cent of the additional income generated by economic growth on provision for increased population, leaving little for raising standards of living or for investment for further growth. In the second place, growth occurs mainly in the relatively small modern sectors of developing economies, while the traditional sectors tend to stagnate. The population explosion, increasing pressure on the land in many countries, and the unfavourable 'backwash' effects of industrialisation on traditional handicraft activities combine to keep vast numbers of people in abject poverty, deprived of any share in the benefits of a rising average income per head. Growth often benefits mainly those who are already relatively well off. Whether or not substantial progress is made in family planning, hundreds of millions of youngsters already born will be flooding the job market in the next two decades. No foreseeable rates of growth of output can possibly absorb these increases in the labour force, let alone reduce the backlog of existing unemployment and under-employment, unless growth in the future is associated to a much greater extent than in the past with increasing labour inputs.

We are witnessing a 'dethronement of GNP' as an adequate indicator of social progress.[1] We need to know not only how fast GNP is growing, but what use is being made of the annual increments to income and how widely they are shared. Not growth for its own sake, but the overcoming of poverty, squalor, disease and ignorance are the objectives of economic and social policy.

[1] The expression comes from the keynote address delivered by David Morse, formerly Director-General of the ILO, at an Overseas Study Committee Conference on Prospects for Employment Opportunities in the 1970s held at the Univ. of Cambridge in 1970, published in *Prospects for Employment Opportunities in the Nineteen Seventies*, R. Rodrikson and P. Johnston (Eds), HMSO, London, 1971, pp. 5ff.

Of the many who share little or not at all in the fruits of growth, some would not be helped by the provision of productive work opportunities because they are disabled or too ill, too old or too young to work. In traditional societies these people are looked after by the extended family or tribe. As societies become more industrialised, they recognise a responsibility of the community as a whole for the well-being of these people, and organise income transfers in their favour through social insurance or other measures.

A redistribution of income through the fiscal system from those who have more than they need to those who have less has a part to play in the fight against poverty in developing as well as developed countries. The vast majority of those in acute poverty in *developing* countries are either able-bodied or belong to families with able-bodied members, and a major reason for their poverty is that they or those who support them cannot find work, or can find only work that yields a very low income. By far the most important single element in a policy for ensuring widespread sharing in the fruits of economic growth must be an effective employment policy. Few developing countries could either afford or administer extensive schemes for the redistribution of income from the well-to-do to the poor. But in all of them there is scope for organising much more extensive opportunities for those able to work to do so productively. Employment objectives and income distribution objectives need to take their place alongside growth targets as major objectives of economic and social development.

The benefits of more employment where many people are in need of work are clear enough. Leaving aside for the present the question of effects on output and growth, more employment in these circumstances not only (i) can make for a more equitable distribution of income, but in addition (ii) can satisfy the human needs for useful and creative activity, (iii) can provide more people with opportunities for acquiring skills and the habit of work and thus participating in the tasks as well as the benefits of economic development, and (iv) for all these reasons can contribute to a reduction of political and social tensions. The fact that the incidence of unemployment and under-employment is so high among young people, and that these form such a large proportion of the population in developing countries, enhances the values of these benefits.

If any country could be confident of having these benefits without cost, it would obviously wish to have them. Even if it were certain that a specific price would have to be paid for fuller employment, the price might be considered well worth paying. But few governments would wish to sign a blank cheque. Hesitation to do what has to be done to promote employment, even in countries that have included employment objectives in their development plans, seems to arise largely out of uncertainty about the costs of employment promotion.

The cost that is most discussed is a possible slowing down of economic growth. The question of the relationship between growth and employment is discussed below.[2] Suffice it to say here that though it is certainly true

2 Pp. 21–27.

that ill-chosen measures of employment promotion could lead to slower growth, there is plenty of scope in developing countries for measures that can be expected to promote employment and faster growth simultaneously – i.e. for measures that put to productive use the resources which developing countries have in greatest abundance and which are increasing most rapidly, namely their human resources.

It is easy to point to the advantages of an employment policy. It is much more difficult in the present state of knowledge to specify, unless in very general terms, of which measures such a policy should consist. The governments of many developing countries have identified unemployment and under-employment as the major problems confronting them. A number of them have included some kinds of employment targets or objectives in their development plans; but few have made any substantial progress towards working out a strategy that will enable these objectives to be attained. And they have thus far received little help in this task from developed countries or from international organisations. This is a reflection of the extent to which growth objectives have dominated thinking about and planning for development until very recently.

This, as suggested above, is now changing. The change is overdue, but appears to be gathering momentum. Examples of growing concern over the employment problems of developing countries can be multiplied.[3] But a very great deal remains to be learned about how to translate general prescriptions for increasing employment into precise policy measures adapted to the needs and possibilities of developing countries in all their variety – the large and the small; the very poor and the not so poor; those heavily dependent on foreign trade and those that are more self-sufficient; those with a shortage of land and those with plenty; those with almost no industry and those with a good deal; those with relatively high educational standards and those with a desperate shortage of educated and trained manpower. The world is still very near the beginning of what may prove to be the most challenging and the most important social task of the last third of the twentieth century.

The problems will have to be solved mainly by the governments and people of the developing countries themselves: but these problems cannot be solved by their efforts alone. They lack capital. They lack markets. They lack entrepreneurial and managerial expertise. They lack technological knowledge. They lack vocational skills and the capacity to impart them. And most of all they lack time: their population of working age is growing at an explosive rate. A world in which visible and perceptible progress towards solving employment problems is not made will become

---

[3] Statements from, among others, the President of the World Bank Group, the Pearson Commission on International Development, the Chairman of the Development Assistance Committee of the OECD, the Director-General of the Latin American Institute for Economic and Social Planning, and the International Development Strategy adopted by the General Assembly on the occasion of the twenty-fifth anniversary of the United Nations are quoted in ILO: *The World Employment Programme*, International Labour Conference, 56th Session, Report IV, Geneva, 1971, Chapter 3.

11

an increasingly dangerous and uncomfortable world for everybody, including the people of the rich countries.

It seems possible that a 'dethronement of GNP' or at least the elevation of an employment objective to a place alongside it, might do more than anything else to overcome what seems to be a growing disenchantment with development aid in developed countries. The difference between 6 and 7 per cent growth of GNP means nothing to the ordinary man or woman and leaves them profoundly unmoved. The difference betwen having a job and not having one means a great deal, and many people are generous enough to be moved by other people's need for jobs as well as by their own, even if the other people live in other countries.

The present volume is an attempt to take stock of experience that has been acquired in a number of developing countries in matters relating to employment promotion. It begins with a discussion of the nature of the employment objective, its role in the development process and with some attempt to quantify the dimensions of the problem. In Part Two employment promotion measures are examined in relation to each of the major economic sectors, while Part Three is concerned with vocational training, migration and demographic policies. Finally, some suggestions are made as to how developing countries might define employment goals and formulate programmes for their attainment.

The raw material for this study was quarried by many members of the Economic Branch of the International Labour Office; their contribution is hereby gratefully acknowledged. Its processing was the work of J. Mouly and E. Costa, also of the Economic Branch of the ILO, and the study was content edited by P. Lamartine Yates. Views expressed are those of the authors and do not engage the responsibility of the ILO.

Geneva
December 1972

Part One

GENERAL CONSIDERATIONS

Chapter 1

Policy Objectives

The Fruits of Economic Development

Only twenty-five years have elapsed since India, Indonesia and Pakistan, the largest of the former colonial territories, became independent; some developing countries have been independent for less than half that time. Even those whose independence dates much further back did not embrace economic growth as a primary objective of national policy in any conscious manner until after the Second World War. By the clock of history twenty-five years is a very short period from which to judge any major trend, hence an evaluation of what has been achieved must be extremely tentative. One cannot yet discern in what ways the period was typical and in what exceptional.

Almost certainly the most striking fact has been the large amount of economic progress accomplished in such a short time. During the 1960s, according to United Nations statistics, the developing countries taken as a whole recorded an average annual increase in total production of 5·5 per cent. For the earlier years figures are incomplete, but it may be surmised that over the period 1947–72 the average annual growth rate exceeded 3 and may have been closer to 4 per cent. In order to appreciate the significance of this achievement it should be compared not with the contemporary growth rates of developed countries but with their performance in the early decades of their industrialisation. None of them sustained a rate of more than 3 per cent over any extended period; indeed, even at a later stage of their development, for instance the period 1900–50, no European country reached a 3 per cent average while the world's two fastest growers, the United States and Japan, average between 3 and 4 per cent.[1]

By this yardstick, for what it is worth, the developing countries have begun brilliantly.

Yet the mood among the leaders of developing countries is more one of disappointment than of satisfaction. Partly this is explained by making comparisons, as they cannot help doing, between living standards in their countries and those prevailing in industrial countries, whereas no possibility of such comparisons existed in the early stages of the industrial countries' take-off. But apart from this, the process of economic development, even though it be in its beginnings, does not seem to be bringing forth its expected fruits. The poor countries still feel overly dependent on

[1] A. Maizels, *Industrial Growth and World Trade*, Cambridge Univ. Press, 1963, Appendix E, p. 531.

the rich countries: for the supply of capital and know-how, for the purchase of the developing countries' exports, for the exploitation of local mineral and other resources. The population explosion which has resulted mainly from improved health services eats up a large part of the growth in national product. What is more, much of the increase in national income has gone into the pockets of a rather small section of the population, a prosperous middle and upper class in the cities, leaving a large mass of the population virtually untouched by the economic progress so far achieved. Especially in the rural areas remote from urban influences, life goes on as before – i.e. at or near subsistence level.

These income disparities have become a matter of widespread social concern, particularly the persistence of a hard core of extreme poverty and destitution which can be found not only in the shanty towns of the big cities but also in regions which are predominantly agricultural. Admittedly the concept of poverty is relative and its definition bound to be in some degree arbitrary. In general terms it can be described as a condition which falls below the 'minimum standard of living consistent with human dignity', to use the language of the first paragraph of the International Development Strategy. In more precise terms a poverty-line income might be determined in the light of a government's best estimate of the cost of a minimum 'basket' of necessities.[2] No reliable estimates have been made of the numbers of persons in the developing countries considered to fall into this category, but they are undoubtedly very large. They are the left-over people – some unemployed, some under-employed, some working full-time but earning quite inadequate incomes.

These large blocks of extreme poverty are found not merely in the least developed countries, those having the lowest average income *per caput*, but equally in the more prosperous among the developing countries; indeed it is in the latter that the problem shows itself more acutely because of the stark contrasts between the local poor and the local rich. When in a national community almost everyone is poor it can be convincingly argued that only short-rum efforts to achieve over-all development will ameliorate poverty, but in the circumstances where a section of the population has rapidly improved its economic position and has become comparatively well-to-do many are inclined to the view that it should be possible in the short-run to initiate poverty-relieving action. In other words, as the national income grows its distribution should also become less unequal. The tree of growth, it is alleged, needs to be pruned and trained if it is to yield good fruit.

Conflict and Consensus in Objectives

There is one school of thought, however, which finds nothing wrong with the tree except that it is young: give it time to grow and the fruits will

[2] See N. N. Franklin, 'The Concept and Measurement of Minimum Living Standards', *International Labour Review*, April 1967.

emerge of their own accord. According to this view, to which many developing countries' governments subscribe, the top priority should be economic growth in the conventional sense of the maximisation of GNP. The national cake is too small; as soon as it has become bigger, the size of the slices going to the lower income groups can be increased. In describing their yearly achievements many governments focus on the tons of ore mined, the yards of cloth manufactured, the megawatts of generating capacity installed. These are the insignia of progress, and by the same token the answer to poverty.

Those who look mainly to economic growth to provide, in the course of time, solutions to the poverty problems of the developing countries sometimes appeal to the experience of the now highly industrialised countries. Their progress towards prosperity, full and productive employment and over a long period probably a less unequal distribution of income has been interrupted, it is true, from time to time by recessions and depressions, some of which have caused appalling suffering. We cannot yet be confident that enough is known about the problems of demand management to ensure that there will never be another bad recession. Problems of adaptation to structural change will always be with us. But by and large the industrially developed countries are now labour-shortage and not labour-surplus countries; they still have poor people but they have overcome the extreme poverty of human degradation. Is it reasonable to see the problem of poverty in the developing countries and its associated problem of labour absorption as a transitional malady which may be expected to respond to patience, aided perhaps by some mild and inexpensive therapy?

It would be very rash to come to any such conclusion without giving full weight to a number of major differences between the circumstances in which the Industrial Revolution took place in Western Europe and North America in the nineteenth century and those in which the industrialisation of the developing countries is taking place today. In the first place, in the developing countries the population explosion appears to have occurred at an earlier stage in their economic growth, making it more difficult to manage; and furthermore, whereas in the nineteenth century the open spaces of North America and Australasia absorbed tens of millions of Europeans – hundreds of millions if we count their offspring – no such safety valve is available to today's developing countries in a situation in which a safety valve is much more badly needed.

Second, the nineteenth-century industries and service occupations were labour-intensive, so that they could and did directly absorb large numbers of unskilled workers released from the countryside. The technology which was later evolved to save labour, and which made heavy demands on capital which the industrial countries became increasingly able to afford, has been transplanted, in many cases prematurely, to developing countries which need capital-saving, not labour-saving techniques.

Third, there is the accelerated rate of technological progress. To take the right managerial decisions today, both in the private and the public sector, requires much more technical expertise than it did in the nineteenth century.

One must not exaggerate: not all the comparisons between the experiences of the developed and those of the developing countries are unfavourable to the latter. Those who industrialised during the nineteenth century had to invent their technologies as they went along, whereas those who industrialise in the second half of the twentieth century have at their disposal a range of technologies already in existence. The pioneers had to find their investment capital entirely from their own savings; today the developing countries can obtain loans and grants from the rich countries, even if domestic savings must still contribute the major part of their needs. Today much more is understood about how the national economy functions, with the result that, by means of planning and economic and social engineering, resources can be more effectively mobilised and social hardships more easily mitigated.

Weighing up the pros and cons of the above-mentioned comparisons it is difficult to deduce whether today's developing countries will find the road of economic development easier or harder to travel, and it is far too early to cite historical experience. What does seem certain is that the single-minded pursuit of growth in the narrow sense of maximising GNP will fail to satisfy sufficiently the social values which contemporary society upholds; in particular it fails to alleviate the economic misery of the poorest sections of the population. In the face of this dilemma there are many who maintain that 'a policy of full employment is the first and most effective component of a programme to eliminate extreme poverty'.[3] In other words, the provision of work opportunities should have high priority in development planning. Poverty, it is pointed out, cannot be satisfactorily dealt with by mere income redistribution though job creation will of course have certain redistributive effects, partly because the rich are so few relative to the masses and partly because mere redistribution on a scale sufficient to make any real impact would almost certainly have too damaging an influence on the rate of economic growth. Employment promotion, on the other hand, provided it be productive employment, can augment production at the same time as it brings income to the needy. It is therefore claimed to be the constructive remedy to poverty by dealing directly with poverty's twin brothers unemployment and under-employment. Through harnessing as much as possible of the surplus labour which abounds in developing countries, poverty is ameliorated and growth stimulated.

However, if developing countries need to concern themselves not with just economic growth alone but a combination of objectives, it is worth devoting a few pages to an examination of the relationship between fuller employment and other objectives, and particularly to the question how far and in what circumstances the different objectives are compatible or in conflict with each other. The following sections discuss, briefly but in somewhat greater detail than was appropriate in the Preface, the relation-

[3] ILO, *Towards Full Employment: A Programme for Colombia*, Geneva, 1970, p. 139. (This Report is hereafter referred to as the Colombia Report or Seers Mission Report.)

ship of employment objectives to two other major elements in a balanced combination of objectives, namely faster economic growth and more equitable distribution of income.

Employment and Income Distribution

We may deal with the latter first since there is relatively little that need be added to what was said in the Preface. Provided it deals effectively with under-employment as well as unemployment, employment policy seems certain to promote a more equitable distribution of income since it will increase the incomes of a very poor section of the community, namely those among the unemployed and under-employed who are provided with work or more remunerative work. The reason for the proviso is that the wholly unemployed may include some people, for example educated young people supported by relatively well-to-do families who are less poor than some under-employed persons whose poverty drives them to compete with others equally poor as porters, street vendors, boot-blacks or in other over-crowded service occupations in which self-employment is possible. Provided it does not confine itself to the wholly unemployed, 'a policy of full employment is the first and most effective component of a programme to eliminate extreme poverty'.[4] 'Schemes (for the direct transfer of purchasing power among individuals) cannot be relevant if no institutional means exist for their implementation, as is typically the case in underdeveloped surplus-labour economies. There the most important if not the only means of redistribution may consist of increasing the rate of employment.'[5]

But there is a two-way relationship between employment and income distribution. Not only does the level of employment affect income distribution but, conversely, changes in income distribution may affect the level of employment. Income transferred from the rich to the poor, through fiscal measures or otherwise, will be used differently from the way in which it would have been used if it had remained in the hands of the rich.

First, the *level* of consumption is likely to rise, i.e. a smaller proportion of income is likely to be saved and invested. This, taken by itself, might be bad for employment.[6] But one may question the practical importance of

---

[4] *The Colombia Report, op. cit.* p. 139.

[5] L. Lefeber, 'Planning in a Surplus Labor Economy', *American Economic Review*, June 1968, p. 344.

[6] Except in countries suffering from a deficiency of aggregate demand. It is frequently said that this does not seem to be a typical condition in developing countries. Though much under-utilisation of physical capital is known to exist in these countries, there is a tendency to explain this rather in terms of a lack of complementary factors and inelasticities of supply than in terms of a lack of demand. Professor H. W. Singer has, however, suggested that:

'In some respects the situation is much more Keynesian than we would imagine, and the complementary factors which are lacking to make Keynesian solutions relevant may be more in the field of planning policies and aid practices or in the field of entrepreneurship and administration than in inescapable shortages of physical capital'. *Dualism Revisited* (unpublished, roneoed), p. 23.

this effect in a number of developing countries. Writing about Colombia for example (and similar conditions seem to prevail rather widely in the developing world)[7] the Seers mission observed that:

'In the first place, notwithstanding the extreme degree of economic inquality that has prevailed in Colombia, total personal savings appear to be quite low. . . . Thus a high price has been paid, in terms of welfare and equity, for a fairly disappointing result in terms of savings. . . . Secondly . . . even if a highly uneven distribution of income did induce a higher rate of personal saving, it would not be obvious that Colombia would benefit. To a considerable but unknown extent savings flow abroad.'[8]

Third, the mission questioned whether, even in the case of a regressive redistribution of income that did lead to higher levels of both savings and domestic investment, employment would benefit when account was taken of the fact that only a part of any increased income going to the rich would be saved, and of the probability that the part that was spent would generate less employment than a similar amount of spending by the poor.

A second and probably more important way in which a redistribution of income may affect employment is through its effects on the *pattern* of consumption. Two such effects are emphasised in the Colombia Report, both favourable to the view that greater equality of income distribution makes for fuller employment. First, there is likely to be a larger import content in the consumption of the rich; where this is so, the greater the degree of inequality in income distribution, the higher the demand for foreign goods and the less foreign exchange is left for the capital goods and intermediate products needed to expand employment. Second,

'the basic goods which are widely purchased by those on low incomes – essentially food and rather simple manufactures like clothing and foot-wear – are precisely the goods which are (or can be) produced with techniques considerably more labour-intensive than those used in the production of the goods demanded by the rich. . . . A given amount of income will thus generate more employment when spent in the purchase of wage goods than in the acquisition of consumer durables.'[9]

There is, however, a third difference between the consumption patterns of the rich and the poor which works in the opposite direction from those stressed in the Colombia Report, namely that rich people in developing countries spend a good deal on domestic and other personal services, and generate a good deal of employment in so doing.

7 Cf. Harry T. Oshima: 'Labor-Force "Explosion" and the Labor-Intensive Sector in Asian Growth', *Economic Development and Cultural Change* (Chicago), **19**, 2, January 1971, p. 174: 'Apparently less inequality under certain conditions does not result in reduced personal savings. . . . A study of personal savings in poor countries must not ignore dissavings when income distributions are highly unequal.'
8 The Colombia Report, *op. cit.*, p. 149.
9 *Ibid.*, p. 147.

We may conclude that, in general, policies to promote fuller employment and policies to promote greater equality of income distribution fit well together and are often likely to reinforce each other; but while we can assert with great confidence that a successful employment policy, provided it deals effectively with under-employment as well as unemployment, will make for greater equality of income distribution, the converse proposition that greater equality of income distribution makes for fuller employment is, as a general proposition, more doubtful. There are forces working both for and against the truth of this proposition, and it is not certain which are the stronger. Their relative strength is likely to vary in different countries and different situations.

Employment and Economic Growth

We may turn now to the question of the relationship between employment objectives and growth objectives.[10] It is important to know whether there is any conflict between maximising growth and maximising employment. If there is none, we need have no hesitation in urging high priority for employment objectives. In circumstances in which there is a conflict, it may still be found worth while to sacrifice some growth in order to achieve some additional employment. For, as was suggested in the preface, employment, if not an end in itself, can serve as a means to other important ends besides production. But there would be a limit to the amount of growth that it would be worth while to sacrifice for the sake of fuller employment, for failure to achieve economic growth at least as rapid as population growth means stagnation and the perpetuation of poverty.

We should begin by noting that it is an over-simplification to speak of sacrificing growth for employment or vice versa. What we are confronted with are alternative time-profiles or combinations of production and employment stretching into the future. Moreover, even in the present, neither maximum output nor maximum employment is an unambiguous objective. At any one time both output and employment are heterogeneous collections of goods and services, and current levels of both may influence future levels. As Stewart and Streeten point out, weighting both at any one time and as between the present and the future, is therefore crucial to the definition of the objectives. And one set of weights may give the impression that we are sacrificing output for employment; another may not.

After an extremely useful discussion of problems of weighting and timing and related problems, Stewart and Streeten conclude:

10 For an extremely useful recent discussion of this subject, to which the following pages are much indebted, see Frances Stewart and Paul Streeten, 'Conflicts between Output and Employment Objectives', in *Prospects for Employment Opportunities in the Nineteen Seventies*, HMSO, London, 1971, pp. 77–94. Also useful is the treatment of the subject in S. Wellisz, 'Dual Economies, Disguised Unemployment and the Unlimited Supply of Labour', *Economica*, **35**, 122, February 1968; and L. Lefeber, *op. cit.*, p. 343. For an earlier treatment of the subject ILO see *Employment and Economic Growth*, Studies and Reports, New Series 67, Geneva, 1964, pp. 52–4.

'On examination the possible conflicts between employment maximisation and growth appear more complex than might be supposed. . . . Not only current but also future levels of employment, as well as output, must be taken into account. Future levels of output and of employment depend partly on the resources available each year for investment. These in turn depend on the level of output and the proportion of that output that is saved. To the extent that lower levels of output lead to lower savings, the rate of growth of both output and employment will be lower, the lower the level of output. Thus choice of a method which maximises current employment, despite a sacrifice of current output, may eventually lead to lower employment at some future date, compared with a technique which maximises current output. But it can also work the other way round with higher levels of employment increasing the productiveness, and the savings capacity, of the economy and leading to higher future levels of output and employment. . . .

'Any conflict arising between employment and output objectives is thus likely to be a question of different preferences for an entire time profile of output and employment, with the preferred output path being associated with a rejected employment path. It is unlikely that this conflict could be accurately described as a desire to sacrifice output for employment or vice versa. It is a more complex question of, for example, the weight given to current as against future output being greater than that given to current as against future employment.'[11]

The ambiguity of the concepts of maximising output and maximising employment, and the complexity of the relationship between them, mean that any simple statement about this relationship is suspect. In what follows we shall, however, ignore these ambiguities, and assume that maximising current output and employment is equivalent to maximising the present value of the entire streams of output and employment over time. We may first discuss the relationship between employment and output, and then between output and growth.

At first sight it may be difficult to see how, in a labour-surplus economy, a conflict between more employment and more output could arise at any point short of one at which so many workers were employed that they actually got in each other's way and reduced each other's output, i.e. had a negative marginal productivity – a point which, we may hope, would seem fairly distant even in densely populated countries. For when output is limited by a shortage of capital (or land) it is the productivity of capital (or land) that has to be maximised in order to maximise output, and the productivity of capital (or land) can be increased by taking on more workers up to the point at which the marginal productivity of labour is zero. Wage-earning employment, of course, will not normally be carried beyond the point at which labour's marginal net productivity equals the wage that has to be paid. But if others can work as self-employed or unpaid family workers on the land or in handicrafts or services, it would

[11] F. Stewart and P. Streeten, *op. cit.*

seem that output and employment should increase together, or at least that increased employment should not *reduce* output. It might seem tempting to conclude that, except perhaps in a few extreme and unlikely cases, institutional or other factors that kept employment below desirable levels would tend to restrict output too.

It is, of course, an over-simplification to speak of capital and land as though they were homogeneous, undifferentiated factors of production. Most of a country's capital is embodied in specific pieces of capital equipment. Many pieces of capital equipment are designed to be operated by a fairly specific number of workers. This number can be varied within limits, particularly if there is a choice between working one, two or more shifts, but also through variations in the intensity of staffing and the amount of maintenance work, cleaning and other ancillary activities. Often, however, the limits within which the amount of labour employed in combination with a given piece of capital equipment can usefully be varied are rather narrow. If additional workers are taken on beyond an upper limit, they will not add to output but at best lighten the tasks of some of the other workers, at worst get in their way. These considerations may suggest that the scope for adding to output by taking on more labour will often be rather limited, but they do not otherwise affect the argument much.

A more important point is that an expanding economy adds yearly to its stock of capital equipment as well as replacing some existing equipment. In selecting the particular pieces of equipment that are to be added to, or are to replace parts of, a community's capital stock, there is likely to be greater scope for varying the amount of labour that can be employed in conjunction with a given amount of capital. One million dollars may be invested in a few bulldozers or in many thousands of shovels. It is in making this sort of decision that conflicts between output and employment objectives are most likely to arise.

When there is a conflict, it arises because a more labour-intensive method, in the sense of a method that uses more labour per dollar of capital, also uses more capital per unit of output than a method that uses less labour.[12] Some theoretical models assume that this can never happen. It would indeed never happen if all techniques were invented and developed simultaneously, since labour-intensive methods that also use more capital never would be developed; but it is quite possible for an older technique to be replaced by a newer one that saves both capital and

[12] A. S. Bhalla, 'Investment Allocation and Technological Choice – A case of Cotton Spinning Techniques', *Economic Journal*, 1964, suggests that the capital – output ratio (including working capital as well as fixed capital) using factory methods in cotton spinning is about three-quarters of that using the hand Ambar Charkha methods. Bhalla's analysis of rice-pounding ('Choosing Techniques: Handpounding versus Machine Milling of Rice: an Indian Case', *Oxford Economic Papers*, March 1965), suggests a similar conflict here; the technique which maximises employment (or has the lowest cost per workplace), the pestle and mortar, requires nearly twice the capital per unit of value added compared with the large shelling machine. The latter requires investment per workplace of about 100 times as great as the former.

labour. If such an opportunity for saving capital is not taken because of a desire to employ more labour, then output has been sacrificed to employment.

Opportunities for simultaneously saving both land and labour may also occur. It seems to be true that economies of scale in farming are typically economies in the use of labour, not land. And economies in the use of labour are important, from a general social point of view, only when the condition of labour surplus has been overcome. Land-saving technology such as improved seed varieties, fertilisers, insecticides and weeding techniques can often be applied as effectively on small farms as on large ones, and there is much evidence from many parts of the world that the productivity of land (though not of labour) is higher on smaller than on large holdings. Most opportunities for saving land (in the sense of increasing yields per hectare) indeed require higher labour inputs per hectare. But the Green Revolution is creating a situation in a number of countries in which yields increase more than labour inputs, so that labour inputs as well as land inputs per ton of crop produced fall off. If opportunities for achieving this result are not taken because of a desire to employ more labour, again some output and growth have been foregone for some short-term employment.

There seems to be no doubt, then, that conflicts between output objectives and employment objectives *can* arise.[13] The interesting question for policy-makers is how important such conflicts are and how much scope there is for measures of employment policy that do not run into them. This is a subject on which extensive empirical research is badly needed. There is, however, already considerable evidence that in many industries and many processes the more labour-intensive varieties do save capital per unit of output.[14] In these cases, maximising output and employment are consistent. Many more cases would no doubt be created by devoting greater research and development (R&D) efforts to developing the efficiency of labour-intensive methods.

'Present possibilities reflect the fact that almost all R&D is concentrated on producing methods suitable for the developed world, in which labour is scarce; the labour-intensive methods currently available are generally the products of earlier and less-sophisticated science and technology.'[15]

The belief that there is substantial scope for measures of employment promotion in developing countries that will promote higher output as well rests not only on (as yet rather scrappy) empirical evidence, but also on certain widespread characteristics of developing economies which tend to cause larger amounts of capital to be embodied in equipment that uses little labour, and smaller amounts in equipment that uses much labour,

[13] Just as some economists operate with assumptions under which a conflict between output and employment cannot arise, others assume that it necessarily must exist. Stewart and Streeten firmly reject both extreme views.
[14] Stewart and Streeten give examples from A. S. Bhalla, A. K. Sen and G. K. Boon.
[15] Stewart and Streeten, *op. cit.*, p. 80.

than would be desirable even from the point of view of output alone, disregarding employment considerations altogether. Measures to counteract these characteristics would serve to promote larger output[16] and more employment simultaneously. To quote from a recent ILO report:

'These features include, in the first place, a possible preference for modern capital-intensive and labour-saving industries and technology on grounds of prestige, as distinct from economic advantage. Secondly, there is assymmetry of promotion of the use of capital and labour respectively. This arises partly from the fact that the managers or directors who decide how much labour to employ may be, or may be advised by, engineers from industrially advanced countries whose training predisposes them to regard "labour-saving" and "efficiency" as virtually synonymous terms, while in countries where labour is plentiful and capital scarce it would be more appropriate to identify efficiency with the saving of capital; but there is the further fact that labour-saving ideas are more often than not embodied in saleable pieces of capital equipment, sales of which are assiduously promoted; nobody has a corresponding interest in promoting capital-saving labour-using ideas (except the unemployed, who are not equipped to do so). Related to the last point, there are also difficulties of handling a large labour force, and lack of experience of the problems of doing so. Further, the vast bulk of technological research is carried out in industrially advanced countries with a view to solving problems encountered in those countries, and the most appropriate technology for countries in which unskilled labour is plentiful and capital is scarce has received insufficient attention. Again, "up-to-date" modern equipment may be imported under foreign aid programmes under which donor countries require that equipment be purchased from them.

'Finally, in most developing countries, the prices which firms must pay for the use of factors of production do not reflect true social scarcities. The cost of labour, at least in some sectors or for some grades, is often fixed by legislation or union agreement at a relatively high level in relation to conditions in the country concerned. Moreover, a parallel distortion can be observed in the price of capital goods. Frequently an over-valued exchange rate combined with various investment subsidies or tax concessions will make imported capital goods relatively too cheap. Interest rates are often also subsidised for those who have access to a privileged market. On the other hand, capital goods manufactured locally, which frequently represent a simpler or more labour-intensive technology, may be relatively more expensive. The combination of these factors adds up to a substantial bias against the use of labour and in favour of the more capital-intensive techniques.'[17]

16 Because the various 'distorting' influences referred to in the text mean that market forces will not bring about situations in which the social marginal productivity of capital or land is equal in all uses, which is the condition for maximising the total social productivity of capital or land.

17 ILO, *Fiscal Measures for Employment Promotion in Developing Countries*, Geneva, 1972, pp. vii–viii.

If for all these reasons there appears in most developing countries to be plenty of scope, as suggested above, for measures to promote more output and more employment simultaneously, this is not of course to deny that ill-chosen measures of employment promotion may check output. But it raises the question how far it will be necessary to resort to such measures even if employment promotion is given very high priority.

We have been discussing thus far the relation between employment and output as the first step in a two-stage discussion of the relation between employment and growth. It remains to look briefly at the relation between output and growth.

With given rates of saving and investment there is a presumption that maximising current output will tend to maximise growth, for out of a larger output and income more will be saved and invested. Thus *with given rates of saving and investment*, if some price in terms of current output is paid for higher employment, the growth rate is also likely to suffer. But it is a familiar fact that people with large incomes are apt to save a larger proportion of their income than those with smaller ones. This means that an allocation of resources that is sub-optimal from the point of view of current output could make for faster growth if it also made for a sufficiently greater inequality of income distribution to bring about larger total savings and investment than would have been achieved from a larger but more equally distributed national income. This could happen if the sub-optimal allocation of capital were associated with larger profit incomes and smaller labour incomes.

This has led some writers to suggest that policy-makers should sacrifice both current output and current employment for the sake of faster growth of both.[18] Others have taken the opposite view that the future will be better able to look after its problems of poverty than the present can.[19] The argument for sacrificing both current output and current employment for the sake of faster rates of growth of both in the future seems likely to carry conviction to policy-makers only if they are convinced (*a*) that it is necessary to induce the community to save and invest more than it would wish to do, given the prevailing level and distribution of income, the

[18] A well-known statement of this argument is contained in W. Galenson and H. Leibenstein: 'Investment Criteria, Productivity and Economic Development', *Quarterly Journal of Economics*, **69**, 3, August 1955, p. 343.

[19] Cf. Sir Arthur Lewis: 'I have taught my children that since their income per head will rise by 2 per cent per year, they are going to be twice as well off as I am. It follows that it is not I who should make sacrifices for their future, but they who should make sacrifices for my present!' 'Summary: The Cost of Unemployment in Less-developed Countries and Some Research Topics', *International Labour Review*, **101**, 5, May 1970, p. 552. Stewart and Streeten (*loc. cit.*) suggest that, on a balance of considerations, it would be rational to discount the value of future employment at a lower rate than the value of future output compared with the present. This would imply that, partly because of the alarming rate of increase in the working-age population, policy-makers should perhaps be more willing to contemplate some check to the rate of growth of output than to that of employment. Since, however, the latter will be heavily dependent on the former, the policy implications of this value judgement are not necessarily favourable to short-term employment.

prevailing level of taxation, and so on, and (*b*) that there are no other and better ways of inducing the increase of savings and investment that are considered necessary. Other instruments that are at hand for operating on the rate of savings and investment include taxation, monetary policy, the price policy of state enterprises, variations in the level of public spending on current services, variations in foreign economic policy, and a host of others. Even if humanitarian considerations were ignored (which of course they should not be) it seems possible to argue rather convincingly that measures enhancing the inequality of income distribution are likely to be inefficient instruments for promoting growth; what might be gained for growth through larger savings and investment by people at the top end of the income scale may be lost or more than lost through impaired productivity of ill-fed, ill-housed workers at the low end of the scale.

The following seem to be the main conclusions emerging from the above discussion: (*a*) measures to promote employment may, but need not, conflict, with growth objectives; (*b*) certain widespread characteristics of the economies of developing countries suggest that the scope for measures of employment promotion that do not conflict with growth objectives is substantial; some (as yet rather scrappy) empirical evidence points in the same direction; and (*c*) much more empirical research is needed to establish the nature and extent of possible conflicts between employment and growth objectives, and to point to practical ways of avoiding these conflicts and promoting both objectives simultaneously.

Employment in a Welfare Strategy

A conquest of wealth which did not include the conquest of poverty would be a hollow victory. Nor are the peoples of the developing countries willing to wait indefinitely for the conquest of poverty when the resources of knowledge and skill for overcoming poverty exist if only they can be mobilised. Surely it is tolerable for, say, three more generations to be born into poverty and to die in poverty and to be given nothing? As Dr Johnson said: 'Poverty is a great enemy to human happiness; . . . it makes some virtues impracticable and others extremely difficult.'[20]

The provision of reasonably remunerative employment must, in the circumstances of developing countries, be the chief weapon in the attack on poverty;[21] their governments do not have the resources that other governments have for assuring minimum living standards through state-financed social welfare programmes. It is for this reason that a World Employment Programme becomes ineluctably the central feature of the social approach to development. Moreover, as will be seen at a number of points below, particularly in Chapter 8 and 10, many of the same kinds of

[20] *Boswell's Life of Johnson*, Vol. IV, p. 157, 7 December 1782.
[21] This will consist partly of creating additional employment and partly of making existing employment, notably in agriculture, more remunerative.

measures (such as promoting a high level of investment, training and market development) that are needed to promote employment are also needed to promote growth.

Because a number of misgivings still persist about the use of employment in the strategy of welfare it was necessary to deal at some length with the contention that the expansion of employment and the achievement of rapid growth are incompatible. That areas of conflict between these two objectives may exist must certainly be recognised, and if governments go about their programmes imprudently such conflicts could become serious. Nevertheless, a harmonisation of the two objectives is entirely possible, and indeed, if skilfully pursued, success in either one can multiply the chances of success in the other. There is considerable scope for augmenting the demand for manpower within the framework of the existing capital equipment of a country; there is even more scope in association with the new equipment that is each year added to the economy. The modernisation of agriculture has been shown by experience to require a larger input of labour per hectare of farm land. The equipment of a country, step by step, with its needed infrastructure comprises a series of projects, almost all of them labour-intensive, which, by means of more vigorous mobilisation of local initiatives, can probably be programmed more ambitiously than at present seems possible. In each of these sectors the opportunities are waiting to be exploited, as will appear from the analysis in the chapters which follow. Nor should the approach be made solely from the labour requirements of the several spheres of economic activity. It is desirable to simultaneously make an approach which starts from the needs of those living in extremes of poverty. These are by no means a homogeneous group. On the contrary, they consist of a number of distinct groups whose problems are different and call for different kinds of policy measures. For many of those occupied in agriculture it is lack of land which is the principal constraint, suggesting a need for land settlement and/or agrarian reform. For others in agriculture it may be lack of capital, lack of know-how or lack of motivation. For many others in rural areas it may be a lack in particular of part-time employment since they cannot be wholly released from farm duties at certain seasons. There are the under-employed in overcrowded urban occupations, notably some service occupations, who need transfer to more productive work; and there are the wholly un-employed. It would be useful to planners to have some information regarding the numbers, even approximatively, in these several categories; but the knowledge that they are all numerically important provides already a solid basis for formulating programmes which take account of the characteristics of the different groups.

Nor is mere job creation enough: it is not just a numbers problem. Attention must also be paid to shaping the quality of the labour supply to match the qualities of manpower demanded. This implies the development of better techniques for the projection of manpower requirements by occupations and the devotion of a larger volume of resources both inside and outside enterprises to vocational training. There are other vital

28

components. In later chapters consideration will be given to ways of accelerating capital formation and to policies aimed at widening national and international markets for the products of the developing countries.

It would be foolish to ignore the political constraints which in each developing country individually influence the manner in which a welfare strategy is formulated and the role of employment in it. Some governments are preoccupied with cementing together into a national entity a population deeply divided by race or creed; some have inherited from the colonial powers territories which cannot be economically viable until they are completely transformed; some are concerned with the maintenance of law and order; some are distracted from the pursuit of development by having to deal with the struggles of groups for political power. Inasmuch as politics is the art of the possible it is recognised that not all the suggestions put forward in the ensuing pages will be feasible in each and all of the developing countries. Some policies will be appropriate in one set of circumstances, others in a different set. Development strategy has many facets. Wealth and welfare, to the extent that they are not identical, both have to be accorded their places in the hierarchy of values; and for the achievement of both the creation of a sufficient volume of productive employment provides the key.

Chapter 2

The Dimensions of the Employment Problem

How serious is the employment problem in the developing countries? What is the quantity of unemployment and under-employment? Has this quantity been increasing in recent years? Is the outlook over the coming years for a further deterioration or for some improvement? Unfortunately, fully satisfactory answers to these questions cannot be given, not only because of the shortage of manpower statistics but also because of conceptual difficulties regarding what is really meant by employment and unemployment in the circumstances of the developing countries. Some discussion of these concepts and some clarification of the way in which they will be interpreted for the purposes of this report is needed as a prelude to the analysis in the subsequent chapters.

Difficulties of Measurement

It is very important that each country should make the best estimates possible of the numbers of people for whom productive work is needed in the present, and will be needed in the years ahead. Those needing work or more work now are – to use what has become the accepted terminology – the unemployed and the under-employed. Looking ahead, it is necessary to add the prospective newcomers to the labour force.

The labour force is usually defined as the sum of the number of people employed (for pay or on their own account or as unpaid family workers) and unemployed; the latter in turn being commonly defined as people who are not at work but are seeking work or available for work.

The rate of growth of the labour force depends upon the rate of growth of the population of working age and upon participation rates, i.e. the proportion of people in different sex and age groups who are employed, or are seeking work or available for work. But it is important to recognise that the distinction between members of the labour force and dependants is not at all clear in most parts of most developing countries. This is particularly true in many rural areas where men, women and children above a fairly young age may all devote a part of their time to productive activities. Even in urban areas there are large numbers of people who carry on certain kinds of work at least sporadically, but who are also at least partly dependent on others.

Another important difficulty about the labour force concept is that there is much evidence that the number of people wanting work varies with the amount of work available. Often 'discouraged workers' who do not bother to look for work when they think there is no chance of finding any start to do so if the chances improve. This may lead to changes in the size of the labour force that are very hard to predict and that depend partly on policy measures taken: the number of people for whom work is needed depends partly on the number for whom it is provided.

Definitions of Unemployment and Under-employment

If the concept of the labour force is not well adapted to analysing social realities in developing countries, this is equally true of the concept of unemployment. In the accepted terminology, a person can be unemployed only if he is a member of the labour force, and if it is not clear who is or is not in the labour force, it will be equally unclear who is or is not unemployed.

Recognition that large numbers of people in developing countries cannot properly be regarded as either fully employed or wholly unemployed has led to widespread use of the concept of under-employment. This is seldom precisely defined. It is commonly sub-divided into visible and invisible under-employment. Being visibly under-employed means working less than a certain number of hours per year. This number of hours may be either the number of hours of work desired at prevailing rates of remuneration (in which case some people working very long hours may be considered visibly under-employed) or a number of hours considered normal or appropriate, e.g. 40 to 50 per week for 46 to 50 weeks per year. But in developing countries many people attending their places of work for a full number of hours may still be said to be (invisibly) under-employed either if they are idle for much of the time or if, though they are continuously occupied, the product of their activity is of unacceptably low value.

Attempts have been made to give more precision to the concept of invisible under-employment by saying that people are invisibly under-employed if more of them are engaged in a certain activity than would be needed to produce the output which they do produce. But the numbers needed to produce a given output will depend, among other things, on levels of nutrition, techniques of production, the size of land holdings and other factors that change over time and in which changes can be deliberately induced by means of appropriate policies. Thus this approach to the measurement of under-employment lacks any precision unless the techniques and methods of production are specified. Controversy about the magnitude of a country's reserve of under-employed labour can be traced largely to difference of views regarding the framework of assumptions about techniques, institutions and nutritional levels that it is appropriate to use. 'A labour reserve', says Myrdal, 'cannot be defined without specifying a time span during which definite policy measures are applied to a concrete situation.'[1]

[1] Gunnar Myrdal, *Asian Drama*, New York, Pantheon, 1968, Vol. II, p. 1010.

It is not clear whether or not the two-fold classification unemployed plus under-employed, even if, despite the difficulties, an attempt is made to express under-employment in terms of its full-time unemployment equivalent, provides the best approach to the problem of measuring the extent of under-utilisation of labour in a country. Another approach[2] would be to distinguish three dimensions in the concept of under-utilisation of labour: the numbers-at-work, the duration-of-work and the intensity-of-work dimensions. Statistics showing numbers at work are available for a number of developing countries, though as pointed out above the distinction between work and leisure is apt to be more blurred in developing than in developed countries. For a few developing countries tables are published in labour force or household sample surveys showing the frequency distribution of hours worked by those at work. The intensity of work seems scarcely measurable in itself, but the productivity of or income yielded by work might be taken as a rough proxy, and surveys of family incomes or expenditure could be designed to throw light on this.

It is in any case clear that the common result of no work, unduly short hours or unduly low intensity of work is no income or low income. What people are mainly interested in is not work for the sake of work but work for the sake of income. The problems of poverty and of unwanted idleness are two distinct problems, but so far as the able-bodied of working age and their dependants are concerned the two problems overlap to a very large extent. Under-employment is scarcely a serious problem if it yields a sufficient income. One might try to cut through conceptual difficulties by thinking in terms not so much of under-employment as of low-productivity or low-income employment, and regarding the number of those whose work brings in an (arbitrarily defined) unduly low income, together with the unemployed, as reflecting the numbers of those for whom work or more work needs to be provided.

But in trying to count these people it is important to bear in mind that very large numbers of people in developing countries, particularly but not only in rural areas, supply work not as individuals but as members of groups – the nuclear family, the extended family, or in some cases still larger groups. Working arrangements that give the best results in terms of work and income for the group as a whole will not necessarily utilise the services of each member of the group as fully as an observer might think they should be used. Likewise, account has to be taken of existing commitments, often of seasonal character, so that persons who would appear to be available for full-time work and who are anxious to work have in fact obligations at certain moments of the day or certain times of the year to assist their family group either as a temporary worker or in some other capacity. The problem of under-employment or low-income employment may be seen in a distorted perspective if it is viewed as a problem confronting a number of atomistic individuals having an indiscrimate capability of being mobilised.

This definition, or better said this redefinition, of the concepts of

2 This has some affinity with an approach suggested in *Ibid.*, p. 1016.

unemployment, visible under-employment and invisible under-employment will, for the later analysis, provide an essential clue as to the *kinds* of work which need to be created. Some of it will indeed be regular full-time employment of the convential type probably in the modern sector of the economy; some will be full-time employment for a specified number of months in the year, e.g. on public works projects during the dry season; some will be part-time work in the sense of a few days' work each week and, for this reason, within easy reach of the worker's home; in some cases the task will be to persuade a self-employed person, particularly the peasant-cultivator, that by devoting longer hours to working with his existing equipment (his land) he could increase his output and income; finally there are the innumerable cases of those, again especially farmers, who work full-time but gain unacceptably low incomes, and whose escape from extreme poverty depends not on working harder but upon being given the know-how (and access to a little more working capital) to modernise their farming practices so that the productivity of their labour is improved. All these avenues have to be explored.

One further complication deserves mention. Poverty and unemployment or under-employment may overlap but are far from being identical: by no means all, perhaps not even the majority, of those below the poverty line, however defined, are under- or unemployed, nor conversely do the majority of the unemployed necessarily come from households in the poverty category. This can be illustrated from an inquiry in Ceylon in 1969 which revealed that more than 60 per cent of the households on rural estates, nearly 50 per cent of the households in the rest of the rural sector and over 20 per cent of households in the urban sector had incomes below Rs 200 per month – which might be considered the poverty line. However, only a minority of these were unemployed or under-employed; the rest were either in regular but poorly paid work or for various reasons did not consider themselves available for work. As to the relationship between unemployment and level of income in Ceylon, only 42 per cent of the unemployed on the estates, 35 per cent of the unemployed in the rest of the rural sector and 19 per cent of the unemployed in the urban sector were from households below this income level.[3] Similarly in the Philippines in 1965 the average income of families whose household head was 'unemployed, without work experience or not in the labour force' was reported to be somewhat higher than the national average for all families. To some extent this is doubtless a distorted picture owing to the fact that registered unemployment tends to be concentrated in towns where money incomes are higher than in rural districts. It is the unregistered, inarticulate under-employment which is characteristically married to poverty.

The Available Evidence

It will be evident from the foregoing discussion that inasmuch as the

[3] P. J. Richards, *Employment and Unemployment in Ceylon*, OECD Development Centre, Paris, 1970; see also, ILO, *Matching Employment Opportunities and Expectations – A Programme of Action for Ceylon*, Technical Papers, Geneva, 1971, p. 64.

concepts of employment and unemployment are vague in the context of developing countries the statistical evidence even if it were prolific could not be precise. In fact it is neither.[4] Probably the most reliable point of departure is the census information relating to the occupational distribution of the population. Data for selected countries are shown in table 2.1.

Considering first the agricultural sector, the proportion of the occupied population which is engaged in farming runs as high as 94 per cent in Tanzania and ranges between 50 and 90 per cent in almost all the developing countries of Africa, the Near East and Far East. Only in the Latin American region is it already below 50 per cent in the majority of the countries.[5] In all countries the percentage share of the agricultural sector is declining, but this does not mean that the absolute numbers occupied in farming are also declining; on the contrary they are still increasing throughout the developing world and are expected to continue to increase until about the end of the century. This is going to pose a problem of finding sufficient productive work for these rising numbers on the limited amount of agricultural land available.

In most developing countries farming is one of the occupations with the lowest income in relation to hours of work performed, and any attack on extreme poverty must include measures to raise agricultural incomes, as will be seen in Chapter 7. Over the past two decades the improvement achieved has been very slight indeed. During this period the volume of agricultural output has been increasing in most parts of the developing world by about 3 per cent per annum (but only 2·5 per cent in the African region) whereas the agricultural population has increased at something between 2·0 and 2·5 per cent per annum.[6] Thus, the output per person occupied in agriculture has risen at significantly less than 1 per cent. But while this roughly measures the growth in the productivity of farm labour, it exaggerates the growth in the living standards of farm people; because throughout most of the two decades the terms of trade between agricultural and manufactured products have turned against the former – in other words, the dollar earned by the cultivator from the sale of produce bought fewer manufactures in 1970 than it did in 1950. It is safe to conclude that improvements in the welfare of farm people have been very small and very slow. So much for the income aspect.

As regards the employment aspect this, as noted above, is extremely difficult to measure on account of the sharing of the work among family members and the great variations in intensity of work at different seasons of the year. Studies which have attempted to examine on a macro-economic scale the general level of activity during both slack and busy seasons

[4] Some of the available statistics have been assembled and commented on by D. Turnham, assisted by I. Jaeger, in *The Employment Problem in Less Developed Countries, a Review of Evidence*, OECD Development Centre, Paris, 1970; see also ILO, *The World Employment Programme*, Report of the Director-General to the International Labour Conference, 53rd Session, Geneva, 1969, and *The World Employment Programme*, Report IV, International Labour Conference, 56th Session, Geneva, 1971.

[5] FAO, *The State of Food and Agriculture 1971*, Rome, 1971, Annex Tables 6–9.

[6] *Ibid.*

Table 2.1 *Structure of Employment (percentage shares of the economically active population)*

		Agriculture	Other Goods producing sectors (1)	Service-type activities
Latin America				
Argentina	1947	26·7	30·2	43·1
	1960	19·8	35·9	44·3
Chile	1952	31·2	30·5	38·3
	1960	29·6	30·1	40·3
Colombia	1951	55·9	18·4	25·7
	1964	49·0	19·6	31·4
Mexico	1950	60·9	16·7	22·4
	1960	54·6	19·1	26·3
Venezuela	1950	45·1	20·1	34·8
	1961	34·3	22·3	43·4
Asia				
Ceylon	1952	56·7	13·5	29·8
	1963	55·7	13·8	30·5
India	1951	70·6	11·1	18·3
	1961	73·8	11·5	14·7
Korea (South)	1960	65·9	9·6	24·5
	1966	57·2	15·9	26·9
	1963*	63·2	11·5	25·3
	1969*	51·4	18·1	30·5
Pakistan	1951	79·5	7·6	12·9
	1961	75·6	9·6	14·8
Philippines	1960	65·9	13·4	20·7
	1960*	61·2	15·4	23·4
	1969	56·4	15·3	28·3
Middle East				
Iran	1956	58·0	20·7	21·3
	1966	47·1	27·6	25·3
Egypt	1947	63·8	12·3	23·9
	1960	58·3	12·1	29·6
	1960*	54·0	13·7	32·3
	1967	50·6	15·6	33·8

Source: Adapted from *ILO Year Books of Labour Statistics*, 1960, 1967, 1968, 1969, 1970 – (1) mining, manufacturing, construction, public utilities.
Note: Census data except where survey data is indicated by an asterisk.

relate to Ceylon, India, Malaysia, South Korea and the Philippines, but there seem to be rather few of them for Africa, Latin America or the western part of Asia. A recent report observes that:[7]

'Perhaps the most striking aspect of the survey (or for that matter census) results is that on the whole they do not conform to a widely held opinion about unemployment and under-employment in rural areas. They provide, in particular, little or no evidence for the commonly expressed view that labour has little or nothing to do for four to six months of the year in the rural sector. In Korea for example (the results show) a 40 per cent utilisation rate in the slackest period in farm households, and this rate undoubtedly exaggerates the amount of unused labour because many additional workers who would not be available all the year round are drawn in at the peak season (June) used here as the "full utilisation" standard.

The interpretation of this finding is however much more difficult. There are scattered but in total fairly numerous studies at the sub-regional or village level which suggest that the seasonal pattern in actual cultivation requirements for labour is extremely marked. Quite a few of these studies also suggest a low over-all rate of working, but these relate mostly to Africa. Perhaps the most important point to emphasise is that we still need a great deal more detailed and extended field work before being able to derive well-founded conclusions.

One problem deserving particular mention is the treatment of activity not directly related to on-farm cultivation – which includes things like marketing, food preparation (basic food processing is often done in the home), maintenance of buildings, irrigation channels, etc. Studies show both that these activities use up quite a lot of time and that they tend to offset the seasonal pattern of on-farm cultivation work.'

Even if this non-farm work is necessary and fills up part of the slack periods, much of it is characterised by very low labour productivity and thus contributes little to alleviating the poverty of these families. To improve their living standards such people need, in addition to agricultural modernisation, to be provided with slack season activities which earn a higher rate of remuneration. From the policy angle what requires emphasising is that in many cases rural employment promotion projects should be organised so as to offer part-time rather than full-time work.

Turning now to the employment situation in the other sectors, one finds a strong contrast between manufacturing and construction on the one hand and the service-type activities on the other. In both sectors the labour force is being augmented partly by natural increase and partly by emigration out of agriculture, but of those who leave the land by far the larger proportion end up in the services sector, as can be seen from table 2.1. Much of this is precarious low-productivity self-employment; indeed, the overcrowding of service occupations that call for neither

7 D. Turnham, *op. cit.*, pp. 79–80.

capital nor skill is one of the most serious features of the employment situation in nearly all developing countries. In Latin America, for example, it is estimated that the average productivity of labour as a whole in service occupations has dropped in recent years notwithstanding the growth of over-all labour productivity. Many of the precariously self-employed in services would no doubt choose to be among the unemployed if unemployment benefits were available to them. In some developing countries, Argentina, Chile and Venezuela for instance, service occupations account for between 40 and 50 per cent of the labour force, a proportion which matches that found in the most advanced countries and which must be considered inappropriate to the present stage of development of the former.

By contrast the manufacturing and construction sector employs a small proportion of the developing countries' labour force: between 10 and 20 per cent according to countries compared with 30 to 40 per cent in the industrialised countries (see table 2.2). The data in the table indicates a faster rate of growth of employment in the developing than in the developed countries, but (a) this growth starts from a very low base in terms of absolute numbers of workers and (b) the total labour force in developed countries is growing at barely 1 per cent per annum compared with around 2 to 3 per cent in the developing countries. Moreover, experience in the latter shows that to generate a 3 to 4 per cent annual

Table 2.2. *Comparison of Construction and Manufacturing Employment Arithmetic Means (in percentages) 1955–64*

Item	Under developed countries (10)	Middle group countries (7)	Developed countries (14)	All countries (25)
Share of economically active population in:				
Construction	3·9	6·7	7·2	5·8
Manufacturing	11·1	18·6	27·5	20·4
Growth rate of employment:				
Construction	1·3(9)	5·1(6)	1·8(13)	1·6(22)
Manufacturing	4·4(9)	2·9(6)	1·6(13)	2·7(23)

Source: W. Paul Strassmann, 'Construction Productivity and Employment in Developing Countries', *International Labour Review*, May, 1970, p. 508.

Note: Figures in parentheses indicate number of countries if less than the total shown at head of column. Developed countries included in the sample were: the United States, Canada, Australia, Norway, the Federal Republic of Germany, the United Kingdom, France, Denmark, Belgium, the Netherlands, Austria, Finland*, Italy*, and Japan*. Classified as underdeveloped were Spain*, Jamaica*, Mexico*, Turkey, Peru, Honduras, El Salvador, Egypt, the Philippines, South Korea, Nigeria and Kenya. Middle income countries are marked with an asterisk, and Puerto Rico is also included in that group.

Table 2.3 *Rates of Urban Unemployment* by Sex and Age*

	15–24	15 and over — Total	Notes
Africa			
Ghana, 1960 (large towns):			
Total	21·9	11·6	Census tabulation
Males	22·1	11·5	
Females	21·5	11·8	
America			
Bogota, Colombia, 1968:			
Total	23·1	13·6	March 1968 survey
Males	21·8	10·3	
Females	24·3	18·5	
Buenos Aires, Argentina, 1965:	(a)	(b)	
Total	6·3	4·2	(a) 14–29 age group
Males	4·3	2·9	(b) 14 plus
Females	9·0	7·0	1965 survey
Chile, 1968 (urban areas):		(a)	
Total	12·0	6·0	(a) 12 plus age group. Survey December 1968
Guyana, 1965 (mainly urban areas):		(a)	
Total	40·4	21·0	(a) Over 14 age group
Males	36·5	18·4	survey data
Females	49·0	27·7	1965
Panama, 1963/4 (urban areas):	(a)		
Total	17·9	10·4	(a) 15–29 age group
Males	17·5	8·9	survey data,
Females	18·5	13·3	1963/4
Puerto Rico, 1969 (all areas):	(a)	(b)	
Total	15·3	10·2	(a) 14–24 age group
Males	16·1	11·2	(b) 14 plus age group.
Females	13·4	7·8	Survey July 1969
Trinidad and Tobago, 1968 (all areas):			
Total	26·0	14·0	Survey data,
Males	26·0	14·0	January–June 1968
Females	26·0	16·0	
Uruguay, 1963 (mainly urban):			
Total	18·5	11·8	Census tabulation
Venezuela, 1969 (urban areas):			
Total	14·8	7·9	Survey data March 1969
Asia			
Bangkok, Thailand, 1966:			
Total	7·7	3·4	Survey data, August–
Males	8·0	3·2	November 1966.
Females	7·3	3·4	Bangkok-Thonburi Municipal areas

Table 2.3—cont.

	15–24	15 and over	Notes
		Total	
Ceylon, 1968 (urban areas):			
Total	39·0	15·0	Survey data,
Males	36·1	12·9	January 1968
Females	48·4	25·9	
India, 1961/2 (urban areas):			
		(a)	(a) 15–60 age group
Total	8·0	3·2	survey data, 17th
Males	8·1	3·4	Round, 1961–2
Females	7·7	3·2	
Korea, 1966 (non-farm households):			
Total	23·6	12·6	Survey data,
Males	25·6	13·2	average of four
Females	21·5	11·3	quarters, 1966
Malaya, 1965:			
Total	21·0	9·8	Survey data,
Males	17·7	7·4	Metropolitan towns,
Females	26·8	16·7	1965
Philippines, 1965 (urban areas):	(a)	(b)	
Total	20·6	11·6	(a) 10–24 age group
Males	23·8	10·8	(b) 10 plus survey data,
Females	16·9	12·9	May 1965
Singapore, 1966:	(a)		
Total	15·7	9·2	(a) 15–29 age group survey data
Syria 1967 (whole area):			
Total	8·6	6·0	Survey data,
Males	10·9	6·2	November 1967
Females	3·7	5·2	
Teheran City, Iran 1966:			
Total	9·4	4·6	Census tabulation
Males	9·3	4·6	
Females	10·3	4·0	

Source: Adapted from David Turnham, *op. cit.*, pp. 58–60.

Note: Where possible, the labour force under fifteen has been excluded.

*Some well-conducted survey estimates which do not distinguish rural and urban areas are included.

increase in industrial employment industrial output has to expand at a rate in excess of 7 per cent per annum. This reflects the fact that under existing circumstances the increments to industrial production tend to be characterised by a capital-intensive 'factor-mix'. It is one of the purposes of the present report to examine to what extent and by what means this situation might be modified.

The statistical evidence concerning unemployment derives mostly from registered unemployment and, for that reason, refers mainly to the employment situation in urban areas. The information presented in table 2.3 shows rates or urban unemployment as high as 21 per cent in Guyana, 15 per cent in Ceylon and around 14 per cent in Colombia (Bogota) and Trinidad; these, of course, are expressed as percentages of the urban labour force which is a concept more easily definable than the total labour force, for reasons noted already. The fact that some countries record for their urban areas rather low unemployment rates (India 3·2 per cent, Thailand 3·4 per cent) does not necessarily imply a close approach to full employment; it more likely reflects the fact that registration has not yet become customary. It is impossible to guess by how much these various percentages should be increased to show the true situation; in all developing countries registered unemployment represents no more than the above-water tip of the iceberg of un- and under-employment, but just as icebergs differ in their configuration so does the difference between recorded unemployment and unrecorded under-utilisation of labour vary from country to country. We only know that the difference is great.

Table 2.3 also reveals almost everywhere a much heavier incidence of unemployment among young people in the 15–24 age group. In several countries the rate in this age group was more than double the national average; as high as 40 per cent in Guyana and 39 per cent in Ceylon. Partly this is accounted for by the heavy preponderance of young people in the migrants from countryside to towns and partly by the fact that the young are more inclined to register for work than the middleaged who may have lost interest or hope in job-seeking. In some countries the ranks of the unemployed contain a large component of persons who have passed through secondary school and are reluctant to accept anything less than relatively well-paid posts. Educated persons also tend to be concentrated in urban areas where there are fewer opportunities than in farm zones for employment as unpaid family workers. None the less, although the contrast may be exaggerated by these statistics, the concentration of the most severe unemployment among the young people is a matter of common observation.

For a few countries sample surveys of unemployment have been conducted regularly over a period of years (published in ILO's *Yearbook of Labour Statistics*, see p. 17). It is difficult to draw any firm conclusions from these time series. In some of the countries the unemployment situation (expressed as a percentage of the labour force) appears to have deteriorated, in others it has improved while in yet others it shows little change. Some of the apparent deterioration (or improvement) may be due to administrative changes during the period. In any case the comparatively small number of countries providing this data cannot be regarded as necessarily representative of developing countries as a whole.

This brief review of the statistical evidence on unemployment shows how fragmentary the material is and how little claim it can make to being representative of the true situation. All one can say with any certainty is that the statistics understate the magnitude of the problem. In many countries they probably do not even cover the majority of those who are wholly unemployed and are seeking work; they make no claim to measure the volume of visible and invisible under-employment. Nor do they throw any light on the question whether unemployment and under-employment are becoming worse. Again, one can say with confidence that whatever the real trend in the magnitudes may be, public opinion is becoming more deeply concerned with the existence of this problem.

Indeed, there is no need to collect any more statistics to prove to the planners and political leaders in the developing countries that un- and under-employment and the extremes of poverty often associated with them have become an urgent social issue which demands a reformulation of many existing policies and programmes. Job creation is being recognised as a top priority alongside that of economic growth. It is a task to which there is no single solution; it has to be tackled by using many different approaches simultaneously. Hence this survey will have to range over a wide subject-field.

Part Two

EMPLOYMENT PROMOTION IN THE SECTORS

Chapter 3

Industry

For the peoples of developing countries industrialisation constitutes a major goal. They see how the industrial revolution of the nineteenth century put today's developed countries on the road to prosperity, and they wish to accomplish the same evolution albeit accelerating the process of transition from agricultural to industrial economy and avoiding the excesses of social injustice committed in the past. They hope to arrive at a position in which they will be manufacturing most of the range of goods now produced in the industrial countries with the beneficent consequence of a large volume of employment not merely in factories but also in the various ancillary activities generated in a modern economy. This is their legitimate ambition.

Unfortunately, things are not yet working out quite as anticipated. During the nineteen-fifties industries output in the developing countries taken as a whole did indeed expand satisfactorily compared with previous periods but industrial *employment* grew much more slowly, as is indicated by the following data from selected countries (see table 3.1).

During the nineteen-sixties the over-all situation in the developing countries was no better. Industrial production expanded at an annual average rate of 7·3 per cent, but industrial *employment* grew at a rate of only 3·2 per cent.[1] Such a modest growth rate contrasts sharply with the expectations fostered by the proponents of industrial development. When it is remembered that industrial employment at present accounts for only a small part of the total volume of employment in developing countries and that in many of them a rate of growth of 3·2 per cent does little more than absorb the annual increase in the *existing* industrial labour force, clearly the absorption of the masses of urban and rural unemployed and under-employed will not occur unless some quite radical measures are taken to modify present trends.

Of course, a major objective must be to step up the rate of growth of industrial production itself, and this in fact is included among the targets adopted by the United Nations for the Second Development Decade; some policies designed to stimulate industry in general are considered in Chapter 8 of this report. But under present circumstances a 1 per cent increase in the annual growth of industrial output generates a less than 0·5 per cent increase in employment. Therefore, in addition to general

[1] Calculations of the Statistical Office of the United Nations cited in *Employment Strategies and Poverty-Reduction Policies of Developing Countries*, Centre for Development Planning, E/AC.54/L.47, New York, January 1972.

Table 3.1 *Annual Rates of Growth in Manufacturing Production and in Employment in same Developing Countries (1950–60)*

Country	Production	Employment
Argentina	4·4	−2·0
Brazil	9·8	2·6
Chile	5·4	1·7
Colombia	7·6	2·5
India	6·8	3·3
Kenya (1954–64)	7·6	−1·1
Mexico	6·5	0·4
Peru	6·6	4·4
Venezuela	13·0	2·1
Zambia	12·5	2·0

Source: Michael P. Todaro, 'An Analysis of Industrialisation, Employment and Unemployment in Less-developed Countries', *Yale Economics Essays*, **8**, 2, Fall 1968, p. 338.

stimuli, it is necessary to examine what can be done to augment the volume of employment within the industrial sector at any particular moment. While numerous possibilities exist, there are three areas which appear to merit detailed consideration: the present under-utilisation of equipment, the choice of more or less labour-intensive techniques of production and finally the choice of products for manufacture in an individual country.

Under-utilisation of Productive Equipment

Surprisingly enough, while industrial programmes provide for the establishment and equipment of all kinds of new manufacturing enterprises, the plant of existing enterprises remains under-utilised. For example, an inquiry made in India in 1967 embracing some 75 per cent of all industrial production showed that the average degree of utilisation of all installed capacity was 74·6 per cent, after taking account of current practices concerning shift systems and hours of work.[2] These current practices, however, were far below the norms currently accepted in the advanced economies; based on these latter the degree of plant utilisation would have been of the order of 60 per cent.

The case of India is by no means exceptional; other countries record even less favourable performances. Thus in 1965–6 in West Pakistan the figure for the manufacturing sector was 63·8 per cent, again on the basis of current local norms.[3] In Burma in 1962–3 the figure was 20 per cent for

[2] M. V. Raghavachari, 'Excess Capacity and Production Potential in Selected Industries in India', *Reserve Bank of India Bulletin*, April 1969, pp. 471–92.
[3] Gordon C. Winston, *Excess Capacity in Underdeveloped Countries: The Case of Pakistan*, Research Memorandum No. 25 Centre for Development Economics, William College, September 1968.

46

vegetable oil extraction plants and 85 per cent for certain food processing factories.[4]

In Afghanistan in 1963 in the textile industry the figure was 43 per cent, and in Ceylon in 1964 in the light consumption goods sector 60 per cent.[5] The Philippines' Five Year Plan for 1962/3–1966/7 explicitly stated: 'The level of industrial output does not exceed 50 per cent of the estimated capacity.'[6]

A comparable situation is found in Latin American countries. Thus in Central America in 1962 less than 75 per cent of the industrial capacity was being used and in Ecuador a few years earlier only 40 per cent.[7] In Chile in 1960 the figuer was 60 per cent for the sector of modern industry.[8]

Similar evidence is available from Africa. In the Sudan the Ministry of Planning has estimated that in the private sector the utilisation of existing capacity is normally between 15 and 30 per cent and rarely exceeds 50 per cent.[9]

In the Republic of Madagascar an inquiry covering ninety-two industrial firms showed a poor utilisation of capacity and that most of the enterprises should be able to increase their output by 50 to 200 per cent.[10] According to a survey of several countries in North and West Africa firms were operating at 30–40 per cent of capacity for a variety of reasons to be discussed presently.[11]

The increasing recognition of this state of affairs has occasioned profound concern on account of its damaging consequences for economic growth and for employment. It results in unnecessarily high unit costs of production leading to high selling prices, which in turn mean restricted domestic sales and lack of competitiveness in foreign markets. It results also in low rates of profit in such firms and consequently low rates of re-investment.

It is worth pausing to consider the direct employment effect. On the supposition that the average plant utilisation in developing countries as a whole is around 60 per cent which seems justified on the available evidence, let it be assumed that this is increased to 100 per cent. (Such complete

[4] *Economic Survey of Burma*, 1963, Ministry of National Planning, The Revolutionary Government of Union of Burma, Government Printing and Stationery, Rangoon, 1963, pp. 60–1.

[5] United Nations Economic Commission for Asia and the Far East, *Industrial Development, Asia and the Far East*, Vol. 1, Doc. 66.II.B.19. New York, 1966, p. 46.

[6] *Five-year integrated Socio-economic Program for the Philippines*, Appendix I, Manila, 1962, p. 69.

[7] Cf. UNIDO, *Industrial Excess Capacity and its Utilisation for Exports*, ID/WG.29/8, pp. 20–1. (Document prepared for the Expert Group Meeting on Utilisation of Excess Capacity for Exports, Rio de Janeiro, Brazil, 25 February–6 March 1969.)

[8] N. Novič and J. Farba, *Un Ensayo de Medición del Excedente Económico Potencial*, Santiago, Chile, 1964.

[9] Ministry of Planning, *Five-Year Plan*, Vol. 1, Khartoum, 1970, p. 10.

[10] *Note sur la conjuncture*, 1966, Institut Nationale pour la statistique et la recherche économique, Tananarive, 1966, p. 3.

[11] ILO, African Advisory Committee, *Employment Policy in Africa*, Geneva, 1967, p. 28.

utilisation is, of course, impossible but these percentages are calculated on the basis of existing norms regarding amount of work performed, norms which could be brought closer to those of industrial countries.) The additional 40 units produced would naturally not require 40 additional units of labour – part would be attributable to economies of scale – but if, say, half required a corresponding addition to labour there would occur a 33 per cent increase in employment from this one innovation.

The above represents a very crude schematisation of a complex subject in which some studies have been made and much still remains to be investigated,[12] but it suffices to indicate the considerable opportunities both for augmenting employment and at the same time for increasing the economic efficiency of industry in these countries. For too long the coefficient of plant utilisation has been looked upon as something about which little or nothing can be done, whereas it should be regarded as a variable susceptible to substantial improvement. The great bulk of equipment in developing countries has been purchased with scarce foreign exchange and the national interest requires that it be utilised as fully as possible. Significant benefit might accrue if agencies responsible for industrial development undertook sample surveys of firms in each major branch of industry with a view to identifying and removing the bottlenecks to fuller and more rational plant utilisation.

REASONS

Among the many reasons for under-utilised capacity the lack of a large enough market is a frequent occurrence. In some instances the plant has been designed for an output far greater than the local demand can absorb, in some the product is not of a type or quality which can find an export outlet;[13] sometimes an entrepreneur, knowing that import licences are difficult to obtain, will order a larger plant than he needs instead of waiting until expanding demand justifies an extension.

However, even when the output could be sold many plants are partially idle because shift working is rarely introduced, or because of breakdowns due to poor maintenance of machinery, or due to delays in delivery of spare parts and/or of raw materials. To quote but one instance: according to an investigation in India in 1966 covering 234 different products, no fewer than 81 suffered from shortage of materials causing their output

[12] For in-depth studies of this topic see: *Measurement of Productive Capacity*, Hearings before the Sub-Committee of Economic Statistics, Joint Economic Committee, 87th Congress, 2nd Session, Washington D.C., 1962; A. Phillips, 'An Appraisal of Measures of Capacity', *American Economic Review*, May 1963; Klein and Preston, 'Some New Results in the Measurement of Capacity Utilisation', *Ibid.*, March 1967; and also *Measuring Industrial Capacity in Less-developed Countries*, Univ. of Pennsylvania, the Wharton School of Finance and Commerce, Department of Economics, Philadelphia, 1969.

[13] R. Vermont, 'Industrialisation Techniques in Ghana', *Africa Monthly* 10, October 1966, p. 75, cites a mango canning plant; the local population did not eat canned mangos and the product was too stringy for any export market. He also mentions pharmaceutical and cement factories out of line with local requirements.

to reach only 47 per cent of capacity.[14] These troubles could be ascribed partly to shortcomings in the labour force and in management, but also partly to deficiencies in supporting services and in infrastructure.

A major bottleneck is insufficiency of qualified personnel of all grades: skilled workers, foremen, repair mechanics, maintenance engineers, draughtsmen, accountants, salesmen, managers, etc. A survey in Tunisia showed that out of every 100 employees, on average, there should be one engineer, three technically qualified persons of the grade of foreman and repair shop manager, 19 office staff (several of whom needed special qualifications) and 77 workers (most of whom would require accelerated in-plant training).[15] In Jamaica it has been estimated that 25 per cent of the workers in the mining industry require training, 10 per cent of those in communications, 50 per cent in construction and 15–25 per cent in general manufacturing.[16] The Economic Commission for Africa has estimated the qualified personnel requirements of Africa, excluding South Africa, for the period 1965–75 at 29,000 managerial, 52,000 scientists, engineers and technicians, 112,000 junior technicians and foremen plus 1,722,000 skilled and semi-skilled workers.[17] The reasons for the inadequate utilisation of equipment, as can be seen, are many and reach down into the whole structure of pre-industrial society. They cannot be removed in a day. Nevertheless, in face of the importance from the viewpoint of employment of exploiting every opportunity which is offered, it is worth examining in some details a series of possible remedies of a practical nature.

REMEDIES

The problem may be approached in five distinct but related ways. Measures can be adopted to stimulate demand for the products in question on the national market; measures of a different kind may also be taken to develop export markets; raw materials and spare parts may be made more readily available; fiscal incentives may be introduced to make a high degree of plant utilisation more profitable; and finally the labour input can itself be made more effective especially through adoption of shift working and provision of training facilities.

As to the domestic market, clearly any measures tending toward a more equitable distribution of incomes will have the effect of increasing consumers' current purchasing power and hence the demand for consumption goods. Unfortunately for the present purpose, such a stimulus is indiscriminate in its consequences, augmenting the demand not merely for goods produced by domestic manufacturers but also for products which

14 R. K. Koti, *Capacity Utilisation and Factors Affecting it in Certain Indian Industries*, 1966–7, Gokhale Institute of Politics and Economics, Poona, 1967, p. 34.

15 M. P. Brugnes Romieu, *Investissements Industriels et Développement en Tunisie*, Cahiers du CERES, série économique No. 1, Tunis, 1966, p. 77.

16 W. A. Lewis, Development Planning, the Essentials of Economic Policy, Allen & Unwin, 1966, p. 226.

17 Economic Commission for Africa, *Some Aspects of Manpower Requirements and the Training of Technical and Managerial Personnel for Industrial Development*, Doc. E/CN.14/AS/IV9. p. 10.

have to be imported (though luxury goods probably have a higher import content and are less easy to manufacture locally than things bought by the poor).

For example, measures taken in the United Arab Republic in favour of the lowest income groups resulted in an upsurge in demand for foodstuffs which could be satisfied only by massive imports with deleterious effects on the balance of payments. It is preferable, by public purchase from national firms or by other means, to encourage selectively the consumption of products locally available.[18] In some countries the expansion of the market is inhibited by the relatively high prices of the locally manufactured commodities because the entrepreneurs, enjoying a high degree of tariff protection, have no incentive to modernise and reduce their unit costs of production, which at one stage was the experience in Argentina.[19] Where scope for such cost economies clearly exists, a reduction or removal of the protection will reduce selling prices and expand consumption, although some restraints on imports may be necessary to prevent too many local firms being eliminated. Retail prices can also be brought down by measures which help to modernise wholesale and retail trade, reduce wastage, promote competition and diminish distributive margins.

In the case of commodities which are produced by the traditional sector, i.e. by artisans, as well as in the modern sector, there may be danger of the 'backwash effect' whereby the cheaper factory product drives out the more expensive hand-made one, perhaps putting thousands of craft workers out of business, people for whom no alternative employment opportunities exist.[20] Such a situation raises policy issues of a delicate nature. On the one hand governments may recognise a need to safeguard at least in the short term their artisan and cottage industries, but on the other hand they want to encourage modern larger-scale enterprises which can serve the emerging mass market and which can in some instances successfully export. Both India and Pakistan in their First and Second Development Plans made special provision for their small-scale industries, which has likewise been the strategy in other Asian countries, notably Malaysia and Ceylon. The case for not handicapping the modern in the interests of the traditional sector becomes much stronger when it concerns a wholly new product or an opportunity for import substitution.[21]

The volume of sales may also be expanded through the development of export markets by fiscal and other measures. Among these may be mentioned: reduction or elimination of export duties; reduction or elimination of import duties on needed raw materials; privileges in the utilisation of foreign exchange acquired from exporting; and, of course, direct export

[18] K. Weddel, 'Promotion of Small-scale Industries Through Government Purchasing', *Industrialisation and Productivity*, No. 12, United Nations, New York, 1969, pp. 7–24.

[19] Arthur O. Little, *Industrial Development in Argentina*, Cambridge, Mass, 1961.

[20] G. Myrdal, *Asian Drama*, op. cit., pp. 1172 ff., also pp. 1225 ff.

[21] See especially: S. H. Fine, 'Employment Effect of Import Duties and Export Subsidies in the Developing Countries', in ILO, *Fiscal Measures for Employment Promotion in Developing Countries*, op. cit., p. 243.

subsidies. For instance, Pakistan after 1959 adopted a number of such devices including granting to exporters free use of part of their foreign exchange earnings, exemption from import duties on raw materials and semi-manufactures, tax exemption on revenue derived from exports and special permission to import certain classes of goods otherwise prohibited, all of which seemed to have stimulating consequences. However, governmental promotion of exports on an aggressive scale entails the risk of retaliatory action by aggrieved parties.

A more prudent course may often be to seek the same ends by means of trade agreements with foreign countries, by a group of countries sharing their manufacturing facilities or by the establishment of regional 'Common Markets'. One such example was the agreement setting up the Equatorial Refining Company (Société équatoriale de raffinage) at Port-Gentil in Gabon in 1967 which enjoys a monopoly of the distribution of petroleum products in the countries of the Customs and Economic Union of Central Africa.[22] Similarly, in the East African Common Market and in the Central American Common Market agreements have been reached for some commodities to establish a single enterprise serving all the member countries rather than competing enterprises in each of them. Despite the difficulties of overcoming certain chauvinistic prejudices[23] such policies offer, especially for small countries, an opportunity of establishing industries of modern scale for which local markets would otherwise be quite insufficient, as a recent study for South-East Asia indicates.[24]

Interruptions in the use of equipment due to lack of raw materials or spare parts may be partially remedied by remission of duties on imports of needed items, but there is more involved than this. In quite a few cases permits are granted for the import of basic equipment but not for the spare parts necessary to keep it operating. For example Malta and Nigeria while conceding large reductions of import duties on basic industrial equipment, impose heavy duties on spare parts and raw materials, thus stimulating an over-purchase of new machinery from abroad. Even when imports of materials and parts are permitted up to the 'normal' requirements of the installed plant, the word 'normal' is interpreted as being the requirements for operation on a single-shift system. In India a sample survey of 276 firms showed 48 having difficulties with imports and for 11 among these the material shortages ranged between 40 and 90 per cent

[22] See J. Baudet, 'Un exemple de Coopération entre Etats', *Chronique Sociale de France*, 5, October 1968, pp. 43–4. The customs and Economic Union of Central Africa comprised in 1967 the Cameroons, the Central African Republic, Congo (Brazzaville), Gabon and Chad. The last named, together with Zaire, is now a member of the Union of Central African States.

[23] See M. S. Wionczek, 'Experiences of the Central American Economic Integration Programme as Applied to East Africa', *Industrialisation and Productivity*, Bulletin 11, New York, 1968, pp. 14–28.

[24] See Yeong-Her Yeh, 'Size of Factory, Market Size and Degree of Concentration in a Hypothetical Common Market for the ECAFE Region', *Economic Development and Cultural Change*, 16, 4, July 1968, pp. 559–73.

of requirements.[25] By contrast, in Pakistan which permitted duty-free entry of such supplies the utilisation of productive capacity rose from 53 to 82 per cent between 1963 and 1965 with undoubtedly favourable consequences for employment.[26] In theory it would be desirable to encourage the local production of spare parts, but usually the requirements for any individual item are small and often some of the necessary materials (and skills) are not locally available; the possibility will emerge when many firms become established in the same branch of manufacturing.

The fourth category of remedies for inadequate plant utilisation consists in tax incentives of various kinds. The simplest is a straight tax rebate on sales as, for instance, in Canada where that part of a firm's production which exceeds a base-year quantity is exempt from indirect taxes provided it does not arise from extensions to the plant.[27] India introduced a similar system experimentally for the years 1965–6 to 1969–70. Exemptions could also be accorded to additional profits arising from fuller utilisation of plant capacity. A more conventional device is to grant more generous depreciation allowances for plant being worked on a two- or three-shift system, as has been tried in Pakistan and India; but apart from these two countries it does not appear to have been widely adopted elsewhere.

Fifth and last come the arrangements inside the plant itself for ensuring that expensive machinery is constantly operating. Even within the single-shift system the machinery may frequently have to be stopped because there are insufficient men working with it. Thus in a factory in Calcutta when there was only one man per machine, the latter being idle 25 per cent of the time whereas when three men were provided for two machines both could operate continuously.[28] In industries with a high rate of absenteeism it has been found efficacious to create a pool of workers who can be drawn upon to keep the machines turning. In local circumstances what will be the more advantageous arrangement may depend on the relative cost of manual labour versus that of the machine operation. Thus, in bottle-making plants the bottles emerging hot from the moulds are transported to the cooling chamber on a conveyor belt which from time to time breaks down bringing the entire plant to a halt. In a Mexican plant two men armed with pincers were always available to replace the conveyor whereas in a Puerto Rican plant where wages were nearly four times as high such provision was not made so that when the conveyor failed the incandescent bottles fell into the waste bin until such time as the belt was repaired or replaced.[29]

25 *Under-utilisation of Industrial Capacity*, National Council of Applied Economic Research, New Delhi, 1966.

26 UNIDO, *Excess Capacity and its Utilisation for Export*, Expert Group Meeting, *loc. cit.*, Doc. ID/WG.29/8, p. 36.

27 R. Bird, 'A Tax Incentive for Sales: The Canadian Experience', *National Tax Journal*, 18, September 1965.

28 M. J. Solomon, *Better Plant Utilisation in India: a Blueprint for Action*, Indian Statistical Institute, 1963, p. 25.

29 P. Strassmann, *Technological Change and Economic Development*. Cornell Univ. Press, Ithaca, 1968, p. 164.

Inasmuch as machine maintenance often falls down for lack of trained mechanics as well as for lack of spare parts, it has been suggested that governments or groups of employers might organise in industrial areas central workshops for the training of maintenance staff and even to provide repair services to individual firms.[30] More advantage might also be taken of after-sales service by foreign firms providing the capital equipment.

Undoubtedly the more dramatic changes can be obtained by moving over to a two- or three-shift system.[31] In any given factory its productive capacity depends on two variables: the total number of man hours (or machine hours) and the level of productivity of the equipment. The latter being already determined by the nature of the installed plant, the volume of output will depend on the input of man hours which in turn depends on the length of the working day, the number of working days per year and the number of shifts per day. Since the first two of these are generally fixed by tradition or by law it is the number of shifts which becomes decisive. The order of magnitude of the possibilities up to a theoretical maximum of 365 working days per year with continuous production can be seen from table 3.2.[32]

Table 3.2 *Working Hours per Year According to Shift Systems*

Patterns of capacity utilisation	Working days per year (approx.) (W)	Average working hours per day (h)	Gross annual working hours (Wh)	Approximate maintenance time $\left(\dfrac{M = 10Wh}{100}\right)$	Net annual working hours $H = (Wh - M)$	Shift co-efficient (Pattern A = 1)
Semi-continuous processes:						
(A) One shift	300	8	2,400	240	2,160	1
(B) Two shifts	300	16	4,800	480	4,320	2
(C) Three shifts	300	24	7,200	720	6,480	3
Continuous processes:						
(A') One shift	365	8	2,920	292	2,628	1·2
(B') Two shifts	365	16	5,840	584	5,256	2·4
(C') Three shifts	365	24	8,760	876	7,884	3·6

Source: M. Kabaj, 'Shift Work and Employment Expansion', *International Labour Review*, January 1965, p. 49.

[30] UNIDO, *Report of the Experts on Maintenance and Repair of Industrial Equipment in Developing Countries*, ID/1, April 1967; see also 'Use of Industrial Equipment in Under-developed Countries', *Industrialisation and Productivity*, Bulletin No. 4, New York, 1962, pp. 44–5.

[31] See particularly, M. Kabaj, *Problems of Shift Work as a Means of Improving Capacity Utilisation*, UNIDO, Expert Group Meeting on the Utilisation of Excess Capacity for Export, Rio de Janeiro, 3–12 March 1969 (roneoed document); also ILO, Marc Maurice, *Shift Work*, Geneva, 1971.

[32] The considerable differences between the actual and the possible have been pointed out by Currie: Generally in Latin American countries, 'the working year is short . . . .

Comparing the single shift working a six-day week with three shifts working continuously throughout the year the difference in number of machine hours worked *net*, i.e. allowing maintenance time in both cases, is between 2,160 hours and 7,884 hours, the latter being 3·6 times the former. Such a difference becomes especially important in those plants where overheads form a considerable proportion of total costs.[33]

Table 3.3 shows that the previous profit from a six-day week had been only 2·25 per cent so that the changeover almost trebled the profit.

Table 3.3 *Results of Change from Six- to Seven-Day Working Week: Modern Textile Plant in South India*

	Lakhs	Per month
Additional sales	13	
Additional labour cost (12% of sales)		1·56
Additional raw material cost (50% of sales)		6·50
Additional power (2% of sales)		0·26
Additional spares (3% of sales)		0·39
Total sales	13	
Total increase		8·71
Additional profit	4·29	

Source: M. J. Solomon, *op. cit.*, p. 25.

It must be recognised that shift working is not possible, or even desirable, everywhere and that it is subject to certain biological, social and technical constraints. For instance, night work is said in some cases to give rise to physiological and nervous disorders reducing the efficiency of work or leading in more serious cases to illness.[34] This may take the form of digestive troubles, loss of sleep and heart ailments. From the several studies which have been made on this subject no definitive conclusions emerge; however, it would seem that where working conditions are good and the diet is satisfactory, night shift work is less likely to have ill effects The most recent studies suggest the significance of psychosomatic effects relating to the family and social life of the workers.

Consequently, even for the urban fully employed, the work year may not exceed 220 days. With a few exceptions, a single shift is the rule. Thus the bulk of equipment, even where it is fully utilised during working hours, is not in operation more than 20 per cent of the year. When we add to this figure the excess capacity resulting from forward planning, mergers, uneven spacing of demand, and the necessity to provide for the peak, it is probable that most equipment is not in use more than 10–15 per cent of the time; or in other words, an enormous excess capacity exists' (Lauchlin Currie, *Accelerating Development: the Necessity and the Means*, McGraw-Hill, New York, 1967, p. 54.).

[33] On this topic see: M. Kabaj, 'Shift Work and Employment Expansion: Towards an Optimum Pattern', *International Labour Review*, September 1968, pp. 251ff.

[34] See: M. Maurice, *op. cit.*, p. 45, and M. Kabaj, *op. cit.*, p. 278.

Indeed the social disturbances have an importance of their own. Two different rhythms of activity in the family may occasion friction particularly where quarters are restricted so that the night worker cannot enjoy quiet for his hours of sleep; the marriage relationship and the father's role in bringing up his children may also be disrupted. Similarly, social life with neighbours and friends may be difficult, sport and other club activities becoming impossible. For all these reasons it is desirable to secure the full concurrence of the workers before introducing systems of shifts.

Table 3.4 *Actual Shift Coefficients and Production Expansion Potential with Optimum Capacity Utilisation in Engineering and the Metal Trades*

Country and branch of industry	Actual shift coefficient	Percentage production and employment expansion opportunities (percentages) with shift coefficient of:	
		1·6	1·8
Developing Countries			
India, 1964:			
Machinery except electrical machines	1·07	50	68
Transport equipment	1·00	60	80
Electrical machinery and appliances	1·09	47	65
Israel, 1966:			
Machinery	1·01	58	78
Electrical equipment	1·02	57	76
Transport equipment	1·01	58	78
Mexico, 1956:			
Manufacture of producers' goods	1·06	51	70
Pakistan (East), 1965–6:			
Basic metals	1·00	60	80
Metal products	1·05	52	71
Machinery	1·02	57	76
Electrical machinery	1·48	8	22
Transport equipment	1·05	52	71

Sources: UNIDO, *Underutilisation of industrial capacity, op. cit.*, pp. 112–14; Meir Merhav, *Excess-capacity-Measurement, Causes and Uses: a Case Study of Selected Industries in Israel*, ID/WG.29/7, 1969, p. 27; *Censo Industrial* 1956, Vol. 1, Estados Unidos-Americanos, Mexico, 1959, p. 28; *Labour Exchanges Statistics*, Eastern Pakistan 1965/6, p. 28.

Managerial problems also arise in arranging the flow of raw materials, the periods of maintenance, the presence of the necessary qualified staff, and in determining the need for bonuses where extra effort is required or extra costs are incurred by workers, e.g. in transport. Taking all factors into account there are numerous cases where a two-shift rather than a three-shift system would appear more advantageous. Certainly in the developing countries wide differences of practice are found between one type of industry and another. For example in India shift working is common in the textile industry compared to the chemical industry where 63 per cent of the firms work only a single shift and 80 per cent of those in the machinery and metallurgical industry. A 1967 survey covering 163 industries of all kinds showed 67 per cent working one shift, 8 per cent two shifts and 25 per cent three shifts.[35]

In a two-shift system the total staff is not of course multiplied by two, because certain sections of the personnel, e.g. the office workers and the transport and maintenance workers can continue on a one-shift basis. By the same token the volume of output will also be somewhat less than twice as large, bearing in mind certain interruptions which even under the best of circumstances may occur and the fact that not every enterprises in the particular branch of industry concerned will be able to adopt shift working. In the experience of the socialist countries of Eastern Europe the actual multiplier for a two-shift system lies between 1·6 and 2·0.[36]

In table 3.4 data are presented from four countries showing for individual industries the current multiplier (using 1·0 to represent the norm of a single shift) and alongside the increases that would be possible by moving to a multiplier of 1·6 or one of 1·8.

The lower multiplier would produce output increases of the order of 50 per cent or more while the higher one would raise output by around 75 per cent, all without additional capital investment.[37]

Before leaving this topic one further observation must be made concerning the bottleneck of skilled personnel which so frequently inhibits the introduction of shift working. While the long-term solution to this problem lies in providing adequate training facilities, as will be shown in a later chapter, nevertheless something could be done immediately by studying how to break down certain complex operations into simpler tasks capable of being executed by less qualified persons. The scope for this, it must be admitted, occurs mainly in the larger firms. In the small businesses which in developing countries provide the vast bulk of manufacturing employment the roles of director/manager/foreman are all combined in one person who is neither able to delegate his responsibilities nor prepared himself to work more than, say, ten hours a day.

Much indeed depends on the quality of management. Success involves

[35] M. V. Raghavachari, *op. cit.*, p. 479.

[36] M. Kabaj, *op. cit.*, p. 282. In effect this means that under conditions of an eight-hour shift the equipment will be working at something between 12·8 (1·6 × 8) hours and 16 (2 × 8) hours per day.

[37] Not surprisingly the ILO Recommendation concerning Employment Policy (paragraph 26) suggests the adoption of measures to 'promote fuller utilisation of existing industrial capacity to the extent compatible with the requirements of domestic and export markets, for instance by more extensive introduction of multiple shifts, with due regard to the provision of amenities for workers on night shift and to the need for training a sufficient number of key personnel to permit efficient operation of multiple shifts' (ILO, *Official Bulletin*, 49, 3, Suppl. I, July 1964, pp. 54–66).

attention to detail in the planning of each aspect of the production process, a policy of selective recruitment of workers, a scheme of associating them with the results through piece-work rates or bonuses for extra achievement or profit-sharing, and also organisation of a smooth flow of inputs and of disposition of the final output.[38] Table 3.5 shows up the contrasts between different systems of management. Between the worst and the best the volume of output can be five to six times higher while the volume of employment can increase, on the same equipment, four- to five-fold. This provides a measure of what could become possible when a sufficient supply of managers has been trained.

Table 3.5 *Output and Employment Indices for Similar Enterprises with Different Systems of Organisations*

Organisation system	Enterprises with hand-fed operational equipment		Enterprises with semi-automatic equipment	
	Index of production	Index of employment	Index of production	Index of employment
Poorly managed (one shift)	100	100	100	100
Well managed, with incentives, conventional staffing (one shift)	150	105	130	100
Well managed, with incentives, intensive staffing (one shift)	195	136–153	143–169	100–130
Well managed, with incentives, intensive staffing (three shifts)	550	408–459	403–477	300–390
Well managed, with incentives, intensive staffing (three shifts, seven days)	642	476–535	470–556	350–455

Source: M. J. Solomon, *op. cit.*, pp. 39–40.

Choice of Production Techniques

If considerable space has been devoted to the fuller utilisation of installed capacity this was not because the objective in itself is controversial; it is not. The difficulties arise in devising appropriate means for achieving the objective, since the obstacles to be overcome have their roots deep in the structure of society in the developing countries. That is after all the main reason why under-utilisation persists. Entrepreneurs are not usually stupid,

[38] See ILO, *Payment by results*, Studies and Reports, New Series, No. 27, Geneva, 1951.

and if they could contrive to take a step which promises so much personal pecuniary benefit they would not hold back. But only a few of the needed measures are their responsibility, far more lie with government and will take time to put into effect, which is of course a good argument for starting now. Quite different is the topic of production technique – labour-intensive or capital-intensive – since the objective itself, the act of preferring one over the other, is highly controversial, many of the concepts involved being still in dispute among experts.

DISTORTION OF FACTOR PRICES

The basic assumption that labour in developing countries is plentiful (and presumably cheap) whereas capital is scarce (and presumably dear) and that therefore wherever a choice is possible between two methods of producing the same product the more labour-intensive method will be preferred, does not always hold good in practice because it happens that in developing countries more than in industrial ones the prices of certain inputs in many instances fail to truly reflect the supply situation of those items; for a variety of reasons the factor prices are distorted.[39] The more noteworthy items here are the rates of interest on loan capital, the prices of materials and equipment purchased from abroad and the levels of local wages.

As regards loan capital a quite normal procedure is for governments of developing countries to borrow abroad at the relatively moderate rates of interest prevailing in industrial countries and then to re-lend to industry at the same or a marginally higher rate, whereas the real price of capital on the local market would be considerably higher.[40] Admittedly, cheap money policies have been pursued deliberately in order to stimulate rapid industrialisation, but it is for consideration whether this has in fact promoted the most desirable kind of industrialisation and whether it has not introduced a bias in favour of capital-intensive production. It might be advisable for governments to make it a general practice (there will always be exceptions) to make loans available at rates which reflect the true local scarcity of capital ('shadow rates' in certain cases). Inasmuch as the governments would still be borrowing from abroad at international

[39] See W. A. Lewis, 'Unemployment in Developing Countries', *World Today*, **23**, 1, London, January 1967, p. 19. See also F. I. Nixon and A. J. Stoutjesdijk, 'Industrial Development in the Kenya and Uganda Development Plans', *East African Economic Review*, Nairobi, **2**, 2, December 1966, p. 70. Minimum wage legislation is especially relevant in this context. The authors of the Kenya plan were fully aware of the matter when they stated: 'The general outline of such a policy must maintain the total value of incentives now available to business firms, while at the same time modifying the components of the incentive package in such a way as to make it profitable to firms to employ more labour in their expansion than they would under present circumstances'. (Republic of Kenya, *Development Plan* 1966–70, p. 72). See also on the same topic *The Colombia Report, op. cit.*, especially pp. 119–20 and pp. 185 ff.
[40] Cf. ILO, Geneva, 1971, 'Price distortion and social opportunity cost', 'Meeting of Experts on Fiscal Policies for Employment Promotion', para. 28 ff.

rates they would make some profit on these transactions which could be used for instance to subsidise the rates on loans advanced to labour-intensive enterprises.

Reference has already been made to the over-valuation of the currencies of a number of developing countries which artificially cheapens imports and thus stimulate the purchase of foreign equipment. In certain instances this distortion is pushed even further: those governments which operate systems of multiple exchange rates usually concede the most favourable rate to the importation of capital goods; likewise those which control imports through licensing systems tend to accord licences most easily to 'important', i.e. capital-intensive industries. There would seem to be a case for reviewing and modifying these policies and also for re-casting the system of import duties so as to discourage the importation of equipment destined for capital-intensive operations. In this context a study of tariffs in Latin American countries showed the duties to be on average lower on capital goods than on consumption goods but higher on the former than on raw materials; the indirect effect on choice of production techniques appeared ambiguous.[41] In India and Pakistan a conscious discrimination in favour of agricultural as distinct from industrial imported equipment has been pursued with this end in view.

Fiscal policy can also be utilised to influence the use of capital-intensive equipment. This may be done (1) by general measures to make the use of equipment less attractive for the producer, relative to that of labour; or (2) by selective measures to make the use of capital-intensive equipment less attractive relative to that of labour-intensive equipment. A further possibility is (3) to make capital-intensive products more expensive relative to labour-intensive products, thus inducing consumers to substitute the latter. As is usually the case, these changes may be secured either by a stick (taxes) or a cavout (subsidies) approach.

Both give similar incentives by changing relative costs on returns, but they differ in their budgetary and distributional implications. Moreover they may have different effects upon the total supply of capital and labour.[42]

Turning lastly to the matter of wages, the actual and 'real' cost of labour, the issues here are complex and delicate. On the one hand it would be inconceivable to impose an all-round reduction of wages; the whole object is to augment the volume of employment income. On the other hand current wage levels may in many instances be high in relation to current labour productivity. This situation is found particularly in those developing countries which possess an extractive industry-petroleum or mining – in which wage levels, not only for expatriate staff but also for local labour, are extremely high in relation to comparable

41 'Customs Duties and Other Import Charges and Restrictions in Latin American Countries: Average Levels of Incidence', *Multi-lateral Economic Co-operation in Latin America*, Vol. I, Doc. E/CN 12/621, paras. 77–9. See also: W. A. Lewis, *The Causes of Unemployment in less-developed Countries and Some Research Topics, International Labour Review*, May 1970.

42 R. A. Musgrave, 'Fiscal Devices to Induce Employment', in ILO, *Fiscal Measures for Employment Promotion, in Developing Countries, op. cit.*, p. 337.

jobs elsewhere in the national economy. The privileged position of this usually well-unionised labour may have unfortunate effects on the supply price of labour for similar occupations elsewhere. Though with more training to overcome skill bottlenecks this might lose much of its importance so far as employment outside the high-wage enterprises is concerned, the incentive it gives to these enterprises to use more capital and less labour would remain. As a general proposition the rising cost of labour which employers face can be attenuated to the extent that governments are able to augment wages and salaries indirectly, for instance by family allowances and by taking major responsibility for the financing of social security. In practice this policy, while feasible in developed countries, implies the availability of larger budgetary resources than the governments of most developing countries possess. Alternatively, it would be possible to grant subsidies to the wages bill of firms which satisfied a given criterion of labour-intensive operation,[43] and the funds for this might be in part derived from the profits on the loan operations suggested above.

It may be asked: what practical results might be expected from these various suggestions for dealing with the distortions of factor prices? Evidently the effect in each individual case will depend on the elasticity of substitution of labour for capital. This elasticity concept can be expressed in simple arithmetical terms: if an increase of 10 per cent in the ratio of interest to wages brings about a decline of 5 per cent in the ratio of capital input to labour input, then the elasticity of substitution will be 5 (effect)/ 10 (cause)=0·5. The higher this elasticity the more effective will be the interventions. In daily life the measurement of these elasticities presents many difficulties both conceptually and in application. Much depends on whether individual firms or whole branches of industry are studied, whether time series are available, whether international comparisons are made. By way of illustration certain calculations are reproduced in table 3·6 (see p. 61).

Note that C. K. Clague considers the methodology he used to have resulted in an under-estimation of the elasticities. For similar reasons the elasticities presented by G. Stigler are probably over-estimated. It may be that on average the typical elasticity may be in the region of unity, which is not very high. However, these studies, it must be remembered, were of existing firms in existing situations. An entrepreneur who already possesses a certain equipment cannot do much to change the ratio between capital and labour inputs *for that equipment* (apart from using it to fuller capacity if he is not already working a shift system.) Even if he happens to be contemplating a major renewal of equipment his choice will be determined by the current relative factor prices, i.e. the distorted ones, not by the 'influenced' prices discussed above. Consequently, it may be said that these elasticities illustrate the problem to be remedied, not the scope for remedying it.

[43] This solution is envisaged by J. R. Harris and M. P. Todaro in 'Migration, Unemployment and Development: a Two-Sector Analysis; *American Economic Review*, May 1970.

Table 3.6 *Capital/Labour Substitution Elasticities in Manufacturing Industry*

Author	Branches of Industry	Elasticity
	Leather	0·176
	Hosiery	0·038
	Cotton	0·279
C. K. Clague	Glass	0·162
	Flour	0·161
	Tyres	0·152
	Cement	0·473
G. Stigler	Industry (average)	4·0
Ph. Dhrymes	Industry (average)	0·94
	minimum	0·72
B. S. Minhas	Industry median	0·9
	maximum	1·01

Sources: (1) C. K. Clague: 'Capital-Labor Substitution in Manufacturing in Under-developed Countries', *Econometrica*, July 1969, Table 1, p. 532. (2) G. Stigler: *Capital and Rates of Return in Manufacturing Industries*, National Bureau of Economic Research, Princeton University Press, 1963. (3) Ph. Dhrymes: 'Some Extensions and Tests for the CES Class of Production Functions', *Review of Economics and Statistics*, November 1965. (4) B. S. Minhas: *An International Comparison of Factor Costs and Factor Use*, Amsterdam, North-Holland Publishing Company, 1963.

There are two further considerations. One is the lack of knowledge among entrepreneurs of the choices available to them. An ILO study of thirity-seven firms in three countries of tropical Africa and covering such varied branches as cement, machinery, electrometallurgy, asbestos, plastics, wood and dairy products, indicated that the labour costs were far from being determinant in choice of technology.[44] The other is the shortage of the *right kinds* of labour, since the use of labour-intensive equipment generally demands an availability of more skilled labour than does the use of automated machines. These shortages will continue to constitute a major impediment until training programmes have been greatly extended to meet national needs. It is this preparation of skills to match the requirements of the economy which lies at the heart of manpower planning, to be discussed in a later chapter.[45]

PROS AND CONS OF CAPITAL-INTENSIVE TECHNIQUES
The classical argument in favour of capital-intensive production is that with less of the firm's income flowing to the workers and more to the owners of capital this will encourage savings and generate future invest-

[44] Z. Svejnar, *The Influence of the Labour Costs on Investment and Employment Decisions*, an ILO Study based on a sample of thirty-seven plants surveyed in a region of tropical Africa, ILO, Geneva, 1971.
[45] On this topic see J. Mouly, 'Essai d'Analyse de Quelques Problèmes Techniques de Planification de la Main-d'œuvre', *Tiers-Monde*, Paris, January–March 1970, especially pp. 71-3.

ments. In reply it is pointed out that in developing countries the owners of capital have a weak propensity to save, spending much of their money on luxury goods which are often imported. Moreover, because capital-intensive enterprises tend to pay higher wages per worker (even though they employ fewer workers) this detracts from the flow of revenue to potential savers.[46]

In the view of some other writers, developing countries wishing to conquer markets for manufactures in advanced countries must use the most up-to-date techniques to ensure uniformity and quality of their products. The Leontieff paradox is also quoted to show how although wage levels may be low in these countries labour productivity is in many instances even lower with the result that labour costs may be high per unit of output, and hence more capital-intensive techniques become necessary if the products are to be competitive in export markets.

Others emphasise the value of the 'shock effect' of ultra-modern industry forcing all the industries and services connected with it (through backward and forward linkages) to adjust themselves to contemporary modes of business.[47] This will in itself help to diversify the nation's industrial activity and reduce its dependence on primary products with their wide price fluctuations.[48]

Other arguments refer to the characteristics of the labour supply, the great bulk of it being not merely unskilled but unaccustomed to working under factory conditions. It has been noted that a factory with automated equipment is in most instances better able to make use of totally unskilled labour than one with non-automated machinery and that labour productivity tends to be higher in 'machine-paced' operations than is 'operator-paced'[49] ones. In such an environment the worker becomes a machine minder with a minimum of responsibility. This is the option that has been chosen in certain industries in Tunisia.[50] A comparable policy is pursued in Nigeria where the industries of the modern sector are assigned

[46] See in particular, W. Galenson and H. Leibenstein, 'Investment Criteria, Productivity and Economic Development', *Quarterly Journal of Economics*, **69**, August 1955: M. Dobb, 'Note on the Degree of Capital Intensity of Investments in Underdeveloped Countries', *loc. cit.*, and 'Second Thoughts on Capital Intensity of Investment', *Review of Economic Studies*, **24**, 1956, pp. 33–42; A. K. Sen, 'Choice of Techniques: an Aspect of the Theory of Planned Economic Development', Blackwell, Oxford, 1960; K. N. Raj, 'Small-Scale Industries – Problems of Technological Change', *Economic Weekly* (Bombay), 7 and 14 April 1956. See also A. S. Bhalla, 'Galenson-Leibenstein Criterion of Growth Reconsidered', *Economia Internazionale*, Genoa, May 1964.

[47] F. Perroux, 'Note sur la Notion de Pôle de Croissance', *Economie Appliquée* 1955, Nos 1 and 2, and *La Coexistence Pacifique*, Vol. II: *Pôles de Développement ou Nations?* PUF, Paris 1958. See also A. O. Hirschman, *Strategies of Economic Development*, Chapter 9.

[48] On these various aspects see: J. Mouly, *op. cit.*

[49] H. Myint, *The Economics of the Developing Countries*, Hutchinson, London, 1964, p. 137.

[50] M. P. Brugnes-Romieu, *Investissements Industriels et Développement en Tunisie*, Cahier du CERES, Tunis, 1966, p. 157. This is particularly the thesis of Hirschman, *op. cit.*, but see also J. M. Healey, 'Industrialisation, Capital Intensity and Efficiency',

the responsibilities for production and development whilst the provision of employment is regarded as the role of services and of the traditional small-scale industries.[51]

Yet a further argument frequently heard in support of capital-intensive types of operation is that with these methods the management is less likely to encounter labour troubles. As the saying goes in one Latin American country: 'menores obreros, menores problemas' (the fewer the workers the fewer the problems)[52] but this represents a somewhat superficial view of the matter. It may well 'be easier to train and manage properly fifty workers than to train and manage 500 workers badly',[53] when the management itself is inexperienced, even in some instances incompetent. Gradually as a higher proportion of managers receive professional training and acquire experience, the force of this particular argument may weaken and indeed turn the other way: 'Plagued by breakdowns and lack of spare parts, many maintenance engineers in under-industrialised countries must have been tempted to develop a slogan "fewer machines, fewer problems".'[54]

This last speculation leads naturally to a listing of the considerations militating against a use of capital-intensive techniques. Aside from the central and obvious objection that such techniques contribute little to the creation of employment their superior profitability frequently turns out to be less remarkable than expected and in some instances may not materialise at all, and this for a number of simple reasons. First, the equipment generally has to be imported incurring freight costs and has to be installed often with the aid of foreign personnel, another heavy expense, so that by the time it becomes operational it has already cost much more than similar equipment set up in an industrial country. It has, for instance, been calculated that the capital cost of a fertilizer factory in India is 140 per cent of the cost of the same factory erected in the United States.[55] Second, in many industries the production units manufactured in industrial countries have an output capacity far in excess of the local market demand in most developing countries, and the capacity is being steadily enlarged. Thus, whereas twenty years ago the optimum capacity for an integrated steel mill was 2 million tons per annum, today it is 6 million tons and twenty years hence will probably be 12 million tons.[56] Furthermore, the

Bulletin of the Oxford University Institute of Statistics, **30**, 4, November 1968, pp. 323–38; Baer and Hervé, 'Employment and Industrialisation in Developing Countries', *Quarterly Journal of Economics*, **80**, February, 1966, p. 99.

[51] United Nations Development Programme, UNDA/ILO, *Vocational Instructor and Supervisor Training*, Nigeria, Geneva, 1968.

[52] P. Strassmann, *Technological Change and Economic Development, op. cit.*, Chapter 5.

[53] P. Strassmann, 'The Response to Automation and Advanced Technology: a Comparison of Developed and Developing Countries', *Automation in Developing Countries*, Round-Table discussion on Manpower Problems, *op. cit.*, p. 21.

[54] ILO, *Human Resources for Industrial Development*, New Series 71, Geneva, 1967, p. 222, note 3.

[55] OECD, *Supply and Demand Prospects for Fertilizers in Developing Countries*, Paris, 1968, p. 83.

[56] N. Kaldor, 'Advanced Technology in a Strategy of Development: The Choice of Technology', in *Automation in developing countries, op. cit.*, p. 15.

operation of modern equipment, especially automated equipment, depends upon the maintenance of a reliable supply of raw materials and of power which presupposes a rather advanced level of development of supporting services.[57] For all these reasons, and others could be cited, the profitability of capital-intensive production is frequently disappointing relative to that of its labour-intensive counterpart.

Data from some Asian countries, notably Japan and India, suggest that comparing traditional with capital-intensive production the profits per unit of capital employed are not less and per unit of output are slightly higher in the former than in the latter.[58] A study covering close to 80 per cent of the manufacturing industry in Karachi showed profit per unit of capital employed varying in inverse proportion to capital intensity, profit per unit of output highest in enterprises using the least capital and re-investment highest in the small and medium-sized firms.[59] Moreover, comparisons of the relative profitability of capital-intensive and labour-intensive techniques may be to a considerable extent falsified by distortions in factor prices already discussed.

Apart from the likely danger, mentioned earlier, of the new mass-produced articles putting the small-scale entrepreneurs in the traditional sector of business, there may well be other adverse consequences. Thus, even in the case where the capital-intensive product is marketed at a lower price than the traditional product, which would appear superficially to be advantageous, the employment effect may be negative if the price elasticity of demand for the product in question is less than the increase in the productivity of labour achieved by the new technique.

From the above recapitulation of the arguments for and against the use of capital-intensive production techniques it can be seen that a number of complicated considerations are involved and that in any particular case a detailed study would be required of the positive and negative effects, both direct and indirect. However, especially in the case of products which do not need to be of an exactingly high quality, demanding the use of precision instruments, there may be a case for using methods which provide a larger volume of employment.

LABOUR-INTENSIVE AND INTERMEDIATE TECHNOLOGY
The contrast between production techniques appropriate to an industrial country and those more suited to a developing one can be illustrated by a practical example. Consider a typical bakery in a country like Nigeria, a

[57] P. Kilby, *Technology and Organisational Requirements Economies*, ILO, Round-Table Discussion, *loc. cit.*, 1970, pp. 7–8.

[58] *Economic Survey of Asia and the Far East 1965*, United Nations Economic Commission for Asia and the Far East, Bangkok, 1966 Chapter 1.

[59] G. Ranis, *Industrial Efficiency and Economic Growth – a Case Study of Karachi*, Monographs in the economics of developmen , No. 5 The Institute of Development, Karachi, 1961; also by the same author, 'Investment Criteria, Productivity and Economic Development: an Empirical Comment', *Quarterly Journal of Economics*, May 1962, pp. 300–2.

family business employing, say, one or two persons.[60] The output per worker averages eighty loaves per day sold at five cobos[61] per loaf. Capital investment per worker is 200 nairas sterling and wages are one naira per day. Allowing interest on capital at 15 per cent per annum the costs of production per loaf would be composed as follows:

	Cobos
Raw materials	2·83
Labour	1·25
Fuel and power	0·25
Interest and depreciation	0·17
Total cost	4·50
Profit	0·50
Selling price per loaf	5·00

Assuming a *per caput* consumption of half a loaf per day, a town of 100,000 inhabitants would require 50,000 loaves daily, signifying a total of some 625 workers in perhaps 125 bakeries.

Alternatively it would be possible to perform the same operation using the most modern equipment comprising automatic mixers of the flour, the rising of the loaves on overhead moving belts, baking in a turbo-radiant mobile oven, the loaves passing through the cooler and then direct to the machines for slicing, wrapping and packing. A single bakery of this type would produce 50,000 loaves per day. Vans would be required to transport the bread to the retail outlets and now shops would be needed to the extent that existing grocers could not be utilised. The total investment would be around 1,200,000 nairas. Labour productivity would be much higher since altogether only some 60 persons would be employed. However, most of them would have to be more skilled – manager, engineer, office staff, book-keeper, maintenance men, van drivers, and so forth – and would therefore have to be paid more, say 200 cobos per day. More raw materials would be used – packing and wrapping materials, office supplies, petrol for the vans – some of which being imported would require foreign exchange (as also the main equipment). The costs of production would work out somewhat as shown on p. 66. In short the whole operation would be uneconomic.

And even if some of the expenditure items could be reduced sufficiently to make the business break even, there are other factors militating against the suitability of this type of mechanisation. For one thing it might prove difficult to raise the necessary capital; for another 565 bakers would be put out of work and would have to be trained for some other occupations at the public expense; the suppliers of oven bricks, the coal merchants

60 K. Marsden, 'Progressive Technologies for Developing Countries', *International Labour Review*, May 1970, pp. 485 ff.
61 1 naira = 100 cobos = 10 old shillings.

	Cobos
Raw materials	3·33
Labour	0·25
Fuel and power	0·42
Interest and depreciation	1·67
Total cost	5·67
Less	0·67
Selling price per loaf	5·00

and the weavers of wicker baskets would find the demand for their products replaced by a demand for imported inputs; the automated equipment is designed to process refined (imported) white flour, more expensive than the mixtures of wheat and maize flour supplied by local mills; as a result the final product would have a different shape, colour and taste, and might not prove acceptable to the consumers. In our hypothetical case it is clear, therefore that the most up-to-date technology would be inappropriate to the socio-economic circumstances of the country.

None the less, even if the entire package would be out of place perhaps some elements of it might be advantageously adopted. For example, to knead the dough an alternating Viennese mixer could take the place of one man in a bakery of five employees, thus raising their productivity by 25 per cent. Similarly, an oilfired oven would maintain more even temperatures, reduce the fuel bill and cut down the losses in burnt loaves. Modest innovations of this kind by cutting costs could contribute to raising the bakery workers' wages, reducing the selling price of bread and/or increasing the baker's profit. This is an example of intermediate technology adapted to local conditions without causing major disruption to patterns of employment.

For manufacturing industry as a whole the attempt has been made to define intermediate technology in terms of the average capital/manpower ratio. Thus, on the supposition that in traditional production of artisan type the value of equipment is reckoned at $1 per employee and in the modern sector using advanced techniques the ratio is $1,000 per employee, then the term 'intermediate technology' could be applied to processes using between $70 and $100. Clearly, other things being equal, a given volume of investment in intermediate technology provides substantially more employment than in processes of the advanced type.[62]

One of the objections raised against the adoption of intermediate technology is that it restricts a country to producing low-value unsophisticated goods. This is not at all necessarily the case. By way of illustration the

[62] E. F. Schumacher, 'Industrialisation Through Intermediate Technology', *Industrialisation in Developing Countries*, Impressions and Papers of the Cambridge Conference on the Role of Industrialisation in Development, 6–19 September 1964, Cambridge, 1965, p. 95.

case may be cited of an Asian country where the government decided to establish a sewing machine industry to replace imports. A basis on which to build already existed in the shape of a number of workshops engaged in making repair parts for the machines hitherto imported. Taking advantage of the temporary tariff protection accorded by the government, a number of local entrepreneurs began to extend and co-ordinate the activities of these workshops, transforming them into assembly plants. Within a few years these workshops, equipped with nothing more than ordinary lathes and drills, were producing sewing machines at 60 per cent of the price of the imported articles. Although these locally made machines were less sophisticated and accomplished perhaps less precise work than the imported models, they found a ready market, on account of their price, among the many small clothing and shoe-making businesses of the country in which, as a result, productivity increased. When in due course the import duty was removed the local industry was already strong enough to carry on a flourishing export of machines to neighbouring countries.[63]

The use of intermediate technology should also not be regarded as synonymous with the use of archaic or inferior production techniques. Frequently the use of a relatively inexpensive piece of modern equipment can bring great advantages, for instance 'improved ways of making or growing things as a result of a deeper understanding of the chemical, physical and biological properties of products and materials.'[64] Similar benefits can be obtained in cases where the manual and material components of the process can be easily differentiated. The use of a specialised machine for a particular part of a process is often consistent with the employment of much labour in the earlier and later stages of the production chain; it may likewise significantly accelerate the achievement of a project.[65] For example, in the building industry by using a gun to apply cement to a lattice a wall can be built in much shorter time and at lower cost, leaving the remaining construction activities, such as the site preparation and the weaving of the lattices, to manual labour. (The cost of the gun may be between $35,000 and $70,000).

Two situations may be mentioned in which the use of a modern technology would appear justified. One concerns the utilisation of 'machines which replace non-existent human skills, or skills which would demand the use of very expensive educational facilities'. The other is where the use of a modern technology 'may be the only effective means of exploiting a

[63] ILO, *Human Resources for Industrial Development*, *op. cit.*, p. 244.

[64] *Ibid.*, p. 210.

[65] Y. Barel, 'Industrialisation et Artisanat dans les Pays en Voie de Développement', *Genève-Afrique*, **3**, 1, 1964, p. 25) notes that, for instance in Africa, it would be more efficient to manufacture cotton yarn on an industrial scale and distribute it to artisan weavers, thereby increasing the profitability of their work. In Tunisia it would be advisable to transfer the dyeing of textiles from artisan to industrial establishments to achieve a better quality product. There is no question of trying to rob the artisan of his market; it is rather one of organising a rational division of labour in place of the anarchy which often results in the ruin of the artisans without any compensatory acceleration of industrial expansion.

country's physical resources, which would otherwise lie idle and which form the basis of other indigenous industries. An example might include the use of colour charts, penetrometers and triaxial compression testing machines for measuring the proportion of soils and clays, leading among others to the manufacture of improved ceramic products.'[66]

The use of intermediate technology has to be viewed and considered in a proper time perspective. Whilst it is appropriate to a particular stage in the industrialisation of a country it must also prepare for the adoption of more modern and capital-intensive methods later on.[67] In fact it is often a question of time horizon, of shorter- versus longer-term considerations; an option between low-productivity employment now and higher productivity employment at a future date. It is thus a choice of the length an option between low-productivity employment now and higher-productivity employment at a future date. It is thus a choice of the length of the period over which employment is to be maximised.[68]

POLICIES FOR INTERMEDIATE TECHNOLOGY
In addition to action to reduce distortions in factor prices already discussed under (a) above, other practical steps may be taken to encourage the use of appropriate technologies. Because so much of modern manufacturing equipment is designed and built for the circumstances of the industrial countries where the relative prices of inputs are quite different, there is particular need for research and development of equipment suitable for developing countries, as has indeed long since been recognised by the United Nations Advisory Committee on the Application of Science and Technology. Already in 1966 there were in the developing world some 500 institutes working in this and in allied fields relating to the processing of local raw materials and the introduction of new types of machinery.[69] These institutes, as they come to extend their relationships with nascent industries, should have an important role in orienting the choice of equipment.

Interesting results have already been obtained in adapting scale of production to the market limitations of developing countries. At the beginning of the 1960s, for example, a normal steel mill was reckoned to

[66] ILO, *Human resources for industrial development, op. cit.*, p. 211.

[67] K. Marsden, *op. cit.*

[68] See: J. Mouly, 'Note sur les Coefficients de Capital et le Sous-développement', *Economie Appliquée*, No. 3, 1963, p. 459; also N. Kaldor, 'Advanced Technology in a Strategy of Development: The Choice of Technology', *op. cit.*, p. 10. On the other hand J. Fei and G. Ranis consider that there need not be any conflict if the dynamism for innovation is sufficiently strong and if innovations are biased in the direction of absorbing more labour. ('Innovation, Capital Accumulation and Economic Development', *American Economic Review*, **53**, 3, June 1963.)

[69] J. E. Stepanek, *Technologies Appropriate for Industry in the Developing Countries*, Fifth Session of the Advisory Committee on the Application of Science and Technology to Development, Doc. No. STD/5/PCA/IND/1, March 1966. This document gives examples of research carried out in various countries and leading to the introduction of new techniques. See also by the same author: *An Engineer Scares the Developing World*, Alin Lectures, Yale Univ., 1–2 October 1969.

be able to produce around 1 million tons of steel per year at a cost of $45 per ton and with an investment of $32,000 per person employed. But at the United Nations Conference on the Application of Science and Technology to Development in 1963 a proposal was presented for a steelworks producing between 100,000 and 200,000 tons per annum, admittedly at the slightly higher cost of $54 per ton but with an investment of only $5,700 per workers employed.[70] The proposal was subsequently realised in practice at a plant established at El-Fouladh in Tunisia. Similarly, small petroleum refineries have been built with a capacity of between 5,000 and 10,000 barrels per day, whereas previously the minimum capacity for economic viability was considered to be 25,000 barrels.[71] One can also mention 'movable' ammonia plants which can be set up in thirty days and can treat 60 tons per day at a cost of $36 per ton compared with 250 to 300 tons per day and $32 per ton at a conventional plant. More than probably, although the cash cost per unit of output is a little higher in the small plants, the 'social' cost taking all factors into account would be lower.

Often a quite simple and inexpensive innovation can bear extremely fruitful results: resourcefulness applied to traditional inefficiencies, e.g. the old woodworking lathe operated back and forth by hand or the potter's oven that has to be destroyed after each baking. Often it may be advantageous to adopt the industrial countries' techniques of a couple of decades ago: for instance, by using the textile machinery of 1950 vintage instead of the most recent automated models, nearly three times as much labour could be employed per unit output, the investment per worker employed was only one-third as much and yet the unit costs of production were only 12 per cent higher.[72] A wide range of opportunities exists in, for instance, the clothing, leather and woodworking industries,[73] in brickyards, in tile-making and in certain branches of the chemical industry. The Cameroons has established a variety of processing activities in the food industry based on the local raw materials – canned meat and fish, fruits and vegetables canning and jam-making, soluble coffee, flour, pasta and malt – but still has much to do in finding the best intermediate techniques.[74]

Research to this end is also being carried on in developed countries by some of the multi-national corporations and by other groups. One example

[70] United Nations Conference on the Application of Science and Technology to Development, *A Low-cost Integrated Steelworks for Emergent Countries*, Doc. E/CONF./39/D/151, 1963.

[71] 'Choice of Capital Intensity in Industrial Planning', *Industrialisation and Productivity*, Bulletin No. 7, New York, 1964, p. 32; for other examples see: *op. cit.*, Bulletin No. 6, pp. 20–1.

[72] United Nations Economic Commission for Latin America: *Choice of Technologies in the Latin American Textile Industry*, Doc. E/CN. 12/746, January 1966.

[73] On this topic see: G. K. Boon, 'Choice of Industrial Technology: the Case of Woodworking', *Industrialisation and Productivity*, Bulletin No. 3, New York, 1960.

[74] Ph. Hugon, *Analyse du Sous-développement en Afrique Noire: L'Example du Cameroun*, Travaux et recherches de la Faculté de Droit et des Sciences Economiques de Paris, série 'Afrique', No. 3, PUF, Paris, 1968, pp. 286–92.

is that of a large electrical group in the Netherlands which has shown the way by establishing at Utrecht a pilot radio assembly plant for training future managers and technicians to man their overseas factories.[75]

The Group for developing Intermediate Technologies, established in the United Kingdom in 1965, publishes an illustrated guide entitled *Tools for Progress* which lists under thirty-one headings tools and materials suited for use in developing countries; and in other places too the problem is under constant investigation.[76]

This leads on to consideration of the vexed question of second-hand equipment. In the developed countries, because of the pace of technological innovation, it is quite usual for machinery to be discarded long before it is worn out. Such equipment is for the most part less complex than that which replaces it, easier to maintain, utilises more labour and, since it can be obtained cheaply, can be written off relatively rapidly leaving its owner free to turn to later models. With such advantages one might imagine that for developing countries the purchase of second-hand equipment in good condition would represent a very attractive buy.

In fact, however, the wisdom of such purchases is widely questioned. For instance, in Pakistan a number of textile firms imported second-hand machinery in excellent condition, but after a time encountered great difficulty in obtaining replacement parts which were no longer being made in the countries of purchase. Moreover, when these firms came to enlarge their scale of operations they had to buy different models, the previous ones being no longer available; consequently, they had then to provide stores and maintenance for two different sets of equipment – an additional expense.[77] The quality of the products coming from the second-hand machines being of slightly inferior quality proved non-competitive in export markets. It was such considerations which doubtless prompted the Government of Peru to forbid the importation of second-hand textile machinery.[78]

Although there is much to be said in principle for using second-hand equipment where appropriate, each case needs to be studied on its merits. There is always the danger that the machinery may be in bad condition though not apparently so at the time of purchase leading to frequent subsequent breakdowns; also it may be more difficult to raise finance for purchasing second-hand rather than new equipment. Nevertheless, in individual cases there may be advantages which fully justify the choice of the second-hand, as was pointed out by a United Nations expert group.[79]

[75] ILO, *Human Resources for Industrial Development, op. cit.*, p. 211.

[76] See J. E. Stepanek, *op. cit.*, especially Chapters 3–6.

[77] K. Ikram, *The Role of Industry in a Long-term Development Plan – a Case Study of Pakistan*, Papers of the Cambridge Conference on the role of industrialisation in development, 6–19 September 1964, Cambridge Univ. Overseas Committee, 1965, pp. 67 ff.

[78] Cf. C. K. Clague, 'Capital-Labour Substitution in Manufacturing in the Underdeveloped Countries', *Econometrica* (New Haven, Connecticut), 37, 3, July 1969, p. 537.

[79] United Nations Centre for Industrial Development, *Report of Expert Group on Second-Hand Equipment for Developing Countries: 7–22 December 1965*, Doc. 66.II.B.9, New York, 1966.

The price may be extremely attractive: the group cited the case of a Latin American country obtaining a gear-cutting plant which new would have cost $300,000 but which was obtained for $100,000 plus $30,000 freight. It stressed the desirability of purchasing a whole factory rather than partial equipment. It pointed out that second-hand plant frequently has a smaller throughput and may therefore be better adapted to the small market of a developing country, one example being that of paper-making machinery where the more recent Swedish and United States models produced 700 to 1,000 metres per minute compared with 350 to 400 metres a minute from the second-hand machines.[80] Because of the many pitfalls in dealings of this kind it is advisable to consult one or other of the agencies specialising in this business.[81]

Since intermediate technology is generally likely to be more appropriate to the smaller-scale industrial establishments, its adoption will be furthered by governments' policies favouring this sector. Although the main discussion of small-scale and cottage industry is reserved for a later chapter, the aspect of their factor-mix and their choice of technology is treated here and ways of giving them support.[82]

In a number of countries the Government organises various forms of central services for the small and cottage industries, services financed from public funds but in some instances with contributions from the firms concerned and in other instances taking the form of co-operatives. Such services may include the setting up of models for firms' accounts, the introduction of quality standards for the products, the creation of a sales organisation for the home market and for export, the conduct of market research, the bulk purchase of the output for distribution through commercial outlets. One example is the 'Cottage Industry Emporium' in New Delhi which maintains a permanent exhibition through which it sells the artisans' products. Such services, which the artisans could not operate themselves, help to make them competitive in a wide market and thus augments their incomes.

Some governments may of course go further and restrict the large firms from competing directly with crafts and cottage industries, as was provided for in India's Second Development Plan; in this case in the textile industry the home market was largely reserved for the cottage industry output and the export market for the large firms. Delicate policy issues may, however, be involved. It may not be wise to encourage beyond a certain limit types of production where the unit costs are so high as to inhibit consumer demand, nor prudent to restrict excessively the expansion of the modern firms with whom the long-term future of the country lies. It may be preferable to seek out, where possible, products for the small-

[80] United Nations Centre for Industrial Development, *Report of Expert Group on Second-hand Equipment for Developing Countries: 7–22 December 1965, op. cit.*

[81] In the United States the Agency for Industrial Development (AID) publishes a catalogue of equipment suited to conditions in developing countries.

[82] Cf. ILO, *Services for Small-scale Industry*, Studies and Reports, No. 61, Geneva, 1961, pp. 22 ff.

scale sector which are complementary to rather than competitive with the products of large-scale industry.

In this connection the practice of subcontracting has peculiar significance. Subcontracting is already widely utilised for the making and the assembly of parts, e.g. for radio and television sets, for bicycles and for automobiles where the labour of the small firm or the family can be fully and advantageously utilised.[83] The Government of India has prepared a long list of industries in which it considers that some parts of the production process lend themselves to subcontracting.

1 Industrial machinery, including among others:
   (a) textile machinery;
   (b) sugar mill machinery;
   (c) chemical plants;
   (d) building and road construction machinery;
   (e) flour mill machinery;
   (f) oil mill machinery;
   (g) paper-making plants and machinery;
2 Agricultural and earth-moving machinery.
3 Machine tools.
4 Industrial, scientific and mechanical instruments.
5 Locomotives, rolling dock, ships and aircraft.
6 Bicycles.
7 Boilers and steam-generating plants.
8 Steam engines, turbines and internal combustion engines.
9 Automobiles.
10 Commercial office and household equipment.
11 Electrical machinery, equipment and appliances.
12 Telecommunication equipment.
13 Industrial instruments (electrical).
14 Radios and electronic equipment.
15 Air-conditioners and cold-storage equipment, including refrigerators.
16 Mineral oil and petroleum industries.

Source: UNIDO, OECD, Development Centre, *Subcontracting – Its Role in Industrial Development*, Expert Group Meeting on the Role and Promotion of Subcontracting in Industrial Development, Doc. ID/WG.41/2, Paris, 6–11 October 1969, p. 27.

[83] See S. Watanabe, 'Subcontracting, Industrialisation and Employment Creation', *International Labour Review*, July–August 1971; and same author, 'International Subcontracting, Employment and Skill Promotion', *ibid.*, May, 1972.
    At the end of 1968 the automobile industry of Argentina, for example comprised ten large assembly plants obtaining their parts from some 2,000 small and medium-sized firms. (M. Lenoble, *Subcontracting in the Argentina Car Industry*, Expert group meeting on the role and promotion of subcontracting in industrial development, Doc. ID/WG.41/BP.1, Paris, 6–11 October 1969, p. 2.)
    See also, Toyoku Ando, 'Inter-relations between Large and Small Industrial Enterprises in Japan', *Industrialisation and Productivity*, Bulletin No. 2, New York, 1959 and 'The Dual Nature of Industrial Development in Japan', *op. cit.*, Bulletin No. 8, New York, 1964.

Subcontracting can be encouraged in various ways. In Japan for example, there exists since 1965 a whole chain of Institutes for the Promotion of Subcontracting whose task is to distribute orders equitably, ensuring a steady level of work for the small subcontractors, supporting and strengthening them in their negotiations, helping them to adapt to changes in production techniques, providing to the large firms information regarding subcontracting opportunities, legal protection of subcontractors in respect to delays in payment, cancellation of orders, changes in prices and forced sales of subcontractors' materials. In the United States subcontracting is of course widespread: in 1968 two-thirds of all military contracts were passed on to subcontractors. France and other industrial countries have subcontracting exchanges centralising offers and demands and an information service supported by the Government. Beginnings along similar lines are being made in certain developing countries, for example in Chile.

An important extension to the principle of subcontracting has been adopted in a number of Asian and Latin American countries. When a government grants permission to a foreign firm to set up, say, an automobile assembly plant the agreement will include the provision that a certain percentage of the components shall be manufactured in the country of assembly, usually by means of subcontract arrangements; more than this, such agreements frequently specify that either yearly or every two or three years the percentage of locally manufactured parts shall rise by a stated amount. This system has two advantages. First, it enables the country concerned to acquire gradually a preponderant share in the operation, though that is a topic different from those under discussion; second, it allows the participation of what are often quite small firms in what would otherwise tend to be a large-scale, capital-intensive enterprise.

Summing up the options regarding choice of industrial technology, a schematic classification of projects into four categories has been made which might be helpful as a guide to policy:

Category A Projects: These are projects in which labour-intensive capital-saving technology, with existing methods and prices, yields money economies in production. In all such projects there is a clear case for choosing labour-intensive technology; the selection of capital-intensive technology for non-economic reasons, such as prestige, would involve an evident misuse of resources.

Category B Projects: These are projects in which labour-intensive techniques, when used carelessly or in traditional fashion or without adequate supervision, involve rather higher money costs than more capital-intensive techniques would do, but in which there are opportunities (through better management, work study, better design of simple tools, etc.) to adapt labour-intensive techniques to produce as cheaply as, or more cheaply than, with more capital-intensive techniques. There is a clear case for doing all that can be done at reasonable cost to transfer category B projects into category A.

73

Category C Projects: These are projects in which, even when all feasible measures to improve the efficiency of labour-intensive techniques have been taken, such techniques still involve higher money costs of production than would more capital-intensive methods, but do not involve higher real costs (i.e. they would be cheaper if shadow prices accurately reflecting real costs could be used instead of market prices).

Category D Projects: The difference between these and category C projects is that the cost differential in favour of advanced technology is greater than the cost distortion produced by the use of market prices instead of shadow prices. There is no case on economic grounds for using anything but capital-intensive technology in category D projects. . . .'

From this the conclusion is drawn that 'a country that chose to confine highly capital-intensive technology to category D projects might thereby save much capital, which could be used to provide more jobs and/or to raise the productivity of labour in category A, B and C projects, resulting in a more even spread of capital throughout the economy and a progressive adaptation of technology to growing markets, knowledge, skill and availability of capital.'[84]

Selection of Products for Manufacture

The number of jobs in industry can be increased by encouraging the selection not only of labour-intensive technology but also of labour-intensive products. Obviously some commodities lend themselves more than others to labour-intensive techniques of production, and various studies have been made which classify branches of industry according to this criterion.[85] It would be possible to tax capital-intensive commodities or subsidised labour-intensive ones, or both, or special government services to industry – counselling, credit, marketing, training – could be confined to or provided mainly in connection with industries producing labour-intensive products.

It is, however, no good producing labour-intensive commodities that cannot be sold. A country's product-mix has to correspond to the structure of demand, including demand from export markets. If the proposition concerns intermediate goods or semi-manufactured goods then, in the absence of reliable input–output matrices which hardly exist as yet in

---

84 ILO, *Human Resources for Industrial Development, op. cit.,* pp. 205–7.

85 See, for example, the tabulation of the 150 most labour-intensive industries in the United States in M. D. Bryce, *Policies and Methods for Industrial Development*, McGraw-Hill, New York, 1965, Appendix I, pp. 275–9. The five industries heading the table were: wooden box-making, pottery, chinaware, seamless hosiery and bookbinding. Tinbergen has classified countries into seven groups according to their physical and human resources per head, and likewise activities into seven categories thus to optimise the international division of labour. This is essentially a theoretical work based on 'heroic hypotheses' and has value more for methodology than for policy orientation. (J. Tinbergen, *On the International Division of Labour*, FSI, Stockholm, 1970, pp. 16–17.)

developing countries, the extent of the market can best be ascertained by contacting potential customers locally and in neighbouring countries. In the case of consumption goods some historical evidence may exist on the size of the local and neighbouring markets, but most would-be entrepreneurs tend to assume, whatever the evidence, that the market is bound to expand rapidly. Unfortunately, they are often ill-informed as to the plans of other entrepreneurs in the same field which may result in the creation of excess capacity in a particular product line. Consultations within the framework of customs, unions or common markets may help to avoid such occurrences.[86] In addition to demand surveys the entrepreneurs will need to assure themselves as far as they can in advance that their products will be cost-competitive in the markets where they sell.

Conclusion

This review of the opportunities for stimulating employment in manufacturing industry in the developing countries has brought out clearly the scope which exists by using existing plant capacity more fully, especially through shift working and by choosing labour-intensive production techniques where choice is practicable. In either of these ways, for a given volume of investment, the amount of employment can be increased, but it has to be recognised that the devising of practical measures to orient the behaviour of employers in these directions is not easy.

The review has also shown that, while ill-conceived measures of industrial employment promotion (e.g. subsidising people to produce articles expensively in cottages that could be produced cheaply in factories) may certainly be harmful to growth, there are numerous opportunities in the industrial field for measures which promote both growth and employment. This would be true of all measures having the effect of minimising unit costs in real terms, and also of all measures that seek to correct, or compensate for, price distortions. Each developing country has in its local situation some factors which are unique and therefore in each case a package of measures would need to be put together in the light of national circumstances.

However, over and above all these considerations the long-run need in developing countries must be for additional employment in the manufacturing sector. In all of them the proportion of the adult population engaged in agriculture is too high and must ultimately be reduced; in most of them the proportion at present engaged in the service industries, although often in the wrong service industries, is already as high as in the most advanced industrial countries. It is the manufacturing sector which, on any international comparison, is currently offering the least employment and where the overwhelming responsibility for expansion lies.

[86] For Latin America see: *El Proceso de Industrialización en América Latina*, United Nations, New York, 1965, pp. 152 ff.

Chapter 4

Services

Because of the lack of employment opportunities in manufacturing industry many people attempt to obtain some income from one or other of the many activities in the services sector. Among the agricultural population those with very low incomes and who are under-employed in many cases work on a part-time basis in local trading or local transport from which they derive some supplementary income. At the other end of the scale are those who, having completed a secondary education, are determined to obtain employment in government administration and who are prepared to remain unemployed until such opportunity materialises or, in any case, for a long time. In between are those who have migrated from rural areas to the cities, who live in the shanty towns and who seek out and accept any sort of casual job – shoe-shining, selling of lottery tickets, window cleaning – in order to have enough to eat. It is often surprising how quickly the new arrivals find themselves work. Surveys have been made which indicate that, for instance in Buenos Aires, more than half the newcomers obtained work within fifteen days; in six cities in Brazil 85 per cent found employment in less than one month, only 7 per cent remaining without work after three months. In Santiago (Chile) 81 per cent were absorbed within three months of arrival. Most of these immigrants were unskilled workers, the proportions being 52 per cent in Argentina, 61 per cent in Chile and between one and two thirds (according to city) in Brazil.[1] The great bulk of the employment which they obtained was in the services sector.

The Nature and Growth of Tertiary Employment

In Latin America between 1950 and 1970 the volume of employment in the services sector increased at an annual (compound) rate of 4·0 per cent compared with a rate of 1·4 per cent in agriculture and 2·7 per cent in industry. During the same period the proportion of the labour force which was occupied in the services sector grew from 25·0 to 33·3 per cent.[2]

[1] Cf. Milton Santos: 'Le Rôle du Tertiaire Primitif dans les Villes du Tiers Monde', *Civilisations* (Brussels), 1968, No. 2.

[2] See ILO, 9th Conference of American States Members of the ILO, Caracas, April 1970: *Review of Progress in the Implementation of the Ottawa Plan*, Geneva, 1970. The above percentages are derived from Table 2, p. 46, of this document combining item B.1 (*d*) Primary Services with item (2) Services. See also 'The Structure of Manpower in Latin America: Evolution During the Last Few Decades and Long-term Prospects', Slawinski, *Problems of Human Resources Planning in Latin America*, OECD, Paris, 1967, pp. 124–37.

In the absence of global figures for Asia and Africa table 4.1 gives data from selected countries.

The percentages represented by the tertiary sector were increasing in all these countries with the single exception of India; and even in India, although the *proportion* fell, the absolute numbers in this sector rose from 19,113,000 persons in 1951 to 30,245,000 persons in 1961 representing an increase of 58 per cent of a cumulative annual rate of 4·5 per cent.

On the basis of this evidence the services sector appears by far the most dynamic in the creation of new employment in the developing countries, and the question arises whether this rhythm of expansion can be expected

Table 4.1   *Changes in the Proportion of Employment in the Tertiary Sector in Selected Countries of Africa and Asia (as per cent of the active population)**

	Tunisia	(1956)	(1966)
		22·5	41·9
Africa	Mauritius	(1952)	(1962)
		32·5	36·8
	UAR	(1947)	(1960)
		24·3	32·1
	Ceylon	(1953)	(1963)
		34·6	37·7
	India	(1951)	(1961)
		18·8	16·0
Asia	Indonesia	(1961)	(1965)
		19·2	23·4
	Philippines	(1960)	(1965)
		20·4	25·7

Sources: ILO Yearbook of Labour Statistics, 1963, Table 4A, and ibid., 1970, Table 2A.

*The data in this table include in the tertiary sector the following occupations: (5) electricity, gas, water and sanitary services; (6) commerce, banking, insurance and real estate; (7) transport, warehousing and telecommunications; (8) services; (9) undesignated activities. The figures differ slightly from those quoted in Chapter 2 of this report owing to small differences in the definitions.

to continue. Here a number of contradictory influences are at work. On the one hand the process of urbanisation in itself stimulates the services sector through the coming into existence of the host of new activities which are needed for the conduct of city life and through the opportunity for a greater division and specialisation of labour than is possible in rural areas.[3] Since in the developing countries the trek to the towns seems certain to continue, even if the growth of the over-large cities can be moderated, a further growth of the sector's employment will be stimulated. A different influence derives from the distribution of income. It is obvious

[3] V. R. Fuchs, *The Service Economy*, NEBR, New York, 1968. See especially the summary of the author's conclusions on p. 3.

that very rich people devote a higher proportion of their consumption expenditure to services than do very poor people; having satisfied their needs in respect to food and material goods, they orient their expenditure towards luxuries – recreation, dining in restaurants, foreign travel and so forth – which contain a large service element.[4] Therefore if future increases in prosperity in the developing countries were to accrue mainly to the upper income groups, this would favour a further expansion of the tertiary sector, whereas if economic growth were accompanied by any significant income redistribution in favour of the lower income groups the effect would be the opposite in the short run though in the much longer run, when these people in turn become really prosperous, their demand for services will expand. What redistribution does immediately is to stimulate a major increase in demand for food and manufactured consumer goods and a smaller increase in demand for services.

A quite different factor generating demand for services is the expansion of public programmes in health, education and social welfare. In contrast to branches whose utility may be questionable and where precarious, unskilled self-employment generally offers nothing better than a *pis-aller*, this branch of the services sector provides employment to professionals, auxiliaries and supporting personnel for tasks which have high development priority.

Indeed, it is important to recall the immense diversity of occupations which are grouped under the portmanteau word 'services'. Various authors have suggested classifying them into categories, for example the tripartite grouping of Katouzian:[5]

(i) New Services which have emerged as a result of modern technology and the mass consumption society. These are expanding rapidly in the advanced countries and are just beginning to expand in the developing ones.

(ii) Old services, being those which existed in the absence of the hardware of modern civilisation, which were associated with a wealthy elite at the top and illiterate masses below. These are on their way out.

(iii) Complementary services which accompany the growth of industry, of cities, of government, of planning. These are expanding rapidly in all countries.

As the evidence cited at the beginning of this chapter indicates, the expansion of the new and complementary services greatly outweighs the decline in the old services, even in the poorest developing countries.

The expansion of demand for services is not necessarily accompanied

[4] This was first noted by Engel in the mid-nineteenth century and later, in the nineteen-thirties, was elaborated by A. G. B. Fisher, *The Clash of Progress and Security*, Macmillan, 1935, and by Colin Clark, *The Conditions of Economic Progress*, Macmillan, 1940.

[5] M. A. Katouzian, 'The Development of the Service Sector', *Oxford Economic Papers*, November 1970. See also A. S. Bhalla, 'The Role of Services in Employment Expansion', *International Labour Review*, May 1970.

by an equi-proportional expansion in the volume of employment. What happens in any particular type of service will depend upon the evolution of the productivity of labour. If this productivity were in fact rising more rapidly than the demand for the service the volume of employment would of course fall; but in most areas of the tertiary sector labour productivity appears to be increasing rather slowly which partially explains the recorded rapid growth in employment. Among the reasons for slow growth of productivity may be mentioned the rather sharp reduction in average hours of work, the very modest qualitative improvement in the labour in this sector, the almost negligible increase in the amount of capital invested per worker employed and the general absence of startling technological innovations,[6] though in respect to this last there are notable exceptions such as the introduction of computers in banking and insurance and of self-service and supermarkets in retail distribution.

For the discussion which follows the various services will be divided into two broad groups: first those for which demand is in general declining, i.e. the old services, and second those for which demand is increasing and can be expected to continue to increase, comprising the new and the complementary services. This approximates closely to Prebisch's distinction between 'labour expelling activities' and 'labour absorbing activities' in the tertiary sector.[7]

The Old Services

Characteristically in this category of activity the supply of labour constantly exceeds the demand. In the developing countries it consists of that mass of persons who live precariously at the margin of existence unable to obtain any better source of income. Their activities are of two kinds: traditional trading and personal services.

Traditional trading extends from the village storekeeper and the itinerant peddler upward through layer upon layer of middlemen sharing the risk and sharing the mark-up.[8] The occupation is overmanned in most countries and its labour productivity is low. Evidence moreover suggests that this productivity is at best stationary and in some instances is declining. Thus in Latin America commercial and financial services accounted for 13·1 per cent of the increase in the labour force in the nineteen-fifties and for 14·1 per cent in the nineteen-sixties, notably more than the increase in the contribution of this category to gross domestic product; and since the group included the 'modern' activities of banking, insurance, etc., where labour productivity has certainly been increasing it would seem likely that productivity in the traditional commercial activities fell.[9] In

---

6 Cf. V. R. Fuchs, *op. cit.*

7 R. Prebisch, *Change and Development: Latin America's Great Task*, Report submitted to the Inter-American Development Bank, Washington D.C., July 1970, p. 90.

8 W. R. Armstrong and T. G. McGee, 'Revolutionary Change and the Third World City: a Theory of Urban Involution', *Civilisations*, Brussels, July–September 1968.

9 ILO, *Review of Progress in the Implementation of the Ottawa Plan, loc. cit.*; see also ECLA, *The Manpower Structure in Latin America*, report to the same conference.

Burma in 1953 some 38 per cent of the urban labour force was engaged in wholesale and retail distribution; and of these 69 per cent of the men and 92 per cent of the females were independent workers or unpaid family assistants of low productivity. In India the labour productivity in commerce is notoriously low compared to the national average, though the gap is less in cities than in rural areas.[10]

An occupation having these characteristics hardly offers much scope for generating new employment. On the contrary its existing volume of employment is more and more menaced by current developments. The establishment of chain stores and supermarkets is already putting many small shopkeepers out of business, as reported from several African and Latin American countries. To quote the ILO's inter-agency team in Colombia:

'The displacement of a large number and variety of small retail shops by a single supermarket is a case in point in the distribution sector. With population growing at a very high rate in the principal cities, and the number of motor cars increasing, the private profitability of supermarkets is bound to rise. It must be remembered, however, that the social *returns* of such investments would be very low, since they would drive out of work a large number of retailers who would not easily find alternative employment opportunities.[11]

At an earlier stage in the evolution of distribution, however, its costs can be reduced by setting up retail shops in villages where none previously existed; for instance, the Plan of the Central African Republic provides for the establishment of 200 such village shops, the chief difficulty experienced being the training of shopkeepers.[12]

The other segment of old services consists of personal services including domestic service, car-washing, shoe-shining, latrine-cleaning. In those countries or parts of countries where standards of living and levels of education are rising fewer people are willing to engage in these occupations; instead they move if possible to the more modern types of service such as dry cleaning, hair-dressing, taxi-driving. Generally speaking the old services act the role of a sponge which still absorbs those who are unable to find work elsewhere. These services do not themselves make much positive contribution to development, indeed they merely spread a given volume of income among an excessive number of people; at the

[10] S. K. Metha, 'A Comparative Analysis of the Industrial Structure of the Urban Labour Force of Burma and the United States', *Economic Development and Cultural Change*, 9, 2, January 1961, p. 178. J. N. Sinha, 'Employment in Trade – the India Experience', *The Indian Economic Journal* (Bombay), 16, 1, July–September 1968, pp. 53–67.
[11] For Africa see ILO, *The World Employment Programme*, 1971, *op. cit.*, p. 43. For Colombia: *the Colombia Report, op. cit.* para. 532, p. 172.
[12] République centroafricaine, *Plan de Développement Economique et Social 1967–70*, p. 125.

same time if they are ousted prematurely by modern services causing widespread unemployment this may create social tensions which spill over into emigration (the cases of Jamaica and Puerto Rico) or into revolution (the case of Cuba).[13] In the longer-term perspective as economic growth accelerates and other employment opportunities multiply, these traditional services will gradually wither away, as has been the experience in Japan.[14] Meanwhile, despite the drawbacks mentioned, these services do perform the role of helping newcomers to the city to accustom themselves to work disciplines and of fostering adaptability and mobility.[15]

The Modern and Complementary Services

All the services in these categories are expanding as part of the process of the modernisation of traditional society. Some, but not all of them, can find room for unskilled and semi-skilled workers; some, but not all, require only modest investment capital per unit of employment.

PUBLIC ADMINISTRATION

The increasing complexity of national economies, the planning of the development process, the organisation of social services and the multiplication of foreign commercial and political contacts all give rise to a rapid growth of employment in public administration which may already in some instances have gone too far. For example, in African countries south of the Sahara the share of government employment in total non-agricultural employment varies between 37·6 and 52·1 per cent (Ghana 46·5 per cent, Kenya 41·4 per cent, Nigeria 37·6 per cent, Tanzania 48·9 per cent, Uganda 52·1 per cent).[16] In Somalia the central government and local authorities together employ 66 per cent of all persons working in enterprises of five persons or more.[17] Moreover, in a number of developing countries it is usual for government servants to practice other professions, indicating that they are either under-employed or underpaid or both.[18] In Latin America, however, the administrations appear to be less overmanned and are expanding at about the same annual rate (5 per cent) as total employment.[19]

13 Cf. W. R. Armstrong and T. G. McGee, op. cit.

14 See G. C. Allen, A Short History of Modern Japan, Allen & Unwin, London, 1962, p. 125; and T. Watanabe, 'Economic Aspects of Dualism in the Industrial Development of Japan', Economic Development and Cultural Change, April 1965, 13, 3. See also: A. S. Bhalla, 'The Role of Services in Employment Expansion', International Labour Review, loc. cit.

15 Cf. Milton Santos, op. cit.

16 Cited by C. R. Frank Jr., 'Urban Unemployment and Economic Growth in Africa', Oxford Economic Papers, 20, 2, July 1968, p. 255. The data refer variously to years between 1961 and 1964.

17 Dr S. B. L. Nigam, The Manpower Situation in Somalia, Somali Republic, Mogadiscio, 1965, p. 33.

18 E. D. Hawkins, 'Job Inflation in Indonesia', Asian Survey, VI, 5, May 1966.

19 ECLA, op. cit., p. 200. But the figures do not embrace the entire public sector, only the administration, justice, police and armed forces.

In many cases the plethora of civil servants has been brought about as a result of deliberate public policy, to ease the unemployment situation. Thus in 1964 the Government of Kenya under a tripartite agreement with the employers and the trade unions expanded the public service by 15 per cent, simultaneously a 10 per cent increase being envisaged for the private sector. The results were disappointing. The new employment prospects stimulated the exodus from rural areas thus creating more urban unemployment than before.[20] Difficulties were likewise encountered in the U.A.R. when in 1962 the Government gave an undertaking to employ all university graduates who presented themselves each year.

Many opportunities exist for setting the additional staff to useful work. For instance, with only a modest amount of preliminary training many of these people could be assigned to rural areas (where staff is grievously short) as para-medical aides, assistant extension workers and school assistants; others could be employed in surveys to collect statistical data the lack of which so seriously hampers economic planning; others could be trained as club managers and leaders of community development programmes.

The policies of governments with respect to the levels of wages and salaries in the public sector and their effects on the quantity and quality of employment have given rise to much discussion and many divergencies of opinion. There are really two separate issues here. The first concerns the general level of remuneration in government service compared to simllar work in the private sector. Although the situation varies from country to country it would appear that in most developing countries public service workers, especially in the administrative grades, are less well paid than their private sector counterparts, for the simple aforementioned reason that governments try to create as much employment as possible with the funds at their disposal. This partly explains why, in Latin American countries for instance, many senior civil servants also teach in universities. The most desirable course is not easily found. On the one hand governments which habitually pay less than market rates will collect a staff less competent than is needed to accomplish the difficult administrative tasks which arise daily in developing countries; but on the other hand the public will not readily approve glaring differences between the living standards of officials (and the spotlight is always more on public than on private sector officials) and those of ordinary people. This leads to consideration of the second issue, namely the *range* of salary between the highest and the lowest paid employees. Again this range may be no greater than, if as great as, in the private sector, but it is more noticed and perhaps more resented. A few years ago, for example, it was calculated in Nigeria that a cut of 10 per cent in the salaries of the highest paid civil servants would

[20] Cf. John R. Harris and Michael P. Todaro, 'Urban Unemployment in East Africa: an Economic Analysis of Policy Alternatives', *Institute for Development Studies*, Univ. College, Nairobi, Discussion Paper No. 71, September 1968; see also F. H. Harbison, *A System Analysis Approach to Human Resources Development Planning*, Nigeria, Princeton, 1967, Studies in labour and industrialisation, reprint No. 39 (offprint from *South Atlantic Quarterly*, **66**, 3, Summer 1967).

permit the employment of unskilled government workers to be increased by 30 per cent.[21] In rather few countries, notably Ghana and Tanzania, attempts have been made to reduce salaries at the top. In Tanzania in 1966 when wage and salary increases were threatening severe inflation the President set an example by reducing his own salary 20 per cent and the salaries of other government officials according to grade by 20 per cent (ministers) down to 3 per cent. The practice of governments often influences the salary scales and thus indirectly the employment opportunities in the private sector.

Of course in many developing countries any lack of quality in the civil service that may exist may be due more to lack of training and experience than to insufficiently attractive salaries. Especially in countries recently achieving independence which have replaced expatriates in their administrations by local recruits, there has not yet been time to organise the training required at the various levels.[22] This deficiency underscores the importance of including in national planning exercises some manpower targets for the various professions and of making provision for training facilities to match those targets.

COMMERCE AND FINANCE

Note merely is this a category of employment which is expanding rapidly but it is also an area in which modern office methods including mechanisation have made great advances in developed countries leading to an export of the same advanced technology to developing ones. The introduction into the latter of computers, for example, has a mixed record. Many are the instances of the purchase of machines far too large for the work available for them in the foreseeable future; many the stories of breakdowns and long delays over repairs; and all this aside from the unemployment-generating consequences.[23] Yet there are also cases where the adoption of advanced technology including computers has not only made services more efficient, thereby underpinning future industrial expansion, but has also actually increased the volume of employment. Thus the Banco do Brazil SA, the largest bank in Latin America, not merely retained all its personnel while transferring its operations to computers, but began to take on additional staff because the mechanisation and improvement of the quality of its services facilitated extensions into new fields of activity resulted in a need to open a large number of new branches.[24]

[21] C. R. Frank Jr., *op. cit.* p. 263, who cited the 1959 *Nigeria Report on the Earnings and Employment Enquiry*, according to which 11·7 per cent of the staff received 41·5 per cent of the salaries while at the lower end of the scale 36·6 per cent of the workers received only 13·9 per cent.

[22] See S. B. L. Nigam and G. E. Eaton, *Utilisation of Manpower in the Public Service in Somalia*, Somali Republic, Mogadiscio, July 1964.

[23] *The Colombia Report, op. cit.*, p. 173.

[24] ILO, *Advanced Technology in Brazil: a Case Study*, Celso Albano Costa, Doc. RT/AUT/1970/6, Round Table Discussion on the Manpower Problems associated with the Introduction of Automation and Advanced Technology in Developing Countries, 1–3 July 1970. See also, ILO: *The World Employment Programme*, 1971, *op. cit.*, p. 43.

There is here a delicate choice for the planners and policy-makers. Not all developing countries are at the same stage of economic evolution. There may be some among the larger countries where the business sector is sufficiently developed and widespread to justify considerable mechanisation of office work, while in others business is for the time being still conducted on a relatively modest scale and it would be in the national interest for governments to discourage the importation of these technologies. This would be especially true in the many countries where unemployment is high among secondary school leavers.

TRANSPORT AND COMMUNICATIONS

In the course of the transition from a subsistence to a market economy the transport and communications sector undergoes a major transformation from a largely manual operation characterised by bicycles, rickshaws, bullock carts and the humping of loads on dock-workers' backs to one which uses cranes, fork-lift trucks, lorries and buses. Although the labour-intensity of each individual operation has diminished, the sector as a whole has been expanding so rapidly that its total volume of employment has increased, as is illustrated in the data from selected countries contained in table 4.2. The further expansion of employment in this

Table 4.2 *Recent Changes in Employment in Transport, Storage and Communications: Selected Countries*

Country	Number of persons employed		Percentage increase
	1960	1969	
Gabon	3,000	3,800	26·7
Israel	43,500	72,600	66·9
Philippines	271,000	384,000	41·7
Puerto Rico	40,000	50,000	25·00
U.A.R.	218,600	324,500 (1967)	48·4

Source: Adapted from ILO, *Yearbook of Labour Statistics*, ILO, Geneva, 1971, Table 3.

group of services depends on the extent to which new investment programmes are initiated partly by private enterprise but mainly by governments. In some countries such activities as road building and docks modernisation were already pursued with energy many years ago, but in others, notably in Africa and to a lesser extent in Asia, so little has been done that the lack of facilities constitutes a serious obstacle to industrialisation.[25]

[25] United Nations, *Development Prospects and Planning for the Coming Decade, with Special Reference to Africa*. Report on the 4th inter-regional seminar on development planning, Accra, Ghana, 4–7 December 1968, Doc. ST/TAO/SER.C./116, New York, 1970.

Furthermore, a wise planning of road and rail networks may lead to the development of profitable trade exchanges with neighbouring countries, though here some inter-governmental co-ordination of programmes would be required. Thus, the four-year (1961–4) development plan of Senegal recognises the relevance of such coordination to the future of employment on the railways: 'the volume of railway employment will depend on the solutions reached with respect to railway connections with the solutions reached with respect to railway connections with the Republic of Mali'.[26] Examples of bilateral agreements between governments regarding their transport policies are those between Cameroon and the Central African Republic and between Tanzania and Zambia.[27] One of the most serious limiting factors continues to be the inadequate financial resources of governments, a topic which will be further discussed in the chapter devoted to public works programmes.

The volume of employment on railways, with few significant exceptions, is declining: thus between 1960 and 1964 it fell by 22·4 per cent in Algeria, 6·9 per cent in Greece, 15·8 per cent in Iran and 9·1 per cent in Spain.[28] This occurred partly because railway traffic has been increasing less rapidly than road traffic – in some countries the former has actually declined – and partly because various technical innovations including dieselisation and electrification have reduced the amount of manpower needed in railway operating. In Argentina it was primarily dieselisation which created labour redundancy on the railways and induced the Transport Planning Group to recommend a cut of between 30–40 per cent in railway staff. However, most governments and railway boards, being anxious to maintain security of employment, have contrived to avoid outright dismissals either by banning new recruiting or by arranging early retirement or by retraining for other types of transport work.

Road transport by contrast is expanding everywhere. A report on Paraguay by the International Bank for Reconstruction and Development recommended that the road network should form the basis of future transport policy. In Peru the National Planning Institute advised devoting 80 per cent of all transport investment to the road system, and this pattern of investment is similar in many other countries. What presents a difficulty is the very large number of small one-man firms engaged in the transport business, firms operating just one lorry or one bus. Many of these operators know little of the maintenance of vehicles and nothing of book-keeping; many are too weak to obtain credit for the renewal of their equipment; many, as in Gabon, are firms which undertake transport only as a side-line.[29] In the Central African Republic a state of near-anarchy developed

26 République du Sénégal, Ministère du Plan et du Développement, *Plan Quadriennal de Développement 1961–64*, Dakar, 1961, p. 40.
27 ILO, Inland Transport Committee, General Report: *Recent Events and Developments in Inland Transport*,1 966, pp. 41–2.
28 *Ibid.*, p. 4.
29 *Résumé du Plan de Développement Economique et Social du Gabon 1966–70*, Monaco, 1967, p. 101.

on the roads, the small operators driving down the freight rates by inter-necine competition to such uneconomic levels that the larger operators retired from the market.[30] Action was needed and the Development Plan of this country provided for the establishment of an office for licensing carriers and co-ordinating their activities.

Elsewhere the creation of co-operatives of small transport enterprises has been attempted. For example, in Tanzania in 1962 the relevant statute was amended so as to give the licensing authority power to grant licences to co-operatives of carriers.[31] In India there are examples of small transport enterprises organised into groups which provide common services in-cluding vehicle repair, training of mechanics and legal assistance.

In telecommunications, as is well known, the developed countries now possess extremely sophisticated, and by the same token expensive, equip-ment; but it does not follow that these systems are necessary to all develop-ing countries at the present stage of their evolution. In most cases the traditional system of communication by wire will be more appropriate except perhaps in certain regions (e.g. large lakes or marshes) which are difficult to traverse with conventional equipment. Similarly, governments should make careful in-depth studies before deciding whether or not to automate their telephone systems. Manual exchanges employ a large number of persons for the retraining of whom, if they are thrown out of work, the country probably does not yet possess facilities.

TEACHING

Education is a sector in which the governments of almost all developing countries have set ambitious targets. The conference of African States on the development of education (Addis Ababa, 1961) determined that by 1980 primary education should cover 100 per cent of that age group. In Latin America the Alliance for Progress not only aims to remove illiteracy among adults but also during the nineteen-seventies to provide six years of schooling to every child.[32] In Asia although the number of schools and the enrolment of children is rising rapidly much still remains to be done. Out of the 28 countries comprising this region there were 15 where in 1965 the primary school attendance ratio was below 50 per cent and in only one country in the region did it exceed 70 per cent.[33]

The positive influences of education on employment are three-fold. First, the provision of secondary and university education retards the arrival of young persons on the labour market. Second, the expansion of

[30] Central African Republic, *Plan du Développement Economique et Social 1967–70*, Paris, 1968, p. 13. Following the accumulation in francophone West Africa during the years 1952 to 1958 of an excessive stock of transport equipment, there has recently been a reduction in the number of vehicles. See, Samir Amin, *Le Développement du Capitalisme en Côte-d'Ivoire*, Editions de Minuit, Paris, 1967, p. 135.

[31] *Modern Transport*, London, 14 March 1964, p. 22.

[32] United Nations, *World Economic Survey* 1969, New York 1970, Doc. E/4841/Add.1, pp. 100 and 109.

[33] United Nations, *op. cit.*, Table II–23.

education at all levels creates a demand for teachers and auxiliary staff associated with running schools and colleges. Employment of nationals may not, however, expand as much as the demand for teachers. Most developing countries face an acute shortage of teachers, despite their efforts at establishing training colleges, so much so that some have large recourse to foreigners. In Ethiopia a recent survey showed that 95 per cent of the teachers were foreign, in Gabon 90 per cent, in the Democratic Republic of Congo 80 per cent.[34] In Latin America in the mid nineteen-sixties it was estimated that 115,000 out of 250,000 teachers did not have the necessary qualifications, and in secondary education the qualifications deficiency was as high as 70 per cent.[35] This was one of the reasons why the Alliance for Progress at its Punta del Este Conference deferred its targets for educational coverage from the nineteen-sixties to the nineteen-seventies.

Third, the expansion of education may contribute to the overcoming of skill shortages and of the lack of professional workers needed jointly with unskilled or low-skilled workers if these are to be provided with productive jobs.

A major obstacle to the establishment of more schools and the employment of more teachers is finance. This relates partly to the endemic insufficiency of the financial resources of the developing countries' governments and partly to the fact that whereas in developed countries the age group five to nineteen represents 20–25 per cent of the total population, in developing ones it represents 33–37 per cent;[36] also the gap between a teacher's average salary and average national income per head is much greater than in developed countries. In fact, governments make noteworthy efforts. In African countries, according to estimates of the Economic Commission for Africa, governments devote between one-quarter and one-third of their budgets to education. In Nigeria the cost of maintaining the five universities takes up one-quarter of the Government's budget. It is argued in some quarters that such outlays could be used more profitably for other purposes and that under present circumstances it might be cheaper to send students to study in Europe,[37] though this entails the risk of their remaining permanently abroad, the risk of a brain drain. One way of economising the costs of higher education is for a group of neighbouring countries to pool their university facilities, each providing a faculty in a different subject field, as has been attempted between the Cameroons and the other French-speaking countries of Equatorial Africa. Whatever the solution the present bottleneck

[34] Economic Commission for Africa, *A Survey of Economic Conditions in Africa 1960–4*, United Nations, Doc. E/CN.14/401, New York, 1968, p. 229.

[35] ILO, Eighth Conference of American States Members of the ILO, Ottawa, September 1966, *Manpower Planning and Employment Policy in Economic Development*, Geneva, 1966.

[36] Gur Ofer, *The Service Industries in a Developing Economy: Israel as a Case Study*, Praeger, New York, 1967, p. 60.

[37] F. H. Harbison, *op. cit.*, pp. 352–6; see also W. A. Lewis, *Development Planning*, *op. cit.*, p. 105.

consists in the supply of teacher training facilities, not in the demand for teachers.

TOURISM

In most developed countries tourism is the fastest expanding sector of the national economy. With rising incomes an ever-increasing proportion of the population is able to take holidays away from home and of these more and more are venturing into foreign travel. A certain number of developing countries are able to take advantage of this, thanks to their location, their sunshine, their natural beauties, their exoticism. Already in 1963 the United Nations recommended that technical assistance programmes should include aid in establishing tourist facilities, since tourism offers the double advantage of providing foreign exchange and generating employment. In Spain in recent years some 40 per cent of all foreign exchange earnings have been derived from tourism[38] and for Mexico the proportion is nearly as high.

As regards the stimulus to employment the Development Plan of the Caribbean island of St Lucia reckoned that for every three hotel beds two persons were employed directly by the hotel.[39] A similar figure is quoted from the neighbouring island of Antigua. But this is not all. A study undertaken in Puerto Rico showed that for every additional hotel job another job was created in the supplying and supporting services outside – in maintenance, building, retail trade and so forth.[40] These figures may be higher than those recorded in other developing countries because the Caribbean tourist trade is essentially a luxury trade requiring very high standards of service.

But tourism also has its less advantageous aspects. For one thing it is a seasonal trade, seldom providing year-round employment. Second, it depends to a considerable extent upon cyclical fluctuations in prosperity in the countries from which the tourists come. Third, it is influenced by the unpredictable vagaries of fashion; for a few seasons a particular country or island may be 'in', but then the jet set moves on elsewhere. Fourth, when a very small country, and one or two of the Caribbean islands are examples, comes to depend heavily on tourism then whatever indigenous economy the territory previously had is abandoned, the workers moving away to the higher paid and otherwise more attractive jobs in the tourist sector. It is important that these difficulties and disadvantages be considered seriously and measures be devised to deal with them, because with the substantial cheapening of air fares which seems certain to occur during the next few years a number of developing countries

[38] Cf. M. Peters, *Internation Tourism: the Economics and Development of the International Tourist Trade*, Hutchinson, London, 1969, Table I, p. 10. However, a number of countries had a negative balance on tourist account, e.g. Argentina, Colombia, Iran, Nigeria and the Phillipines.

[39] *Economic Development in the Eastern Caribbean Islands–St Lucia*, Institute of Social and Economic Research, Univ. of the West Indies, March 1967.

[40] *Report of the Tripartite Economic Survey of the East Caribbean*, HMSO, London, 1967.

which hitherto have been remote from the tourist circuit will find themselves becoming centres of attraction. With prudent economic and social engineering a tourist industry can bring many blessings, not least that of paying for the infrastructure upon which a diversified industrial economy can subsequently be built.

Chapter 5

Industry in Rural Areas

There can be two approaches to the promotion of industrial employment in rural areas: one is by stimulating and expanding the handicrafts and small-scale industries which have already long existed and the other is to promote the decentralisation of urban industry to new locations away from the large towns. The two objectives need not be mutually exclusive, and indeed in several developing countries they are being pursued simultaneously. However, their problems and the programmes for attaining the objectives are different, so it will be convenient to discuss each separately.

Small-scale Industry

Neither in English nor in any other language does there appear to be a single word which covers all the types of production being reviewed here. We speak of handicrafts, of cottage industry, of artisanal activities, of small-scale manufacturing. Each of these concepts differs to some extent from the others. What they have in common is that all of them offer to people in rural areas employment in some branch of manufacturing, as distinct from agriculture or commerce, and all of them are modest in scale compared with the large factories of so-called 'modern' industry. This sentence has included the words 'offer to people in rural areas'. Now, of course, it is perfectly possible for small-scale enterprises of the type described here to be located in towns; indeed in some developing countries the town-based small industries have greater economic importance than those based in rural areas. But the general employment aspects of industrial development have already been discussed in Chapter 3 without any limitation as to size of firm but with an implication that the firms would be mostly located in urban areas; hence it appears convenient to focus the present discussion of small industries on their capacity to generate employment in rural areas.

Various attempts have been made to define the size of enterprise which entitles it to be classified as 'small-scale'. Thus in Paraguay and Uruguay it is any establishment employing less than 50 persons, in Trinidad and Tobago the ceiling is put at 25 and in the secretariat of the Central American Common Market at 14. In Chile those establishments employing 10 to 50 persons are classed as small-scale while those employing less than 10 persons are 'artisanal'. In India the upper limit is 50 persons for a mechanised and 100 persons for a non-mechanised manufacturing activity. Clearly the differences between countries are considerable, and

90

even within a country experience shows that the drawing of any fixed frontier is impracticable. Neither can a differentiation be based on the type of commodity manufactured. While there is certainly a range of articles in the 'arts and crafts' category typically produced by rural artisans it is equally true that cottage industries turn out products, notably in textiles, which have to compete with the same products produced in large modern factories. In fact the range of products emanating from this small-scale sector is very wide.

It is a sector which has received a great deal of attention in the literature of development planning partly because a flourishing and expanding small-scale industry in rural areas could be expected to retard the too rapid migration to the cities and partly because this form of production, being labour-intensive, should be able to contribute significantly to the provision of employment. In this latter aspect its attractions are manifold. Not only does it create remunerative work while requiring a minimal amount of capital and, hitherto at least, of expertise, but it also offers the important advantage of providing employment *on the spot* in the villages so that those taking up this work can continue to live in their own homes, thus obviating the re-housing expenses involved when rural people go to seek employment in the cities. More than this, in a large number of instances it offers *part-time* employment, particularly convenient in agricultural districts where anything approaching full employment occurs only at one or two peak moments in the year leaving many persons wholly or partially unemployed for the rest of the time.

Despite its many attractions, experience has shown that this type of industrial activity is not easy to maintain, still less expand, in countries which are undergoing rapid economic growth. The upheavals caused by the modernisation of traditionalist society, the disruption of long established family and social relationships, coupled with the rising expectations for access to the range of consumer goods available to the inhabitants of industrial countries, all this has called into question the role and the chances for survival of the handicraft and cottage industries. The present discussion will focus first on the problems connected with making these industries viable and subsequently on the experiences of those countries which have made the greatest efforts to support this sector.

THE PROBLEMS OF VIABILITY

Consider to begin with the question of markets for the commodities produced by this sector. There are several different kinds of small firm, mostly producing for different kinds of markets, whose prospects need to be separately evaluated. First is the market within the village itself: the demand of the local peasants for hand tools and for their repair, the demand for building of simple structures and for building materials, the demand for furniture and for cloth, the demand in villages where a division of labour has evolved for bread and cooking oil and other simply processed farm products. A second and completely different market is that for the 'arts and crafts' products bought by richer people in the towns and by tourists – the hand-made jewellery, the wood-carving, the metal trays, the embroidered cotton and woollen fabrics, etc. A third market is the nationwide one for general consumption goods such as clothing and simple household utensils wherein the small-scale producer has to compete with the large factory. These three markets correspond to the categories adopted for the analysis of small-scale industry in India's first Five-Year Plan. To these should be added a fourth having rather different characteristics, namely that of subcontracting already referred to in Chapter 3, the chief difference being that the outlet for the produce is assured in advance.[1]

Apart from the first market which he knows intimately and the fourth where he has no sale responsibility, the rural entrepreneur cannot easily acquaint himself with the changing nature of market demand. He may persevere with the same handcarved book-rests that his father produced before him, only to find suddenly that they are being manufactured at half the price by a large firm in Japan or the United States. He may be producing workmen's trousers which for a long time sold well in the urban market but after a while finds himself competing against a large modern clothing firm whose establishment has been partly subsidised by his own government. He has no market research organisation to help him, no trade journal; if he is not to go out of business he needs to be helped.

In India, which among all developing countries has elaborated the most far-reaching programmes in support of cottage and small-scale industries, subsidies were granted to a number of products facing this kind of competition, the funds being obtained from taxes levied on the large enterprises of the modern sector. This is not necessarily an uneconomic procedure when it is remembered that many large-scale enterprises receive advantages equivalent to substantial subsidies in the form of low interest rates and foreign exchange policies that make their imported machinery and materials uneconomically cheap. Moreover, in respect to certain varieties of cloth of central importance to the small sector, the large firms were banned from producing or had the volume of their production strictly limited. In Ceylon the Five-Year Plan of 1965–70 divided textile weaving into three classes, manual looms, machine looms and large-scale production, many common articles such as sarongs, camboys, pyjamas and silk saris being reserved for the manual class of enterprise. Likewise importers of textile goods were instructed to obtain a certain proportion of their supplies from local sources. In India the Government assumed the role of central purchaser of some types of craft goods.[2] Yet it gradually became apparent that direct subsidies did not in themselves improve the competitive strength of the small producers and that it might be preferable

[1] For a general examination of the opportunities for small-scale rural industries see: *Services for Small-scale Industry*, Studies and Reports, New Series 61, ILO, Geneva, 1961, pp. 13 ff.

[2] For further information on these various methods of protection see: ILO, *Meeting of Experts on the Role of Handicrafts in the National Economy in Developing Countries*, New Delhi, November 1968; J. Patel, *Government Policy on Village Industries in Developing Countries*, Doc. MEH/1968/Final Report (roneoed), pp. 26–30.

to devote the money to helping the producers to modernise their methods, to provide research, credit, training and marketing services.[3]

To begin with it is necessary to study closely the production techniques currently in use with a view to determining what modifications might be introduced which would improve the quality of the goods and/or the productivity of labour without throwing people out of work. For example, in villages where an electricity supply was available it was found that the provision of small electric motors to the craft-workers' machines could significantly increase the volume of output. Patel, in the study referred to above, noted that in cotton weaving the introduction of semi-automatic pedal-looms produced an output as high as that of fully automatic looms; in the preparation of fruit juices the use of a simple press gave more employment and was just as efficient as grading machines and mechanical juice extractors. The most advantageous modifications in techniques will differ from commodity to commodity and, even for the same commodity, from district to district.[4]

For this purpose a number of governments have set up regional bodies charged with the responsibility of assisting in all aspects of the modernising and strengthening of small industries. For instance, in Chile such bodies were established for the northern zone and for the province of Magallanes, and in Peru for the departments of Puno, Arequipa and Moquega. These bodies help the small entrepreneurs to obtain the most appropriate machines, to acquire their raw materials more advantageously; they assist in improving the packing and presentation of the articles, they find new market outlets in the cities and undertake, perhaps through a central institute, research as to new lines of production which might prove profitable, the latter may be particularly rewarding in countries already exposed to foreign tourism. The staff of such bodies also give advice to individual producers as to the adaptation of their traditional designs to meet current tastes and as to their production and selling problems.

One constantly pressing need is for credit which at the village level is normally available only at exorbitant rates of interest. Because the artisan needs credit, albeit often in quite small amounts, to buy a new machine or to change over to new packaging materials several governments have created separate credit institutions especially for this purpose. In some areas artisans can obtain loans from the general-purpose credit co-operatives. Since these small family businesses are in most cases a poor risk, it is usual for the government to guarantee such loans. Sometimes, as in parts of India, in Ceylon and in Tanzania, the artisans themselves establish co-operatives to furnish the services which they need and which they cannot provide individually.[5] In other instances they join forces with the traditional agricultural or consumer co-operative organisations.

[3] Government of India, Planning Commission, *Third Five-Year Plan*, p. 431.

[4] D. N. Saraf, *Development of Artistic Crafts*, and J. Patel, *How to Modernise Handicraft Technology for Developing Countries*, both from Doc. MEH/1968/Final Report (roneoed) *loc. cit.*

[5] J. Patel, *Co-operation in Village Industries*, Doc. MEH/1968/II (roneoed), ILO, *loc. cit.*

It will be clear from the foregoing that if the artisans and small-scale entrepreneurs are to remain viable while industrialisation goes on around them they need help, perhaps more in kind than in money, and above all they need training. Not too many experiences are yet recorded in this respect, though mention must be made of the centres established in 1967 at Lomé and at Sokodé in Togo.[6] Training needs to embrace the constant re-adaptation of designs, acquaintance with new production techniques and some elementary knowledge of business methods – stock-taking and book-keeping, for example. But the provision of training courses presents difficulties. Such centres as exist are almost all located in towns and therefore serve primarily the urban rather than the rural small entre-preneurs. To establish a multiplicity of such centres throughout the rural districts would be extremely expensive. In some countries a system of itinerent teachers has been introduced, though only the most gifted of these succeed in forming good contacts and in overcoming the conser-vatism and suspicion of the local craftsmen. In some quarter the traditional method of apprenticeship is still recommended. While it is true that communication will be easier between master and pupil both stemming from the same social background, this may mean that the pupil learns the customary rather than the modern ways of operating his craft. But when economic and market incentives to introduce improved technology exist, traditional apprenticeship systems have not proved to be barriers to change. Apprentices can be taught how to use new tools just as well as old ones. A group of African experts has suggested that apprenticeship should be combined with a course of training provided from outside the village.[7] A somewhat different approach has been adopted in the Philippines where certain large firms in Manila send their own specialists out to the country districts to teach the desired styles of embroidery for goods which in due course are purchased by these city firms.[8] This practice, which amounts to a form of subcontracting is found also in Latin America where mail order houses and supermarket chains, especially from the United States, farm out to rural families the fabrication of a variety of articles according to predetermined designs and quality standards and under the supervision of intinerant advisers who at the same time collect and pay for the finished goods. Whatever the means resorted to, what has to be accomplished is the integration of the craftsmen and the small-scale entrepreneurs into the modernising market economy without at the same time detaching them from their local roots and, which may be commercially important, their local sources of artistic inspiration.

COUNTRY EXPERIENCES

In India in the first two Five-Year Plans covering the period 1951 to

[6] J. K. Hadzi, *L'Artisanat dans le Développement Togolais*, Diplôme de l'Ecole pratique des Hautes Etudes (roneoed), Paris, 1967, pp. 123–4.

[7] ILO, *Report on the Meeting of the ILO Advisory Working Group on Rural Employment Problems*, Lagos, November 1965, Doc. D.11(2), 1966 (roneoed), p. 18.

[8] Y. C. J. Yen and G. M. Feliciano, *Rural Reconstruction and Development*, Praeger, New York, 1967, p. 183.

1961 considerable prominence was given to programmes supporting labour-intensive rural industries such as hand weaving, tanning, silk production and manually-operated vegetable oil extraction. The subject was of major importance since it had been estimated, according to a sample survey, that 'household enterprises smaller than registered factories' provided rural employment for 12,911,000 persons and in addition employment for another 4,407,000 in urban areas.[9] These programmes, it was hoped, by encouraging activities in which the capital–output ratio and the capital–labour ratio were relatively low would maximise production and employment during a period when investment capital was very scarce. The subsidies were regarded as in some sense a form of unemployment benefit which would have particular justification if simultaneously they brought down unit-costs in the industries being supported.[10]

The results proved disappointing, at least in part. It is true that new or additional employment was created during the Second Five-Year Plan for some 3 million weavers and for some 500,000 artisans and workers in other trades and crafts, but the expenditure involved seemed out of proportion to the results obtained. In particular, the improved spinning technique known as 'Ambar charkha' which was expected to raise labour productivity and to create employment for 2,240,000 workers by 1959–60 resulted in an increase of no more than 371,000 persons.[11] More generally it became apparent that village industries, although labour-intensive, had a capital–output ratio no better than that of comparable industries using modern technology.[12]

In the Third Five-Year Plan for India a number of conclusions were drawn from the accumulated experience:

'An important lesson of the past decade is that where individual small industries, including village industries, have failed to adopt improved techniques or to achieve economies of scale or to organise themselves into co-operatives, production costs have remained relatively high and problems of unsold stocks and of decline in production and employment have arisen.

Hence, the future objectives of programmes in this field should be:

'. . . to improve the productivity of the worker and reduce production costs by placing relatively greater emphasis on positive forms of assistance

[9] *The National Sample Survey, Fourteenth Round: July 1958–June 1959*, No. 94, Cabinet Secretariat, Government of India, Calcutta, 1965, p. 5.

[10] See: *Report of the Village and Small-scale Industries (Second Five-Year Plan) Committee*, Planning Commission, Government of India, Chapter 3.

[11] *Khadi and Village Industries Commission, Annual Report, 1959–60*, Khadi and Village Industries Commission, Bombay, 1967, p. 30.

[12] In this context see, V. M. Dandekar, *The Role of Small-scale Industry in Economic Development: the Indian Experience*, paper prepared for the Conference on Education, Employment and Rural Employment, University College, Nairobi, 1966; see also, L. K. Mitra, *Employment and Output in Small Enterprises of India*, Bookland Private Ltd, Clacutta, 1967, especially pp. 78–132.

such as improvement of skill, supply of technical advice, better equipment and credit, etc. . . .'

The Plan also indicated that:

'for many years the greatest scope for utilising manpower resources in rural areas will lie in agricultural development programmes and in projects for road development, village housing and the provision of rural amenities.'

Clearly the authorities were voicing a concern as to the backwardness of small-scale and village enterprises and as to the difficulty of expecting them to provide major opportunities for the expansion of employment unless something were done to change the situation.

In the light of all this the Plan proposed the application of 'intermediate technology' to the village industries. This policy, though requiring investment and accepting the need for the processes to become somewhat more capital-intensive, seemed to hold out the prospect of making this sector viable. It was estimated that the new programme would create during the plan period some 900,000 additional full-time jobs plus additional part-time employment for 8 million people including both rural and urban areas; while the target for part-time employment was reached, the other one was not completely achieved, the new full-time jobs amounting to 630,000.[13] Meantime and as a result the incremental capital–output ratio in this sector rose to 2·2 compared with a ratio of 1·8 for the economy as a whole during the same period. (In the previous planning periods the ratio in the small-scale sector had approximated to the national average.)[14] To cite the example of one much-published activity, the Khadi programme, i.e. the hand spinning and hand weaving, between 1956–7 and 1962–3 the capital–labour ratio doubled while the annual rate of growth in output of cotton textiles rose from 4·57 per cent to 8·84 between the Second and the Third Five-Year Plans.[15] These policies were maintained during the Fourth Five-Year Plan.

The success of the part-time employment component of the programme was perhaps the most significant. Thus the activities coming under the auspices of the Khadi and Village Industries Commission gave part-time employment to 2,259,100 persons in 1965–6 and full-time emp oyment to only 353,700 persons.[16] This contrast probably has two explanations. First, the great majority of the village people are not wholly without work; they are needed in the fields at peak seasons of the year but are available for other work during the remainder of the time. Second, the fact that most of them are members of households whose total income is extremely low means that a strong incentive is present to augment these earnings

[13] Government of India, Planning Commission: *Fourth Five-Year Plan, a Draft Outline*, p. 238.
[14] L. K. Mitra, *op. cit.*, pp. 84–5.　　　　　　　　　[15] *Ibid.*, pp. 80 and 91.
[16] *The Khadi and Village Industries Commission at Work 1965–66, op. cit.*, p. 7.

especially in cash. That is why the handicraft and village industries operating largely with part-time employees are better able to recruit labour, at least in the early stages of economic development, than modern industries, *even when the latter are located in rural areas*, because these require labour that works full-time. In the East Pakistan inquiry it emerged that persons working in family or mainly family manufacturing enterprises, many of them probably part-time, constituted 2·3 per cent of the total population whereas those working in the remainder of the industrial sector, i.e. in modern larger-scale industry, constituted only 0·65 per cent.[17] The experience suggest the importance of adapting organisational forms to the local situation when promoting manufacturing and craft activities in rural areas.

This conclusion is confirmed in the work of the National Cottage Industries Development Authority in the Philippines (NACIDA) which was created in 1962. At a time when small artisan-type enterprises were establishing themselves rapidly in the towns where they had access to electricity, raw materials, transport, repair facilities, markets and so on, NACIDA experienced the utmost difficulty in implanting similar activities in rural districts. During the first years of its operation it achieved only 57 per cent of its target of creating 22,400 new jobs per annum.[18] In spite of reinforcing its efforts by setting up an Emergency Employment Administration to put across a crash programme, it was plagued by the problems of how to make the village enterprises economically viable. The lack of local purchasing power, the lack of contact with more distant markets, the difficulty of getting local people to assimilate even the rudiments of intermediate technology, all combined to emphasise the weakness of the cottage industries.

In the overall employment programmes of developing countries handicrafts and village industries certainly have a role. Many writers, noting the almost total absence of quite elementary consumption goods in millions of rural families on the one hand, and the widespread rural unemployment and under-employment on the other, believe that by setting these people to work consumers' needs could be to a large extent satisfied. There are the difficulties that the craftsmen's neighbour's in the village do not yet have sufficient purchasing power to acquire the articles which may be produced; but as soon as these producers orient themselves, as they must, towards markets outside their own areas they encounter all the problems of an ordinary industrial enterprise without having the know-how or financial resources for coping with those problems. Consequently many of these businesses cannot pay their way. These difficulties mean that village industries can be expected to thrive only on two conditions. First, their encouragement must be part of a broader policy seeking to promote rural development and raise rural incomes by all available means such as agricultural extension work, agricultural price policy and

[17] *Survey of Cottage Industries in East Pakistan, loc. cit.*, pp. 1 and 22.
[18] A. Lorenzo, 'Employment Effects of Rural and Community Development in the Philippines', *International Labour Review*, November 1969, p. 425.

fiscal policy public works and the building up of the rural infrastructure. Second, village craftsmen need to be aided by the provision of a range of technical services helping them to assimilate the intermediate technologies which may make them economically viable. This is worth while because by these means an important volume of employment, especially of part-time employment, can be generated. This transformation of traditional village industries into semi-modern enterprises will at best be a slow process; old customs die hard. But for rural people it constitutes an important stepping-stone in the modernisation of society.

The Decentralisation of Urban Industry

Some readers may be surprised to find in a book devoted to studying the promotion of employment a section on the decentralisation of industry. After all a firm of a given size and using a given technology will have the same staff wherever it may be located; and since in most if not all developing countries there is plenty of unabsorbed labour in urban areas why, *on employment grounds*, should any effort be made to encourage location specially in rural areas? (Our questioner would willingly recognise that many urban agglomerations have become too large and that their further expansion should be discouraged, but this is a different issue.) Yet in spite of superficial appearances to the contrary, there are at least two *a priori* reasons why manufacturing industry well scattered generates more employment than the same volume of industry concentrated in one or two metropoli. First, the firm is more than likely to opt for a more labour-intensive technology if it locates in an area where wage rates are lower than in the city; consequently its staff will be more numerous. Second, the multiplier effects may be more substantial outside a metro-politan zone, partly because supporting services have to be created instead of using those which already exist and partly because once a firm has become successful in a new area other firms may decide to choose a location in the same vicinity; but this will be further considered presently.

Before proceeding to the main discussion it is important to realise how difficult is the task of decentralisation, how strong are the centripetal forces driving prospective entrepreneurs to seek an urban, preferably a big city, location. The advantages have been analysed by many writers since the beginning of this century.[19] They include availability of skilled labour, easy transport of raw materials since most rail and road links converge on big cities, presence of spare parts and repair services, proximity of banks, credit houses, advertising agencies, access to government depart-ments for licences, etc., a large market on the doorstep for the firm's output, agreeable social life for the top echelons of the staff – and the list could be extended. In a developing country the contrast in all these respects between a metropolitan and a provincial location is far greater, for the

[19] See, for example, A. Weber, *Über den Standort der Industrien*, Tübingen, 1909; also E. M. Hoover, *The Location of Economic Activity*, New York, 1948; also P. Sargent Florence: *Investment, Location and Size of Plants*, Cambridge, 1948.

reason that developing countries have not yet been able to afford to equip more than the capital and perhaps one or two other major cities with the infrastructure and other facilities which modern industry desires. Only in these few islands of modernity does the technological apparatus and the sophisticated society exist, which make the centripetal forces even more powerful. It is against this background that the problem has to be examined.

DECENTRALISATION POLICIES

The pros and cons of decentralisation can be viewed from a macro-economic standpoint, i.e. its effects for the country as a whole, and from a micro-economic standpoint relating to the particular locality and/or to the firm itself. As regards the former, since so much is uncertain in the long-term future of economic development, a government and its planners can utilise only the broadest general considerations in attempting to influence the geographical distribution of economic activity.[20] They may wish to check the speed of urbanisation, they may have strategic considerations for stimulating settlement and economic activity in border areas, there may be districts of dense habitation where it would be good to create employment, and so forth. But it is the micro-economic considerations which bring policy of decentralisation into precise focus.

Among these considerations one of the first and most obvious is the location of heavy or bulky raw materials: the initial processing of most minerals has to take place at or near the mine itself, a pulp mill has to be sited near its forest, a sugar mill near its cane fields. Even in a small country like Israel, well provided with roads, it was found that a sugar factory could not be profitably situated more than 30 to 40 kilometres from the beet fields.[21] Likewise in the case of perishable raw materials, such as fruit and vegetables for canning, the plant needs to be within short trucking distance from the growing areas. In all these cases a decentralisation imposes itself and there is unlikely to be any conflict between the interests of the firm and those of the community.

The opportunity of access to an abundant labour reserve which is probably willing to work at lower rates than in the city constitutes an attraction for those branches of manufacturing which, even while using modern technology, remain relatively labour-intensive – examples being furniture making, certain lines of clothing, and accessories such as hand-bags, hats and gloves. This alleged advantage does not always materialise in practice. As noted earlier in this chapter most of the rural people tend to be under-employed rather than totally unemployed and may not clamour for full-time jobs. Also although their hourly wages may be less

[20] L. H. Klaassen, *Méthodes de Sélection d'Industries pour les Régions en Stagnation*, OECD, Paris, 1967, pp. 49–71. R. B. Ogendo, 'The Significance of Industrial Zoning to Rural Industrial Development in Kenya', a Study of the Facts and Methodology, *Cahiers d'Etudes Africaines*, Ecole pratique des Hautes Etudes, Paris, Mouton, Vol. 7, 3rd ed., 1967, pp. 444–84.

[21] R. Weitz, 'Sur le Principe du Développement Rural Intégré', *Economie Rurale*, Paris, No. 61, July–September 1964, pp. 3–14.

than in the city their lack of skills and experience may be such that the labour-cost per unit of output comes h gher in the rural than in the urban area. Many employers find, indeed, that their first task is to train their labour force. Because of the training problem it may often be easier to implant in rural areas those branches of manufacturing which require a minimum of skilled labour or, at least, skills which can be quickly learned. In speaking of rural areas a distinction has to be made. It is one thing to set up a factory in a small town which it is hoped will in due course become a pole of economic growth, and quite another thing to establish it in the depths of the countryside where the nearest settlements are a few villages and hamlets lacking electricity, water supplies and surfaced roads, not to speak of other services. Apart from the special cases where this latter solution is dictated by the nature of the manufacturing process – the pulp mills, the sugar mills, and so forth referred to above – its adoption is an invitation to failure. First, this alternative is much more expensive: a whole infrastructure has to be created embracing housing, roads, street lighting, water, drains, electricity, schools, police, clinics, telephones, transport, all for the one or two plants being established; whereas when a site is chosen in an existing small town the nucleus of these services is already present and they can be added to as the demand for them grows. Second, there will be personnel problems: for a factory in a rural location all the skilled workers have to be imported from other regions and in many cases are not 'accepted' by the local people; worse still the administrative and management staff have no social life except within their own restricted group and therefore tend to move away whereas in a town, even a small one, they could make contact with a pre-existing circle of professional people. Social factors quite as much as economic ones can bring disaster to decentralisation projects. Many governments have had such experiences; to mention but one example, the attempt of the Mexican Government to create in a very poor rural area a new town, Ciudad Sahagún, north of Mexico City, which was expected to become a growth pole but which never had more than three plants, two of them directed there by the Government and losing money.

Much more successful have been those decentralisation policies which take the form of laying out industrial estates on the outskirts of a small or medium-sized town which has begun to demonstrate a capacity of its own for dynamic growth. This formula has been adopted in most Latin American countries: in Mexico with success at Irapuato, and Guadalajara, in Ecuador at Cuenca, Ibarra and Tulcan, and in Venezuela at Barquisimento, Guarenas, Maracay and Santo Tomé de Guayana.[22] The usual procedure is for the Government in collaboration with the municipal authorities to select a site suitable from the viewpoint of town-planning, to equip it with roads, street lighting, water supply, drainage, electricity, telephone links and perhaps a sports ground and then to rent out factory plots to entrepreneurs. This policy has been used in Brazil for the development of the north-east by the SUDENE which established an iron-ore

[22] *Boletin Económico de América Latina, op. cit.,* **12,** 1, May 1967, pp. 75–7.

smelter in the Reconcavo region and gave assistance to small and medium-sized firms to locate there. Similarly in the U.A.R. Aswan has been developed and established in order to put a brake on the excessive industrial concentration around Cairo and Alexandria. Likewise in India a new metallurgical industry was set up in the small towns of Bhilai, Durgapur and Rourkela, situated between densely populated rural areas on one side and Calcutta on the other; also in the Punjab new industries were located in such small towns as Bahadurgarh, Hissar and Sonipat; in all these cases the intention being to canalise the rural exodus away from the big cities and towards the smaller towns.[23]

Having decided when they want to encourage industrial development, governments have a whole range of policies (e.g. tax rebates and holidays, investment grants, labour subsidies, etc.) which they can use to encourage investors to establish plants in particular regions.

EMPLOYMENT EFFECTS

As mentioned, it is generally easier to persuade enterprises using labour-intensive techniques to establish themselves away from the big cities. For example, under India's Fourth Five-Year Plan the granting of licences for new factories favoured those committed to the use of labour-intensive technologies and those which would be in some sense complementary to the large-scale industries, e.g. firms manufacturing spare parts or components. At the same time, care has to be taken not to encourage activities whose first consequence is to put out of business the village industry enterprises in the selected district. Either the newly implanted undertakings should be in a different branch of manufacturing or, if in the same branch, should be such as can subcontract some of their operations to village enterprises, thus having a stimulating rather than a damaging effect.

Generally speaking better employment effects are recorded with medium-scale enterprises than with large industrial complexes. Thus, the building of the three large steelworks in India generated additional direct employment for only 13,000 to 17,000 persons per project whilst the investment exceeded 2 billion rupees for each works, equivalent to an average of $28,000 per worker at the pre-June 1966 exchange rate. Not merely are investments of this type conspicuously more costly in rural than in urban areas, but they usually prove disappointing in their secondary effects in generating employment in the neighbourhood.

These secondary effects occur in two phases. First, there arises a temporary demand for local labour in the course of construction of the new plant, a demand for building labourers, for additional food supplies

23 For Brazil see, SUDENE: *III Plano Diretor do Desenvolvimento Econômico e Social do Nordeste 1966–8*, 2nd ed., Recife, 1966, pp. 119–25. For the U.A.R. see, *Rural Employment Problems in the United Arab Republic*, UNIDO, Report of the Interregional Seminar on Industrial Location and Regional Development, Minsk, 14–26 August 1968, Doc. E.69.II.B.22, p. 31. For India see, M. S. Khan, 'Industrial Employment Policy in India', *Indian Journal of Industrial Relations*, New Delhi, 1, 2, October 1965, pp. 185–94; also the *Fourth Five-Year Plan, A Draft Outline*, Chapter 10.

from the locality, and there will be a new injection of purchasing power into the local economy. But this stimulating influence lasts only during the period of construction; those who built the factory, the new dwellings, the roads, the school and the clinic are no longer wanted, and the district has to settle down to the level of economic activity generated by the staff of the new plant or plants, a level higher than in the past but not always so very much higher.

This will depend on the so-called 'linkage effect', i.e. the extent to which other firms are attracted to establish themselves on the same industrial estates or otherwise in the vicinity of the new plants. The extent to which this effect may materialise is a question which seems to have been insufficiently studied hitherto, which is strange considering that of the various positive effects which decentralisation may have on employment this is by far the most important. Experience indicates, for instance, that the establishment of plants near mines for the treatment of the ore extracted seldom attracts any other form of manufacturing to those neighbourhoods – the smelters remain geographically isolated; the same is true of steelworks, though not quite so pronouncedly, the manufacture of locomotives and other heavy machinery. On the other hand, the linkage effect of certain consumer goods industries may be considerable, especially those which demand an increased volume of production of local raw materials, those which can subcontract the making of components to village enterprises, those which require ancillary products that can be locally made, e.g. boxes and other packaging materials, and those which generate transportation activity in moving materials into and finished or semi-finished products out of the district. In short, the industries which will contribute most to employment creation are for the most part those which have strong backward and forward linkages.

But this does not in itself suffice. Much will depend on the local reaction, on the ability of local people to take advantage of the new opportunities: whether the farmers can adjust themselves to meeting the demand of the newly arrived population for additional foodstuffs, whether the village industries have the capacity to undertake subcontracting and so on. This can be illustrated by the case of Sicily, where for some years a major industrialisation effort has been in progress. Comparing two neighbouring districts in which industrial investments were made, in Gela the response of the local population was minimal, partly perhaps because the investment concerned an oil refinery and petro-chemicial complex, whereas in the Syracuse district where a wider variety of plants were installed the local people quickly took advantage of the new opportunities.[24] The industrialisation of the coastal zone between Syracuse and Augusta which has been in progress since 1949 has undoubtedly had favourable employment effects, both direct and indirect. Thus between 1951 and 1961 the population of this province increased by 7 per cent compared with a growth of 5·2 per cent for Sicily as a whole and 6·5 per cent for the whole

[24] P. Sylos-Labini, 'Precarious Employment in Sicily', *International Labour Review*, March 1964, pp. 302–21.

of Italy. Since 1960, as one by one the new plants have come into operation, the former emigration has ceased and indeed the migration out of the rural communes of Sicily now is directed not solely to northern Italy and to foreign countries but also to the province of Syracuse. The manpower required in the new factories comes partly direct from agriculture and partly indirectly via the stepping stone of the newly stimulated ancillary trades. The agricultural labour force has diminished sharply, indicating a diminution in the hitherto prevailing under-employment. The factories, which at first had to rely on skilled and semi-skilled workers obtained from the north, now increasingly use local labour – up to 70 per cent of the staff in one typical case. The entrepreneurs themselves took on the responsibilities of training partly by organising courses and partly by in-plant training.[25] Such examples are encouraging but they confirm the conclusion that the modernisation of a society through industrialisation is inevitably a slow process; the benefits to employment and to the general level of prosperity become apparent only over a considerable period of time.

It should perhaps be stressed that the benefit need not be confined to an increase in employment opportunities; it can be equally worth while if it takes the form of augmenting the incomes of the local population. Thus the increase in demand for food on the part of the new industrial labour force may increase the sales and incomes of the farmers in the province without necessarily adding visibly to the volume of farm employment; likewise those engaged in the village industries may find a larger outlet for their products, or for new products, and thereby increase their incomes without needing to take on additional staff. The betterment of social and economic welfare can come about in numerous different ways.

Integrated Regional Policies

At the beginning of this chapter reference was made to the desirability of the governments of developing countries determining a geographical as well as an economic strategy for growth. The localisation of industry should be related wherever possible to broader considerations of national policy. But to this consideration is added another, namely that policies designed for one particular purpose, such as the decentralisation of industry, are the more likely to succeed if they are allied and combined with policies in other fields which may impinge upon them. It is with ideas such as these in mind that a number of governments have required their Planning Ministries to produce integrated regional development programmes.[26]

25 Geneviève Bibes, 'La Formation de la Main-d'oeuvre dans une Région d'Industrialisation Récente: le Cas de la Sincat à Priolo-Mellili (Province de Syracuse)', dans *Mobilité de la Main-d'oeuvre et Développement Économique dans le Bassin Méditerranéen*, Fondation nationale des Sciences politiques, Paris, Centre d'études des relations internationales, Recherches, No. 13, September 1967, pp. 7–23.

26 See, W. Isard, *Methods of Regional Analysis*, New York, 1960. See also: J. R. Meyer, 'Regional Economics: A Survey', in *Surveys of Economic Theory*, Macmillan, London, and St Martin's Press, New York, 1967, pp. 240–71.

Regional development may be based on any one of a variety of physical or economic concepts. In Africa, for example, six different concepts have been distinguished: river basin or lake area development (the Sebou valley in Morocco and the lake of Chad), association with major constructional projects (dams such as Aswan, Volta, Kariba, or road or railway projects in TransCameroon and Zambia–Tanzania), integrated rural development (Central Tunisia, Nigeria, the Rif in Morocco), use of existing administrative units (Libya and Zambia) or readapted units (Madagascar) or newly created ones (Mali and Senegal), creation of growth centres (Kenya), or lastly the approach of multi-disciplinary investigations (Ethiopia).[27] For Latin America we have a report which distinguishes between firstly decentralised general purpose development authorities (the North-East and Amazon regions of Brazil and the provinces of Peru), programmes designed for backward or stagnant regions (Papaloapan and Oaxaca in Mexico and the north-east of Venezuela), zones recently opened to settlement (Guayana in Venezuela and certain provinces of Paraguay), frontier zones (Chiloe in Chile and Patagonia in Argentina), and lastly the selection of new focal points (growth poles) for development.[28] In Israel the motivating influence was the need to absorb rapidly a flood of immigrants into an economy in which agriculture and industry were already closely intermingled.[29]

Some of the considerations determining the selection of particular regions for development were spelt out by the Government of Paraguay in collaboration with the Latin American Institute for Economic and Social Planning: homogeneous physical and climatic conditions, homogeneous potential for agricultural and other branches of production, respect for existing boundaries of the administrations through which the programmes would be excuted, homogeneity of the population of the region, existence within the region of poles or possible poles of economic growth and a stimulus to activity radiating outward from these.[30] In fairness it must be mentioned that some authors take the opposite view, namely that it is more efficient to concentrate industry in large cities and to deal with rural unemployment through public works programmes.[31]

[27] United Nations Research Institute for Social Development, *Regional Development Experiences and Prospects, Preliminary Report on Africa*, Vol. 1, prepared by R. von Gersdorff, Geneva, 1968.

[28] *Materials on Regional Development in Latin America: Experience and Prospects*, by W. Stöhr, United Nations, Economic and Social Council, document ST/ECLA/Conf. 34/L.4, 29 October 1969.

[29] R. Weitz and A. Rokach, *Agricultural Development: Planning and Implementation (Israel Case Study)*, Reidel, Dordrecht, Netherlands, 1968, pp. 253–328.

[30] G. Fogel, 'El Desarrollo Regional y el Cambio Rural en el Paraguay', *Revista Paraguaya de Sociologia*, Asunción, 5, 11, April 1968, pp. 96–122. For discussion of the general issue see R. S. Kaynor and K. F. Schultz, *A Practical Guide to Industrial Development*, especially Part I, 'The Regional Development Corporation Concept'. For India see: J. P. Lewis, *Quiet Crisis in India*, Brookings Institution, Washington D.C., 1962, Chapter 7.

[31] L. Lefeber, 'Regional Allocation of Resources in India', in P. N. Rodenstein Rodan (Ed.), *Pricing and Fiscal Policies*, Allen & Unwin, London, 1964. See also: V. Nath,

There can be no doubt that integrated development programmes for regions tend to be expensive in respect to investment, provision of infrastructure, mobilisation of human resources. In experience of the Cassa per il Mezzogiorno in Italy, at any rate up to 1962, the capital–output ratio of its investments was between 5 and 6 whereas for the rest of Italy it was between 3 and 4.[32] Similarly, in Madagascar the Development Corporations for the Sakay and for the Bas-Mangoky scored technical successes with their projects but from the financial angle could expect to amortise their investments only over the very long term.[33]

One lesson to be drawn from national experiences is that integrated development must on no account neglect the agricultural sector. Farmers' incomes must be raised either by increasing output or by syphoning off some of the labour, or both; otherwise a hard core of poverty will remain in the midst of the modernising activities. Insufficient attention to this aspect explained much of the disappointment with the industrialisation programme in Slovakia in the years 1948 to 1953.[34] Another lesson is to avoid choosing a region which it would be too expensive to equip with sufficient infrastructure. The initial failure of the programme in the Lakish region of Israel and the unemployment in the town of Kiriat Gat were ascribed to the insufficient infrastructure and social services causing entrepreneurs to hesitate to establish themselves there. By contrast the successful regional development in the Central Punjab in India and along the Gujarat coast between Ahmedabad and Surat appeared connected with the good communications, the hydro-electric power, and the school and medical facilities.[35]

Yet another lesson, and perhaps the most fundamental one, is the need to consider these programmes as investments in human resources, just as much as in production facilities. Thus the above-mentioned SUDENE in north-east Brazil put the accent on schools, training and housing. In Venezuela the Corporación Venezolana de Guayana set up primary schools, adult education classes, teacher training courses, training centres for metallurgy and for electricity workers and a centre for programme research.[36] The Cassa per il Mezzogiorno in Italy and the Agency for the Planning of the Aswan Region in the U.A.R. both have emphasised

'Regional Planning in the National Plan', *Artha Vijnana*, Poona, 9, 1, March 1967, pp. 44–72.

[32] H. B. Chenery, 'Development Policies for Southern Italy', *Quarterly Journal of Economics*, 76 (1962), pp. 515–47.

[33] M. Penouil, 'La Région dans la Planification Economique des Pays en Voie de Développement: l'Example des Nations Africaines d'Expression Française: Développement Economique Régional et Aménagement du Territoire, numero special de la *Revue d'économie Politique*, Paris, January–February 1964, pp. 413–38; see also E. Costa, 'Employment Problems and Policies in Madagascar', *International Labour Review*, March 1968, pp. 217–50.

[34] P. Hoffmann, 'Employment Problems of Regional Development: The Case of Slovakia', *International Labour Review*, March 1964, pp. 257–67.

[35] V. Nath, *op. cit., loc. cit.*

[36] República de Venezuela, Corporación Venezolana de Guayana, *Informe Anual 1966*, Chapter 7.

105

education and training to enable local people to participate in the economic developments.[37] In some cases, the community development approach has been used, for instance in the Lerma project in Mexico and the Africa project in Chile. When the planners move into a region with an integrated development programme the kind of human resources considerations which they should have in mind have been described as follows:

ANALYSIS OF DEMOGRAPHIC CHARACTERISTICS AND BEHAVIOUR
Statistical study of demographic structure and its evolution by regions; urbanisation patterns; migration flows; socio-economic studies of the decision to migrate; labour force participation-rates; dependency ratios; etc.

HUMAN RESOURCE ANALYSIS
Studies for manpower requirements of regional programmes; studies of the educational and technical skill levels of regional populations in light of future requirements; institutional conditions for meeting the requirements; special problems in the full development of human resource potentials; policies and programmes; etc.[38]

When all these aspects of regional development are given their due attention, quite clearly regional integration programmes must be carefully planned and generously financed. As to the latter, since most developing countries' governments are perennially short of funds, an ingenious device may be cited from Brazil. It was decreed that firms could claim a 50 per cent reduction in their liability for corporation tax if they were willing to invest this amount plus an additional sum three times as large in establishing an enterprise in the north-eastern region, the new business being entirely under the parent firm's control though having to be approved by the Development Authority. This offer proved so attractive that between 1962 and 1967 no less than 84 per cent of all industrial investment in the region derived from private sources in other parts of the country. In addition, the new enterprises enjoyed fiscal exemptions in the north-east for ten years.[39]

The employment-generating programmes reviewed in this chapter, whether they be for the encouragement of village industries and crafts, or for the establishment of new industries in rural areas and small towns, or more ambitiously for integrated regional development, all have one

[37] A. R. Abdel Meguid and R. D. Loken, 'Pragmatic Economic Development: A Regional Approach', *International Development Review*, **9**, 3, Washington D.C., September 1967, pp. 7–11.
[38] J. Friedmann, 'Education for Regional Planning in Developing Countries', in *Papers of the Proceedings of the Workshop on Regional Development Planning*, Institute of Social Studies, The Hague, 5–7 October 1967 (roneoed).
[39] SUDENE, *IV Plano Diretor, 1969–73*, Recife, 1968, Vol. I; also A. O. Hirschman, 'Desenvolvimento Industrial no Nordeste Brasileiro', *Revista Brasileira de Economia*, December 1967; also A. C. Antunes, 'La Politica de Industrialización del Nordeste Brasileiro', *Boletim Economico SUDENE*, **3**, 1; and Lacerda, 'Nordeste: Industrialisaçao e Absorçao de Mao-de-obra', *ibid.*, October–December 1968.

thread in common, namely to deflect industrial activity from excessive concentration in the larger cities, thereby achieving a more equitable geographical spread of employment opportunities. They are not easy programmes. They have to enlist the willing co-operation of the villagers on the one hand and the urban entrepreneurs on the other, they have to promote enterprises which in the not too distant future will be economically viable, they have to include rather heavy expenditure on the infrastructure and they have to ensure that the prosperity which results will be shared reasonably fairly among the various segments of the local population. Nor is this all. Such programmes, especially those for the integrated development of selected regions, raise political problems, because inevitably they involve discriminating as between different parts of the country. Those which are selected for this treatment will enjoy economic benefits if the projects succeed, while other regions will have to wait their turn. This is to a large extent an inescapable feature of the development process. The same consideration applies to attempts to ameliorate the source of unemployment and under-employment. In many cases it is not possible to tackle the whole country at once; the task must be undertaken by stages. Moreover, it can be argued that the act of concentrating investment and supporting services in a few areas holds out greater hope of overcoming the many daunting difficulties; the lessons so learned can then be applied to other areas with greater chances of success. The stimulation of employment in rural areas and small towns requires a rare combination of social, economic and political skills which can be acquired not by conning a theoretical treatise but only in the hard school of experience. But it seems very important that the development effort should be spread more widely than has been usual in most developing countries in the past.

Chapter 6

Construction and Public Works

Economic Needs

In developing countries the almost unlimited need for construction and public works activities of various kinds is something which no one contests. The cities need more schools, more hospitals, administrative buildings, low-cost housing, improved water supplies, main drainage, electricity extensions, parks and playgrounds – the list could be greatly lengthened. The small towns and the villages need all these things too. The country as a whole needs a network of major roads supported by feeder roads from villages to market centres. Much of the agricultural land needs improvement either by terracing or by drainage or by irrigation involving the building of dams and irrigation canals and the sinking of wells. Some of it should be afforested. Apart from their intrinsic value, the provision of at least some of these elements of a modern infrastructure is essential, as noted in the previous chapter, to the economic viability of the new industrial activities advocated for the rural areas and small towns.

Writers on development problems have long been attracted to public works programmes as a means of harnessing unused resources, especially labour, and at the same time accelerating the pace of economic growth. W. A. Lewis asserted that human labour could produce roads, viaducts, irrigation canals and buildings with the aid of hardly any capital. R. Nurkse took the same position, adding that surplus or under-employed manpower could be mobilised in community development programmes, diminishing the numbers dependent on agriculture without curtailing the volume of food production.[1] Unlike manufacturing which had to be coaxed into adopting labour-intensive techniques, the construction industry with few exceptions was by nature labour-intensive. All that was necessary, therefore, was to prepare projects and set to work rapidly to build the runway

[1] W. A. Lewis, 'Economic Development with Unlimited Supplies of Labour', *The Manchester School*, May 1954, pp. 160–1; R. Nurkse, *Problems of Capital Formation in Developing Countries*, Blackwell, Oxford, 1955. See also, Ch. Ayari, 'La Théorie de l'Épargne-travail de Nurkse et les Politiques de l'Emploi dans les Pays Sous-développés', *Planning and Economic Development*, I. Sachs (Ed.), Panstwowe Wydawnictwo Naukowe, Warsaw, 1964, pp. 199–257; also W. P. Strassmann, 'Construction Productivity and Employment in Developing Countries', *op. cit.*, May 1970, p. 504.

for industrial take-off.[2] Strassmann, in his *International Labour Review* article, calculated that during the period when GDP *per caput* was rising from around \$20 to around \$400 the construction industry would be expanding in most countries half as fast again as the rest of the economy. Most of this expansion represented a natural response to the pressing demands of organisations and individuals in the private and public sectors, yet particularly since the middle of the 1960s, there has also been an element of employment-creation in several governments' decision-taking regarding public works programmes.

Social Significance

For although the provision of a modern infrastructure was recognised as basic to economic development this was not in itself a conclusive argument since the cost of nationwide public works programmes would always far exceed any volume of financial resources which governments could expect to mobilise. In the 1960s certain countries began to realise that such programmes might have major social advantages which were not being revealed by the simpler techniques of cost-benefit analysis.

One such advantage is, of course, the income redistribution effect. Just as the orientation of manufacturing industry toward more labour-intensive technologies redistributes income in favour of the workers, so for the same reason does the execution of public works programmes. But there is another advantage which goes beyond those offered by an expansion of manufacturing, even in the form of small-scale industries. Public works offer opportunities for employment to those whom J. P. Lewis has described as the 'left-over people'.[3] In the villages these are the people who have no land to cultivate, who rarely obtain work and then only for brief periods and who live on the margin of subsistence. In the towns they are the immigrants from the countryside who have failed to find themselves jobs. They are people whom the present system of economic development appears unable to use; and they are the poorest. It is probable that even vigorous prosecution of the policies recommended in the previous three chapters would not make much of a dent in this hard core of poverty, whereas in construction and public works projects a large number of them could be utilised and as a result could set foot on the first rung of the ladder. More particularly, in the villages appeals can be made for volunteers to work together in community development programmes; young people can be mobilised at local and national level for youth service activities; both these approaches will be discussed later. There is so much to be done, there are so many people capable of doing it; somehow they have to be brought together.

[2] B. Ducros, 'Mobilisation des resources productives et développement', *Revue économique* (Paris), March 1963, pp. 216–41; see also G. Ardant, 'A Plan for Full Employment in the Developing Countries', *International Labour Review*, July 1963, p. 18. 'Full employment must be made not an end in itself but a means to an end'.

[3] John P. Lewis, *The Public-Works Approach to Low-end Poverty Problems*, United Nations, Committee for Development Planning, Doc. E/AC.54/L.42, December 1971.

Programmes of Selected Governments

Before presenting some of the experiences of individual governments it is necessary to sound a note of caution. These programmes cover different things in different countries: in some they include all forms of construction and public works; in others they exclude construction unless undertaken by the public sector; in yet others they refer only to projects for which the Public Works Department is responsible; in some cases they refer exclusively to special programmes for rural development or exclusively to the activities of an employment creation agency. Thus, international comparisons would be inappropriate, though much can be learned from successes and failures in each of the various types of programme.

In the Philippines the construction sector, which includes public works, was recorded in 1967 as employing 2·5 per cent of all employed persons, a rather low proportion considering that the average for ten developing countries (of which the Philippines was one) was 3·9 per cent. The Philippines' Development Plan envisages increasing this to only 3·1 per cent by 1974, a rather modest target. Apart from building which is in private hands, the other activities are divided among various government agencies. Some are carried out under the various Public Works Acts, notably highways, schools, airports and harbours; some under the National Irrigation Administration; some under the Authority for Community Development and some under the privately sponsored Philippine Rural Reconstruction Movement. In addition for two years (1962–4) an Emergency Employment Administration put over a crash programme, employing 262,000 persons in the first year and 133,000 in the second; but as the policy was to spread the work each individual was given only thirty days work per year. The over-all achievement amounted to less than 6 per cent of the number of workdays available in the agricultural sector, and the project has not been repeated.[4]

In India the Third Five-Year Plan envisaged employment in public works programmes at 100,000 in the first year rising to 2,500,000 in the final year of the Plan, on the basis of 100 days work per year during the dead season in agriculture; and this all additional to employment under the community development programmes. In the event the target was not attained, only 400,000 jobs being given in the final year; this was reported due to lack of technical staff, foremen, vehicles and materials and to insufficient planning.

A voluntary work organisation in Ceylon, the Shramadana, may have expansion potential, but until now it has generated little more than 2 million days of work per annum whereas it has been calculated that if each of the underemployed were hired for only seven working days per year a programme of 20 million working days would be required. East Pakistan possessed one of the most widely acclaimed rural development programmes starting in 1962–3. Over a period of seven years the annual average

[4] A. Lorenzo; *op. cit.*, also C. Hsieh, *Employment Problems and Policies in the Philippines*, Employment Research Papers, ILO, Geneva, 1969, pp. 78, 86.

number of jobs created was equivalent to 166,000 man years, employing actually between 600,000 and 1,000,000 persons for periods ranging from two weeks to four months. It had been planned to double this performance during the period 1970–5. None the less the volume of employment created was equivalent to not more than 1 per cent of the farm population of East Pakistan, nor more than 3·1 per cent of those reckoned to be wholly or partially unemployed.[5] This is not a criticism of the effort and its efficacy but rather an indication of the magnitude of the task in such a country. West Pakistan had a programme on similar lines, more modest in scale, and less successful perhaps because administratively centralised. The ideas of the Rural Programme were applied also to the cities. Here the object was to mobilise the urban unemployed for constructing low-cost dwellings, preparation of building sites for private construction, erecting schools, community centres, museums and administrative offices, laying out parks and recreation areas.[6] The labour-intensity was extraordinarily high, it being claimed that the investment was only 600 rupees ($127) per worker for a 150-day work year, compared with 5,250 rupees in the rest of the economy.

In Tunisia the Work Schemes Campaign against Underdevelopment has always been regarded as a transitional measure needed until such time as the unemployed and under-employed could be absorbed into the regular labour force. At its height between 1961 and 1963 this campaign provided work (on a basis of 200 workdays per year) for 280,000 to 300,000 persons compared with a total male population for the whole country of 828,000 in the age group twenty to fifty-nine years.[7] During the nineteen-sixties one-third of these people graduated to becoming permanent agricultural workers, so accordingly the numbers involved in the campaign declined until in 1970 they were 40 per cent below their peak. Even in that year, however, the campaign was taking care of about one-third of the country's unemployed. The main barrier to integrating a larger number into the economy was their lack of skills.

In Algeria the Full Employment Scheme in the early 1960s was providing rather less than 8 million days work per year, on a basis of 100 days work per person, which implied an absorption of some 5 per cent of the numbers estimated to be underemployed. By 1970 the Scheme was giving 12 million days work, while the 1970–3 Plan envisaged further expansion to 35 million days. In addition the reforestation programme was providing work for some 30,000 persons working in rotation ten days in every six weeks.

In Morocco the *Promotion Nationale* projects expanded from 14 million workdays in the early sixties to over 20 million by 1970, equivalent to

[5] J. J. Stern, *Background Paper on the Unemployment Estimates in Terms of Man-years*, Government of Pakistan, Planning Commission, December 1969, Appendix, Table 1 (mimeo).
[6] *The First Five-Year Plan, 1955–60*, National Planning Board December 1967 (Karachi, 1968), p. 623; see also *Community Development in Urban Areas*, Doc. 61.IV.6, The Third Five-Year Plan, June 1965, p. 515.
[7] Secrétariat d'Etat au Plan et aux Finances, *Plan Quadriennal* 1965–8, **3**, p. 21; also *Perspectives Décennales de Développement, 1962–71*, République tunisienne, p. 24.

about one-quarter of the estimated amount of underemployment; and this was additional to on-going public works activities of the classical type. Its comparative success has been ascribed to careful advance planning and to emphasise on enlisting the co-operation of the people at local level.[8] According to a report by the Bank of Morocco the *Promotion Nationale* was particularly successful in the rural districts. Indeed, only 15 per cent of its activity was oriented to urban areas – drainage, construction of schools, hospitals and low-cost dwellings. Here the operations encountered greater difficulties: costs were high and labour productivity low, many of the workers regarding the wages as a dole in return for which work was not necessary. Nevertheless, unemployment remained high, 800,000 in 1970 expected to rise to 900,000 by 1973 or 14 per cent of the active population.[9]

In Senegal the first plan (1961–4) provided for an expenditure equivalent to just over $5 million over the four years providing 4·4 million days of work. Had this target been realised it would have met about 1·5 per cent of the estimated seasonal unemployment in agriculture, but in practice it was onty partly accomplished. Recent reports indicate a slow improvement.[10] The programme has also been extended to urban areas.

In Dahomey the target was 4 million working days per annum which was achieved in the years 1966 to 1969, but it represented only 2·6 per cent of the estimated rural unemployment. As usual the employment was on a part-time basis and was oriented mainly to road building but also to earth dams, bunds for the paddy fields, construction of markets, wells, silos, schools and dispensaries. In urban areas the Department of Public Works was encouraged to put in tenders to the municipalities alongside those of private enterprises. Where these tenders were successful the projects required five hours work per day from each employee, four hours being paid and the fifth regarded as voluntary; free meals were provided. As in Morocco the labour productivity was low. It was even said that the scheme took work away from regular construction workers and, by not paying full wages, reduced the standard of living.[11]

In Madagascar the programme was based on the rural commune with the participation of the traditional *fokonolona*. Over the three Five-Year Plans from 1959–63 to 1969–73 the programmed expenditure varied between $11 million and $16 million per annum equivalent to 8–9 per cent of the total national investment. The target of employment to be generated

[8] *Le Plan Quinquennal 1968–72*, Ministère des Affaires Economiques, du Plan et de la Formation des Cadres, Rabat, 1969, p. 171. For an account of the programmes in Tunisia, Algeria and Morocco see, A. Tiano, 'Human Resources Investment and Employment Policy in the Maghreb', *International Labour Review*, February 1972, pp. 109–34.

[9] *Current Economic Position and Prospects of Morocco*, IBRDIDA, September 1971.

[10] République du Sénégal, *Plan Quadriennal de Développement* 1961–4, p. 194; also, E. Costa, 'Employment Problems and Policies in Senegal', *International Labour Review*, May 1967, p. 427.

[11] 'Back to the Land: the Campaign Against Unemployment in Dahomey', *International Labour Review*, January 1966, p. 34.

amounted to only ten days per year per head of active population in rural areas, rather modest considering that in many regions the people had work for only fifty (out of a maximum of say 250) days per year.[12]

Turning now to Latin American examples, the Co-operative Rural Works Programme in Mexico has been providing some 8 million days of work per annum. But in such a large country a programme of this magnitude only marginally affects the problem; for since it is calculated that the 6 million persons active in agriculture are on average unemployed for 100 working days per year, the Rural Works Programme has been absorbing only 1·3 per cent of the under-employment.[13] In Peru the employment creation effort bore a rather similar relation to the needs. The popular co-operation projects, reckoning to give each employee ten days of work per year, have been providing just over 3 million workdays annually, equivalent to 1·18 per cent of the estimated rural underemployment.[14] In Venezuela work creation has been oriented especially toward housing and main drainage in urban areas. Between 1961 and 1967 employment in the construction sector rose from 51,500 to 142,500 and its output approximately trebled.[15] Particularly in housing where the expenditures can be largely reimbursed there would seem to be considerable scope. Thus an inquiry in Medellín (Colombia) in 1969 showed that one-third of the owners of dwellings wanted better accommodation and were prepared to devote a higher proportion of their income to it if it were available – suggesting an opportunity for credit institutions.[16]

The general impression conveyed by these diverse attempts at launching special works programmes is that they have as yet been developed to only a very modest extent. Aside from one or two countries such as Tunisia they meet only a fraction of the needs and the opportunities; and in only a few cases does it appear that the most recent efforts are on a significantly larger scale than those of fifteen years ago. It is natural, therefore, to ask what are the constraints which apparently make it difficult to adopt this approach to employment creation more widely. There are indeed a number of obstacles encountered in virtually all the countries which merit closer examination.

The Labour Supply

It is necessary to begin by removing certain misunderstandings regarding

[12] Commissariat général au Plan, *Rapport sur le Développement de Madagascar*, Tananarive, October 1962, p. 22; see also. E. Costa, 'Employment Problems and Policies in Madagascar', *International Labour Review*, March 1968, pp. 217–50.

[13] *Interim Evaluation Report, Project Mexico 283 – Programme of Rural Works*, World Food Programme, Intergovernmental Committee, 17th Session, New York, April 1970, Doc. WFP/IGC: 17/10 Add. 2, Annex IV.

[14] Instituto Nacional de Planificación, *Plan de Desarrollo Económico y Social, 1967–70*, Lima, 1967, Vol. I, pp. 134 and 319.

[15] Instituto Latino-Americano de Planificación Economic y Social, *La Utilización de los Recursos Humanos en Venezuela*, Santiago de Chile, 1968, p. 32a.

[16] E. A. Aristizábral, *Estudio de la Demanda de Vivienda en la Ciudad de Medellín*, quoted in ILO, *The Colombia Report, op. cit.*, Appendix 7, pp. 395 ff.

the supply of labour. It is too often assumed that when a sample survey shows the agricultural labour force working on average say fifty days per year the peasants are unemployed and hence are available for work on the remaining 200 working days; but this makes the mistake of applying to the village the concepts of an urbanised population in industrial countries. Not only do many rural regions of developing countries still have a subsistence economy, or a subsistence economy just beginning to have market aspects, and not only is the marginal productivity of farm labour positive (although low) at some periods of the year and zero at other periods during which the individual may still not consider himself available for work, but the whole attitude toward work differs from that which has evolved over the centuries in industrial countries. Large numbers of persons, members of or living in cultivators' families, give a helping hand from time to time but over the year as a whole consume more than they produce; nothing wrong is seen in this, it being a family obligation to maintain them. There are also large numbers, perhaps particularly in Asian countries, who consider it a loss of status to engage in work of any kind, who if they possess land hire someone else to cultivate it or if they possess kinsmen expect the latter to support them. These matters including the question of definitions of visible and disguised under-employment will be examined at greater length in the chapter on agriculture which follows. For our present purpose it may be useful to distinguish, as Myrdal does, between the 'readily available labour supply' and the 'labour reserve.'

'In South Asia, the readily available labour supply represents only a very small proportion of the real waste of labour.'

Furthermore, because of traditional attitudes and the institutional framework

'part of the labour force that is wholly or partly idle or engaged in unproductive work is excluded from the pool of the readily available labour supply for reasons that cannot even be thought of in terms of the rationalistic conceptions of voluntariness or involuntariness. And even those members of the labour force who could be assumed to want to work . . . may be prevented from working . . . during certain periods of the year, or from working with other than certain employers or associates, or from working in other localities. In addition, they may be conditioned to working very short hours and with low efficiency.'[17]

Of course there exists no hard and fast demarcation between the two categories; they merge into one another. What is important for public works programmes is to recognise that a quite complex package of incentives, which will differ from country to country, is required in order to mobilise workers even in areas where unemployment and under-

---

[17] G. Myrdal, *Asian Drama, op. cit.*, Vol. II, Chapter 21, pp. 999–1000.

employment are clearly acute.[18] Though by no means all of them will be economic in character, these incentives will generally have to be strong to be effective, except in cases where the workers have a personal interest in the work to be performed, which is a reason why successful community development projects tend to be limited to improving the participants' own property. Even in towns the recent immigrants from rural areas still retain some of their traditional attitudes, so that in many cases nothing less than the going rates of wages will compensate in their eyes for a sacrifice of leisure.

In this context two lessons strikingly emerge from the country experiences recounted above. The first indicates the very limited scope for voluntary labour; wages in cash or cash-and-kind are generally necessary. The second is that most of the labour is available only on a part-time basis, at least initially; this, however, fits in with the desire of the authorities to spread the available work among as large a number of persons as possible. But it raises organisational difficulties, as will be seen presently. Having emphasised these points it remains true that in most developing countries the existing works programmes still only mobilise a fraction of even the 'readily available' rural labour supply.

Another constraint is the dearth of skilled, even of semi-skilled, labour of all kinds. No expertise may be necessary for digging a ditch but a little skill is necessary when it comes to laying a pipe at the correct gradient and effecting proper joins; much more when it comes to bricklaying or carpenters' work; there is an endemic lack of foremen, surveyors, mechanics and administrative personnel. Most of these have to be supplied from outside the rural area, and there are many unwilling to accept engagements under conditions of discomfort in remote places. That is why in a number of countries the army has been asked to loan personnel having these skills, e.g. in Morocco. In some Latin American countries technical instructors from the army lead the training courses. Wherever possible team leaders and foremen should be chosen and trained from among the workers themselves to ensure better communication with the labour force; these must be prepared to remain for the duration of the project because with the rapid turnover of the unskilled labour it is the foremen and the technical staff who provide the sole element of continuity. The amount of training given to the labourers depends partly on their nature and origin. In cases where the labour force on a project consists of a youth group the training element may be substantial – as much as one-quarter or more of their time in the National Service in Kenya, compared with only one hour per day for the rural people mobilised in the Tunisian programme, it being assumed that most of the youth are destined to be absorbed subsequently into the modern sector of the economy. In every

[18] P. N. Rosenstein-Rodan, 'Disguised Unemployment and Underemployment in Agriculture', *Monthly Bulletin of Agricultural Economics and Statistics*, FAO, Rome, **6**, 7/8, July–August 1957; see also E. M. Godfrey, 'Measuring the Removable Surplus of Agricultural Labour in Low-Income Economies', *Journal of Economic Studies* (Glasgow), **2**, 1, 1967, pp. 50–72.

115

case the lack of skills and the imperatives of training add significantly to the costs of the programmes.

As regards conditions of work it is the practice in most developing countries to exempt the labour engaged in these work projects from the provisions of the national labour codes in respect of sickness and accident benefits, pensions and even wage rates. Nevertheless certain minimum standards of safety, hygiene and labour inspection are usually required. This policy, without which incidentally the programmes would become excessively costly, has its justifications. For a large proportion of the workers it is their first experience of organised work in groups, they are receiving indirectly a training in how to adapt to the employment customs of the modern sector; their lodging and nutrition, if simple by urban standards, is almost always superior to what they have been accustomed to; and their length of stay on-the-job is generally brief. The problem becomes much more delicate where programmes operate in cities, because here it is natural for the workers to draw comparisons with the frequently unionised private enterprise labour – as occurred in Morocco for instance. Experience suggests the advisability of dealing with urban unemployment by means of the more conventional activities of Public Works Departments.

Yet in practice in rural areas too the wages paid on workcreating projects by now in most cases approximate to prevailing local rates, if only because of the need to provide incentives to participate. Thus in Tunisia and Morocco the workers on rural projects are now paid the going rates for hired agricultural labourers, though it may be part in cash and part in kind, the latter in Morocco never more than half the total. (The role of food aid will be discussed presently.) Such rates are already a strong incentive since they notably exceed the income of the small peasant. In certain community development projects in the Philippines the rates of pay actually exceed the farm labourers' wages.[19]

For the manner of payment of wages various devices have been tried with the object of stimulating higher productivity and/or discouraging absenteeism or total abandonment of the job. In some programmes part of the cash wage is held back to be handed over upon completion of the project. This form of forced saving is used for example where workers are clearing land for subsequent settlement by themselves or where the participants come from a youth corps whose services are largely voluntary. In the land settlement and clearance schemes in Dahomey those workers who are not owner-cultivators are given their held-back wages in the form of shares in the co-operative which will subsequently be established. Sometimes remuneration is on a piece-work basis, or 'finish and go' as it is called in certain countries. In Morocco this system is used by the *Promotion Nationale* and by the Forestry Department for afforestation projects but not by the Public Works Department on account of trade

[19] Draft Final Report, ILO Research Project, *The Impact on Employment of Community Development Programmes in the Philippines*, Vol. II, p. 416.

union opposition.[20] Many rural workers regard the additional leisure acquired by finishing the task quickly as more satisfactory than a money bonus.

The utilisation of youth groups in public works schemes, as distinct from land improvement schemes to be discussed in Chapter 7, has not become widespread: for instance the National Youth Service in Kenya has never used more than 3,000 persons at any one time. While it is true that young people are mostly mobile and willing to work in remote places, they need considerable training and their productivity is often low. In Afghanistan and several Latin American countries (Bolivia, Brazil, Colombia, Ecuador and Peru) the young people reporting for their military service are used by the army for such tasks as the building of roads, railways and dams.

One other topic has to be considered, namely what happens to the workers when a project is completed? Probably the majority, as has been seen, only wanted temporary employment between two agricultural seasons and will go back to cultivate their land. Others who have worked on clearing new land for settlement will occupy the farms when they are ready. Members of the youth service, having worked on these projects, receive priority in obtaining permanent posts in the public service (Singapore) or in private enterprise (Congo–Brazzaville, Kenya, etc.). For the rest the chances of permanent employment depend on the extent to which the workers have had access to and have profited from training in some skill while on the project. Those who have become proficient at a trade will find it relatively easy to get a job. Over 100,000 workers in the Tunisian programme have passed on to full integration in the modern sector of the economy. Those who for lack of opportunity or of aptitude have remained unskilled will probably revert to being underemployed in their villages, perhaps to join another project a year or two later. The better structured projects include provision for some vocational guidance before they are terminated.

Programme Financing

Inadequate financial resources present the most obstinate bottleneck to a larger-scale adoption of works programmes. Most governments of developing countries are already exploiting to the limit all possibilities of raising money for purposes of national development, and most would reply negatively if asked whether they thought the financial barriers could be pushed further back. The leaders of several governments have furthermore assimilated enough economic advice to fear that ambitious spending will cause inflation bringing in its train social, and perhaps political,

[20] J. P. Arlès, 'Manpower Mobilisation and Economic Growth: an Assessment of Moroccan and Tunisian Experience', *International Labour Review*, July 1966, pp. 1–21. Also Royaume du Maroc, Ministère du Développement, *Trois Années d'Aide Technique à la Promotion Nationale*, scei Coopération, November 1966, p. 48. Also, 'Back to the Land: the Campaign Against Unemployment in Dahomey', *International Labour Review*, January 1966, pp. 29–49, especially, pp. 41–43.

unrest. These considerations are likely to remain pertinent for some time to come.

Theoretically if the whole of the additional public works expenditure were covered by addition foreign aid there need be no inflationary effects, but such a situation hardly ever occurs. Indeed most of the governments of developed countries, and still more private capitalists, have been loath to lend for works programme purposes. If on the other hand, the expenditure is financed from internal sources much depends upon the method chosen. One extreme, the most inflationary, is simply to create the amount of money required. The other extreme, following the path of financial rectitude, is to impose additional taxation for every additional dollar of public expenditure. Yet even this austere alternative may have *some* inflationary effect, depending on the elasticities involved, because essentially it involves an income transfer from richer people who pay the taxes to poorer people who will obtain the employment. The former have a higher propensity to save than the latter, hence consumption will rise; and as most of the projects included in these works programmes are not ones which produce consumption goods, though they may facilitate an expansion of agricultural or industrial production at a later stage, a certain degree of inflation may be unavoidable.

Because food accounts for such a high proportion of expenditure in the lowest income groups the situation regarding food supplies tends to be the critical factor. Since for decades, even centuries, the volume of food production in most of these countries was stagnant or rising imperceptibly, it followed that any injection of purchasing power giving rise to a greater demand for food must lead either to increased food imports or to a rise in domestic food prices. But perhaps the situation is beginning to change, at least in those countries where the Green Revolution is making possible at long last an expansion of food output. In such circumstances an increase in purchasing power in the lowest income groups would not merely be without danger, it would be positively necessary, for otherwise the expanded food supplies could be marketed only by reducing their selling prices, thereby depriving the farmers of most of the benefits hoped for from the new techniques. Thus, to the extent that food output grows and the old bottleneck is removed, to this extent it will become not merely possible but desirable in the future to expand public works programmes.

Meanwhile, much the same result can be secured by means of food aid. It has become an accepted principle of both bilateral and multilateral food aid policy to grant food supplies in support of infrastructural projects of the various types described in this chapter, and while the conditions attached in some food aid legislation remain unfortunately restrictive, it seems certain that a much larger volume of food could be channelled to developing countries for these purposes. It should not be a necessary condition that the food thus imported be distributed to the project workers as part of their pay, though this may be found convenient in many cases. The anti-inflationary effect will be the same if the food is sold by the Government on the market and the proceeds used to finance the works projects, though care needs to be taken as to the manner and timing of such disposals so as not to affect adversely the prices being received by local food producers. On the developing countries' side governments should not find it difficult to have always at hand a much larger list of requests well-qualified for food aid support than the donor bodies are capable of meeting.[21]

In mountainous Lesotho, many villages that could formerly only be reached on foot or on horseback are now linked to the rest of the country by 1,000 kilometres of 'access tracks' negotiable by 4-wheel-drive vehicles. These have been constructed or improved by voluntary labour, with a minimum of machinery, remunerated only by food rations supplied by international programmes. Since many of the men of this country work in the neighbouring Republic of South Africa, the workers are mainly women who, without these programmes, would have almost no opportunities for useful work apart from their domestic labour and working in their fields. In recent years an average of about 5,000 people at a time have been employed on these roadworks. They receive food rations for themselves and for dependants. Besides providing work and food the access tracks programme has brought considerable economic and social benefits to many remote villages. The people have benefited as consumers (the prices of goods in shops have come down) and producers (their wool, mohair and other produce is conveyed to markets more quickly and cheaply and with less risk of rain damage than when carried on the backs of pack-horses: and supplies are delivered more easily and cheaply to maintain schools, hospitals and clinics.

While the short-term effects of food aid can often be very beneficial both to output and employment in receiving countries, doubts have sometimes been expressed as to whether the longer-term effects are always beneficient. Necessity, it can be argued, is the mother of hard work as well as of invention. It is possible that the availability of food aid may in some cases serve as a disincentive to food production and agricultural development. If they know they will have food in any case, some cultivators may plant less or neglect to weed their fields. There may also be some negative effect on the motivation of governments to bring about structural changes in such matters as land distribution and the availability of water and draft power.

However vigorously food-aid possibilities are exploited, there remains for governments a basic financial problem. In many countries it is hard to believe that the conventional sources of tax-raising have been exhausted; there seems still to be much conspicuous consumption of luxuries part of which could be taxed away. There is also scope for augmenting the yields on *existing* taxes by tightening up on evasions. A large potential source of

21 A. Dawson, 'Food for Development: the World Food Programme', *International Labour Review*, August 1964, pp. 99–129. Also J. Shaw, 'The Mechanism and Distribution of Food Aid', *Journal of World Trade Law*, Special Issue, 'Development Aid', 4, 2, March–April 1970, pp. 207–37.

tax revenue lies in the increases in land values resulting from urbanisation. Although it is recognised that these windfall capital gains could be taxed without weakening private enterprise, few developing countries have actually attempted to tap this source of revenue.[22] Another promising approach should be to exploit more fully the local potentialities for revenue raising. It might mean decentralising more than some governments are willing to do the design of and responsibility for the projects themselves, but perhaps many local communities would find ways of making a financial contribution as a price to be paid for greater physical participation.

Quite a number of projects are suitable for auto-financing at least to the extent of covering part of their cost: for instance, irrigation projects where water rents can be charged, terracing and field drainage which improve the yield-potential of the land and for which a contribution from the beneficiaries would be justified, land clearance for new settlement and, of course, low-cost housing which is made available for rent or purchase. While in all these categories of projects the recuperation of a smaller or greater proportion of the expenditures would be appropriate, yet it has to be recognised that work-creating programmes tend to be operated in backward parts of a country where poverty is most acute, as the Governing Council of the *Promotion Nationale* in Morocco has remarked,[23] and where the 'ability to pay' may be non-existent.

Yet another approach is to devise cost-reduction procedures so that for a given sum of money a larger number of projects can be undertaken. While it would be false economy to cut out such features as the training of the workers in certain skills, it should be possible to economise on items of equipment, on supporting services and by in general more efficient planning and organisation to ensure that, for instance, an expensive machine which has been hired by the day is not sitting idle for several weeks because a complementary piece of equipment has not arrived. Although government-operated programmes for the most part have a bad reputation in this respect, examples can be cited in which their performance compares favourably with that of private enterprise, especially for projects located in remote regions. For example, in respect to road-making and surfacing the jobs carried out by the *Promotion Nationale* were cheaper than comparable work carried out by contractors in remote provinces such as Beni Mellal and Marrakesch but more expensive in more urbanised regions such as Casablanca, Rabat and Meknés.[24] For small-scale waterworks in the province of Kaar-es-Souk the *Promotion Nationale* prices were 60–75 per cent of those quoted by private firms. In Peru the Popular Co-operation Programme has reported the following relationship between its prices and those of contractors:

22 J. P. Lewis, *op. cit.*, pp. 30–1.

23 Délégation générale à la Promotion nationale et au Plan, Moroc, *Promotion Nationale au Maroc (1964,)* p. 133.

24 M. D. Layachi, *Technical Meeting on Productivity and Employment in Public Works in African countries, Conclusions and Documents*, ILO, Geneva, 1964.

Roads	1/6
Irrigation canals	1/3
Drinking water conduits	1/2·4
Schools, clinics, etc.	1/2
Bridges	1/1·5

Admittedly the Programme's prices included nothing for materials furnished by the villagers, but these were negligible especially for the last items on the list.

One aspect of financing that sometimes is overlooked relates to subsequent maintenance. It is no good building roads if they are not afterwards kept in passable condition or drainage ditches if they are allowed to become blocked. Normally maintenance charges should be borne by the individual or the community which is the beneficiary, but they need to be foreseen and the shouldering of responsibility for them negotiated in advance.

Project Organisation

It has been noted how comparatively modest has been the scale of operations of even the most energetic governments in employment-creating programmes and how the stringency of funds has been a major factor. But there has been another factor causing governments to hesitate, namely the poor reputation of the responsible agencies in matters of organisation. Programmes have been run either by *ad hoc* boards amateurish both in approach and in execution or by Public Works Departments which with rare exceptions do not attract the best abilities in government service. Without doubt the disappointing results of many of the projects must be attributed largely to poor planning and indifferent administration.

One deficiency has been in the quality and quantity of technical personnel – the failure to consult planners and social scientists, insufficiency of civil engineers, surveyors, accounts, failure to provide each project with repair facilities for its machines with the consequence of much loss of time and accumulation of expense when they were out of action, and so on. These faults have been conspicuous especially in projects operated by volunteers and in those where the watchword was 'hurry'. Another source of trouble has been conflict between departments. Since many projects are multi-disciplinary in character they naturally relate to the subject-field of two or more ministries, for instance, education, health, agriculture, interior, transport, finance and, of course, also public works. In cases where a single ministry is given supreme responsibility for a particular project the other ministries, because of professional jealousy, will be reluctant to co-operate, while if responsibility is vested in an interdepartmental committee the project's operations may be held up for long periods until disagreements are resolved.

These troubles are themselves related to another deficiency which is the almost universal tendency to over-centralisation, and in this context the Provincial (or State) Government of a large country is as much a 'centre' as the Central Government of a small one. Administration, especially day-to-day administration from a central point of operations in a remote area inevitably causes delays and confusions; it also affords the temptation to make appointments to supervisory posts in the programme the reward for political services as well as facilitating cruder forms of corruption. By contrast the virtue of decentralisation is that it enlists the participation of local bodies in the districts and the villages. This participation is of importance at all stages: in the selection of the project, in planning it, in administering it and in providing for after-care and maintenance. The local people need to feel that it is *their* project, not something imposed from outside.[25] The success of the programme in East Pakistan has been attributed to the fact that it was perhaps the most decentralised programme on record and the most successful in arousing the enthusiasm of the local people. This is not to deny the necessity of elements from the outside. The project leader may frequently be an outsider – Tunisia they were in many cases furnished by the Néo-Destour party; outside equipment and materials are also needed. The legitimate role of the central authorities is to lay down the key procedures within which the responsible local agencies have to operate, to set minimum technical standards as to the quality of the work done and to enforce both procedures and standards by means of frequent inspection. The central authorities could indeed use these opportunities to arrange for the training of local officials in such matters and in financial accountability.[26]

A characteristic of the most efficient programmes, those in East Pakistan and in Tunisia, has been their systems of inspection. In East Pakistan this service was provided by the Basic Democracies and Local Government Department and embraced all aspects of the projects – technical, administrative and financial. Inspectors were authorised to consult the local officials with a view to immediate correction of shortcomings, the reports to headquarters being for the record or for the few more difficult problems. In the Tunisian campaign against underdevelopment a regular reporting service was introduced between the projects and the State Secretariat for Planning and Finance.[27] These two represented perhaps the happiest examples of combining local initiative with central supervision.

As already mentioned a defect of many projects has been insufficient advance provision for maintenance. Even in East Pakistan where Union (district) councils were instructed to spend one-quarter of their total revenue on maintenance and risked losing future projects if they failed to

[25] 'Civic Service and Community Works in Mali', *International Labour Review*, January 1966, pp. 50–65, especially p. 60.

[26] J. P. Lewis, *op. cit.*, p. 35.

[27] A. H. Khan, 'The Works Programme in East Pakistan', in ILO, *Technical Meeting on Productive Employment in Construction in Asia* (Bangkok, 1968). Management Development Series, No. 8, Geneva, 1969, pp. 134–47. 'Manpower Mobilisation for Economic Development in Tunisia', *International Labour Review*, January 1966, pp. 5–18.

do so, some of the recently built roads were reported badly maintained.[28] In the Philippines where no authority either local or central was required to undertake maintenance, the roads and canals rapidly fell into disrepair. Moreover, maintenance and repair are ongoing activities which generate employment: in certain developed countries it has been calculated that these activities occupy some 40 per cent of the entire labour force in the construction sector,[29] and while in developing countries the proportion would naturally be lower this type of work would provide openings for some of the project workers wishing to continue in permanent paid employment.

Integration into National Plans

The utility of public works programmes needs to be evaluated within the framework of the national plans and policy objectives. At the least the programmes and their projects should not conflict with over-all objectives nor compete for the use of scarce resources; at best the projects should complement and support the activities in related fields.

Consider first the physical priorities. Where a government is pursuing a vigorous policy of agricultural modernisation either in a particular region or over the country as a whole, there are types of projects which support and further that modernisation will have special utility – irrigation and land improvement works. Where manufacturing plants are being encouraged to establish themselves in provincial growth centres, useful supporting projects would include housing, drainage and road improvement. Where the emphasis is on the integrated development of a selected region the works projects might also, for the time being, be concentrated in that region. If such complementarity is organised both programmes are likely to yield more fruitful results.

Consider next the choice of techniques, as between more labour-intensive or more capital-intensive. This choice is usually considered to be the exclusive concern of the project and those responsible for it. But there is also a national aspect in as much as the works programmes are competing for national funds. Thus in Tunisia where the Campaign Against Under-development was at one time consuming one-sixth of the national budget the government found it necessary to limit expenditure on materials and equipment to 10 per cent, later 15 per cent, of each project's cost, exception being made for very large works requiring heavy equipment for which special subsidies were granted. Or again, the project manager's interest being to maximise the productivity of his resources, he may in many operations prefer mechanical to manual methods, whereas from the national point of view it may be preferable to accept a lower level of

[28] J. W. Thomas, 'Rural Public Works and East Pakistan's Development', in W. P. Falcon and G. F. Papanek (Eds.), *Development Policy II – The Pakistan Experience*, Harvard Univ. Press, 1971, p. 199.

[29] E. J. Howenstine, *Compensatory Employment Programmes*, OECD, Paris, 1968; also *Report of the Committee of Inquiry Concerning Labour in Building and Civil Engineering*, HMSO, London, 1968, pp. 25–7.

economic efficiency in the interest of generating a greater volume of employment. This relates back to the factor price distortion mentioned in an earlier chapter. Close co-operation between those in charge of public works programmes and the national planners should promote a wider utilisation of shadow prices in determining the choice of project technology.[30]

Some projects require support from concurrent activities on other fronts for their success. For instance, the terracing, irrigation and drainage of agricultural land may create insoluble conflicts as to land and water rights, often of absentee proprietors, unless accompanied by land reform measures. Also the co-operation of local cultivators is unlikely to be enlisted if the benefits are expected to accrue to landlords. In Morocco agrarian reform was found to be a pre-condition to the implementation of land improvement schemes.[31]

Co-ordination of programmes is not something to be undertaken solely at national level; it needs to be taken care of at local and district level too. This involves more than just the decentralisation of responsibilities for operations referred to above, important though that is. It involves integration with the other activities of the local authorities at their several levels. The outstanding success achieved in the Comilla district of East Pakistan was in large part due to deliberate incorporation of the programme into the regular activities of the village councils the district authorities and above them the provincial authority. The project proposals were formulated in these various bodies with the collaboration of the people's leaders at each level.[32] In Morocco the provincial councils of the *Promotion Nationale* include, in addition to technical and administrative representatives of the parent body, representatives elected by the communes. In Algeria the projects are formulated in the councils of the communes and then go up through the normal administrative channels of government to the district, the department and the ministry.

A further desideratum is to provide a high degree of continuity in the works programme as a whole. It is recognised that many individual projects may be of short duration and that within projects there will usually be a rather rapid turnover of the labour force, but just because of this it is important to arrange that as one project terminates another takes its place so that the technical and administrative personnel who are gradually acquiring valuable experience will be assured of continuous employment. To achieve this requires careful forward programming and budgeting at the centre; but it will also reduce costs by ensuring, for

[30] N. N. Franklin, 'A Note on Opportunity Cost, Shadow Prices and Labour Intensive Employment', in ILO, *Technical Meeting on Productive Employment in Construction in Asia*, Management Development Series, No. 8, Geneva, 1969, pp. 40–4.

[31] A. Tiano, 'La Lutte d'un Pays Agricain Contre le Sous-emploi: le Maroc', *Annales Africaines*, Paris, 1962, No. 2, pp. 406–50.

[32] R. V. Gilbert, 'The Works Programme in East Pakistan', *International Labour Review*, March 1964. pp. 241–75. Also: *The Works Programme in Comilla, A Case Study*, Pakistan Academy for Rural Development, Kotbari, Comilla, November 1966, pp. 29–42.

example, the full and continuing utilisation of such equipment as tractors and bulldozers. In all these ways the programmes are more likely to be efficient if they are meticulously planned and if at the same time they are co-ordinated with the plans in other spheres of national development.

Choice of Projects

Much of what has been said above in effect spells out the criteria which should serve as a guide in choosing projects. Thus those with a high labour content have *a priori* a strong claim. In fact in Algeria it was required that labour costs must constitute at least 65 per cent of the total costs of each project and in Morocco the minimum was set at 75 per cent, though in both countries some exceptions were permitted for projects which clearly had high economic value. In the Philippines preference was to be given to projects in which the labour cost exceeded 60 per cent.

A related criterion has been the amount of on-going employment which would be provided after the project's termination. This was a particular preoccupation of the *Promotion Nationale* in Morocco which, using both criteria, classified in projects as in table 6.1. In the course of time the

Table 6.1 *Employment Creation by Type of Project*

Type of project	Immediate, temporary employment	Permanent employment days per annum
Field banks and bunds: per hectare	180 days	30 days
Reforestation: per hectare	130–60 days	6 days (increase in output after 12–15 years)
Clearing undergrowth: per hectare	25 days	30 days
Scarifying land: per hectare	10 days	
Clearing stones: per hectare	30 days	
Small irrigation works: per hectare	450–550 days	Maintenance 10–25 days Agricultural benefit: 10–80 days
Dirt roads: per kilometre	18,000–41,000 days	Maintenance 50–540 days (economic gain positive or negative according to intensity of use)
Buildings for village industries	Not calculable	Not calculable
Public buildings	Not calculable	Negative benefits, maintenance expenses

Source: A. Tiano, *La Politique Économique et Financière du Maroc Indépendant*, Institut d'Etude du Développement Economique et Social, Etudes Tiers-Monde, PUF, Paris, 1963, p. 38.

Moroccan authorities have come to give greater priority to land improvement projects than to infrastructural ones. Similar priorities were established in Algeria but varying according to region: irrigation in the pre-Sahara districts but roads and soil conservation in the mountains.

In India experience accumulated over several years gave the following relationships between labour costs and total costs: 90 per cent for reforestation, 70 per cent for soil improvement, local roads and small irrigation works, 50 per cent for large-scale irrigation, housing and other buildings, 20 per cent for harbour works, 15 per cent for railway construction and 5 per cent for erecting plants for heavy industry.[33] A similar ranking was established in East Pakistan, namely 94 per cent for excavating cisterns, 90·3 per cent for making farm roads (kutcha roads), 86·9 per cent for small canals, 84·8 per cent for embankments, but only 18·7 per cent for main roads, 16·4 per cent for buildings and 14·7 per cent for bridges and culverts.[34] The relative labour-intensity of the different types of projects is roughly the same in the different countries cited.

Efforts have been made to present the main factors affecting the choice of works projects in the form of cost-benefit analyses. Sometimes these focus rather narrowly on financial costs and benefits. A more ambitious approach is to try to measure costs and benefits from the point of view of society as a whole, using shadow prices where appropriate. The Three-Year Plan of Morocco (1965-7) it was stated: 'the major concern of the *Promotion Nationale* should be to ensure the profitability of its projects, taking into account the needs for production, the available human and material investment resources and the chances of success'.[35] It was assumed that most of the benefit would accrue from increases in production potential, agricultural or other, and from the permanent additions to the volume of employment. This, however, left more than one question unanswered. Apart from the choice or projects, already alluded to, on the basis of their employment – generating capacity, there was, and is, a choice within each project between using more manual labour or more mechanical equipment. The social objective of maximising employment often conflicts with the economic objective of achieving the maximum for a given expenditure. Moreover, as between these two alternatives the preference curve is constantly changing its shape. To the extent that it becomes necessary in rural districts, and still more in urban areas, to offer incentive wages to obtain the needed manpower, the argument becomes stronger for using at least intermediate technology and associating a certain amount of mechanical aids, e.g. earth-moving equipment with the manual labour of the project. Otherwise the programme authority runs the danger that the tasks could be performed more cheaply by contracting firms, in just the same way as it was seen that village industries

[33] J. M. Healey, *The Development of Social Overhead Capital in India, 1950-60*, Blackwell, Oxford, 1965, p. 126.

[34] *Performance Report 1967-8*, The Basic Democracies and Local Government Department, East Pakistan.

[35] Royaume du Maroc, Délégation générale à la Promotion nationale et au Plan, *Plan triennal 1965-7*, Rabat, 1965, p. 25.

may be unable to compete unless they assimilate a certain quantity of intermediate technology.

Considerations of type of technology and type of project are inextricably interrelated. There are some types of project where the choice of a labour-intensive technology will have comparatively few adverse effects on costs: notably afforestation, land improvement, small-scale canals and drains – in East Africa one reckons ninety work days per hectare for planting conifers, in Arab countries an average of 150 days.[36] When it comes to road building the choice beings to expand. Manual methods are justified in the building of dirt roads with only small bridges, cuttings and embankments. The clearing of the land and the earth-moving operations are something with which the local people are well-acquainted. Even the spreading of gravel and the asphalting can in some circumstances advantageously be done by hand. But when it comes to main roads which have to be given strong foundations and reinforced bridges the use of machines becomes overwhelmingly more economical, e.g. the excavation of rock, the in-filling of marshes and the construction of viaducts.[37] Thus it has been calculated that in the task of cutting away soft earth and transporting it to the other side of the road manual methods are cheaper than machine ones only if each labourer can move at least $3 \cdot 5$ m^3 per day and if his wage is very low. Loading the earth with shovels onto a lorry is even more uneconomic. In Jamaica the road maintenance authority recognises that mechanical methods are cheaper though it uses them minimally in order to contribute to the generation of employment. In many instances the comparison made is not a true one. In Kenya, for example, the main road from Nairobi towards the Ethiopian border and the Thika-Seven Forks road were built with the help of the National Youth Service at a cost approximating to that quoted by private contracting firms, but the youth were paid very little and a considerable amount of equipment was employed. In Morocco the 'Route d l'unité' was allegedly built at one-quarter of the cost required by private contractors, but much of the manual labour was performed by unpaid volunteers while the heavy equipment was loaned by the army. Similarly the Séoul–Pusan road in South Korea, 428 km long, was built in twenty-nine months at a cost per kilometre of five times less than the recently constructed Central Highway in Japan, but again much of the labour force consisted of agricultural workers (paid very little) in the dead season and of the military.

In the case of irrigation projects frequently the most successful combination is to employ machinery for the major works and manual methods for the minor canals, ditches and drains, also for making the access roads to

36 *Forestry and Forest Product Industries*, Conference on Industrial Development in the Arab Countries, Doc. CIDAC.KUW/II/FAO-10, 17 January 1966, p. 52.

37 M. S. Ahmad, 'Some Aspects of Road Construction in Developing Countries', *Technical Meeting on Productive Employment in Construction in Asia, op. cit.*, pp. 70–86; also G. S. Glaister, 'The Construction of Roads in a Developing Capital Deficient Environment', *ibid.*, pp. 118–33; also J. Müller, 'Labour-Intensive Method in Low-cost Road Construction: a Case Study', *International Labour Review*, April 1970, pp. 359–76.

the dam site, for making wooden coffer-dams, for stone embankments, and so on. Such combinations were utilised in the construction of the Bakhra, Gandak and Chandan dams in India, the Sonaichari dam in East Pakistan, and others.[38]

The time factor also plays a role here; it certainly did in the Indus basin project in West Pakistan which had to be completed in ten years. Where the duration of a project is deliberately spread out by using manual methods the machine costs (always *some* machinery has to be employed) will be higher because the machines have to be retained on the project for a longer period; also there is delay to the commencement of the increased output from the improved farm land or the improved market access on the newly-built road.[39] Rare is the case, though there was one in Nepal on the Kosi project, where because of special local circumstances the manual methods are quicker and cheaper than the machine.[40]

In these calculations of comparative costs it must always be remembered that most of the machinery in question has to be imported, as also its replacement parts, that to keep it in running order assumes the availability of skilled mechanics and that unless it can be used almost continuously its amortisation will be a heavy burden on the project costs.

Often a simpler and more acceptable solution to the problem of choice will be found in improving the efficacy of the hand tools used by the labourers. In a particular case in India it was found that the mere replacement of the traditional 'mumtys' by shovels and of baskets by wheelbarrows increased labour productivity by from 30 to 100 per cent. Similar modest changes effected in Nigeria and in Tanzania also had the effect of doubling productivity.

Local housing projects offer an opportunity to utilise mainly manual labour accompanied by economical deployment of scarce skills. For example, in the village of Akyar in Turkey where houses were to be erected under the Village Reconstruction Scheme, two architects and five artisans took care of the designing, the concrete work and the specialised installations while the villagers prepared and laid the foundations and performed all the other manual tasks, using almost entirely local materials.[41] What appears not to function well is the recruitment of youth groups for the construction of dwellings, proving to be more expensive than the employment of private enterprise. This has been the experience in Kenya, Tunisia and elsewhere.

[38] K. Sain and K. Phonekeo, 'Policy and Economy Considerations in Choice of Construction Techniques and Procedures', *Technical Meeting on Productive Employment in Construction in Asia, op. cit.*, pp. 45–54. Also J. S. Jain, 'Employment Possibilities in Irrigation, Power and Land Development Projects', *ibid.*, pp. 14–17 and 87–104.

[39] A. Waterston, *Development Planning – Lessons of Experience*, John Hopkins, Baltimore, 1965, p. 305.

[40] H. W. Singer and D. Dreiblatt, 'Infrastructure Development and Employment Promotion in Development Planning', *Technical Meeting on Productive Employment in Construction in Asia, op. cit.*, pp. 67–8.

[41] C. N. Grummitt, 'Utilisation of Unskilled Labour Resources: A Systematic Approach to Repetitive Housing', *Technical Meeting on Productive Employment in Construction in Asia, op. cit.*, pp. 162–78.

Conclusions

This review of employment generating programmes, especially rural works programmes, has demonstrated both the scope which exists and the many difficulties which are encountered. There are difficulties in mobilising the labour and in finding the investment capital, difficulties in choice of projects and of technologies, difficulties of organisation and of integration into other aspects of the development effort. Some writers are therefore inclined to write off the idea itself as a non-starter. Myrdal put his own view bluntly when he wrote: 'Every effort to mobilise and organise under-utilised labour for investment purposes has been a failure or a near-failure.'[42] He supported this statement by citing the political impossibility of imposing income-redistributive taxes, the insufficient supply of technicians and organisers, the unwillingness of most villagers to work except for their personal advantage. However this is an exaggeration.[43] Even in Asia, with which Myrdal was primarily concerned, the East Pakistan programme has been more successful than he would have admitted possible. The successes in Tunisia and Morocco also suggest that the difficulties are not all insuperable. Indeed, other writers, such as J. P. Lewis, believe that governments could accomplish far more along these lines and have spelt out some of the steps necessary for a more rapid advance. In their view the millions of 'left-over people' and the millions of left-over jobs could be brought together, additional sources of financing could be tapped, administrative organisation could be tightened and the enthusiasm of local people could be awakened by giving them a greater voice in the preparation and execution of projects.

Until now most of the national works programmes have been on a scale which can only be described as trivial in relation to the needs and opportunities. Yet they construct facilities to which private investment will not be attracted and they can employ a section of the labour force which private enterprise will not be able to use, at least in this generation. Some of the difficulties are diminishing as a result of the advance of technology, e.g. the Green Revolution which is beginning to remove the inflationary bottleneck of inadequate food supplies; the overcoming of many of the other difficulties is being learned through the act of operating the programmes. While important obstacles still remain there would seem to be solid grounds for optimism, for believing that in the years immediately ahead these programmes can be substantially expanded. A concerted attack on the worst pockets of poverty through the vehicle of works projects may soon become a normal feature of each developing country's national development plan.

[42] G. Myrdal, *Asian Drama, op. cit.*, p. 1359.
[43] N. N. Franklin, 'Asian Drama and the World Employment Programme', *International Labour Review*, November 1969.

Chapter 7

Agriculture

Population and Output

The agricultural population accounts for 68 per cent of the total population of the developing countries, according to the estimates of the United Nations. The proportion is around 50 per cent in Latin America but as high as 80 per cent for Africa, Asia falling between these two; yet in some Asian countries the figure is extremely high, e.g. in 1965 it was 92 per cent in Nepal and 80 per cent in Thailand.[1]

As a proportion of the total, the agricultural population is falling in almost all developing countries (see table 2.1). Thus during the nineteen-fifties it fell from 26·7 to 19·8 per cent in Argentina, from 45·1 to 34·3 per cent in Venezuela; between 1956 and 1966 from 58·0 to 47·1 per cent in Iran and between 1960 and 1969 from 65·9 to 51·4 per cent in South Korea; however, in India it actually increased from 70·6 to 73·8 per cent between 1951 and 1961. A fall can be expected to continue throughout the process of industrialisation, since the percentage engaged in agriculture is inversely correlated with the level of GDP per caput.

Yet a falling percentage does not imply a decline in absolute numbers; on the contrary in all these countries the farm population continues to increase. Taking the developing countries as a whole it is expected to increase by 13 per cent during the nineteen-seventies and to continue increasing until the end of the century. What are the prospects for agriculture offering employment to these growing numbers of people? Already, as is well known, there exists in agriculture much unemployment and an even greater amount of under-employment, so that farm employment would have to expand even more rapidly than the rural population increase in order to ameliorate the employment situation.

On the side of agricultural production the recent record is far from encouraging. During the nineteen-fifties the volume of agricultural output in the developing countries rose at a rate of 3·5 per cent per annum, though in the earlier part of the decade the growth rate was inflated by the element of recovery from wartime dislocation in many countries; for the nineteen-sixties the rate of growth was only 2·7 per cent. Growth was above average in the Near East, below average in Africa.[2] It was as high as 5·1 per cent per annum (1939–59) in Mexico but as low as 0·9

[1] Asian Productivity Organisation, *Expert Group Meeting on Agricultural Mechanisation, December 12–18, 1967*, Tokyo, Vol. II, October 1968, Table 10, p. 20.
[2] FAO, *The State of Food and Agriculture*, Rome, 1971, p. 2.

per cent in Indonesia, 0·4 per cent in Burma and 0·2 per cent in Algeria (all three for the period 1934–8 to 1961–5).[3] When the growth in agricultural output is related to the growth in population in the developing countries the picture looks much worse. Thus during the decade of the sixties there was no growth at all in output *per head*. The conclusion is unavoidable that on the side of production there seems to be as yet no dynamism which could make a significant contribution to employment.

Under-employment and Low Productivity

In attempting to apply the notions of employment and unemployment (or under-employment) to the agriculture of the developing countries one encounters basic conceptual difficulties, as already pointed out in Chapter 2. Under the circumstances of a subsistence economy – and the situation is not essentially different when the peasant has some relation to the market but does not sell more than a minor part of his output – the number of persons living on farms has resulted not from any 'decision to employ' but rather quite simply from the excess of births over deaths in the family; in the absence of alternative employment opportunities its upper limit is set by the number of mouths that can be fed. If the level of living becomes unbearably low the more venturesome move away to the towns in search of work.

Because for any particular family the amount of land is limited, and because of the particular techniques of production known to the cultivator, in the short run, it often appears to him that nothing is gained by the family members putting in more hours of work per day or per week; in other words that the marginal productivity of his labour is zero or close to zero. In the view of the cultivator the amount of labour which can be profitably applied to the available land is limited and this labour is shared out among the family members. The sharing will usually be unequal, one or two doing most of the field work while others lend a hand at peak seasons; but on the typical mini-farm even the busiest workers put in rather a small number of hours per year measured by industrial standards. There is another factor: in a number of countries because the undertaking of manual work in the fields is associated with lower caste or social status, the head of the family may contrive to work as little as possible; if he has sufficient land or can otherwise afford it he will hire someone else to cultivate his land.

The system has considerable flexibility. Although there is normally an over-supply of manpower in the villages, yet they are capable of absorbing an influx of people, as for instance during the Great Depression of the nineteen-thirties when labour was being discharged from the plantations, or at other times when civil commotion causes a movement of refugees.

[3] K. N. Raj, 'Some Questions Concerning Growth, Transformation and Planning in Agriculture in Developing Countries', *Journal of Development Planning*, United Nations, New York, No. 1, pp. 15–38; see also P. Bairoch, *Diagnostic de l'Évolution Economique du Tiers Monde* 1900–68, Paris, Gauthier-Villars, 1970, p. 25.

On the other hand the over-supply can exist simultaneously with acute labour shortages at certain times and in certain places due to geographical seasonal or social rigidities in labour mobility, which incidentally is a reason why paradoxically the volume of employment can be increased in some situations by the introduction of machinery because this breaks the bottleneck of labour shortage at the peak seasons of the farming year.

While the major part of the agriculture of the developing countries is operated on the basis of family farms with these blurred lines between employment, under-employment and unemployment, nevertheless in some countries, especially those in which plantations and/or large estates still have importance, more than half the agricultural labour force consists of hired workers as the figures given in table 7.1 indicate. Whether a

Table 7.1   *Hired Workers as Percentage of Agricultural Labour Force: Selected Countries*

Country	Date	Percentage	Country	Date	Percentage
Mauritius	1962	90	Reunion	1961	58
Martinique	1967	70	Ceylon	1963	55
Salvador	1961	64	Uruguay	1963	54
Chile	1970	61	Mexico	1960	54
Algeria	1966	59	Costa Rica	1963	53

Source: *Yearbook of Labour Statistics*, ILO, Geneva, 1971.

hired agricultural worker is employed or unemployed on any particular date can of course be enumerated, but the concept of the extent to which his services are needed in the enterprise may be far from distinct. Many large estates and even some plantations have an employment policy which embraces an obligation to maintain the resident families whether or not at certain seasons or in certain years the amount of work really requires that number of people. There is also the previously mentioned case of the small cultivator who hires a man so that he himself may work less. It must therefore be concluded that even in countries where hired labour predominates in agriculture the criteria of employment and unemployment differ markedly from those applicable in other sectors of the economy.

Over the past two decades many economists have given attention to this farm employment problem both in its theoretical and its practical aspects. Already in 1954 Arthur Lewis was discussing the conditions in which a super-abundance of manpower could cause the marginal productivity of labour to be insignificant, zero or even negative.[4] Nurkse, arriving at the same conclusion, pointed out that the idle or semi-idle family members were in effect being supported by the product of the

[4] Sir W. Arthur Lewis, 'Economic Development with Unlimited Supplies of Labour', *The Manchester School of Economic and Social Studies*, May 1955, pp. 139–91.

labour of the other members.[5] Leibenstein by another route arrived at a similar conclusion.[6] Georgescu-Roegen sought to define over-population as being when a proportion of it could be transferred elsewhere without diminishing the volume of output.[7] All these writers adhere to broadly the same school of thought, but there are others who take the opposite view. Schultz, for example, has always rejected the notion that the marginal productivity of labour in farming could be zero.[8] Viner and Myrdal put the same point another way by insisting that even without any change in techniques or in the quantity of land at his disposal the cultivator could obtain an increase in output by increasing the input of labour,[9] though Myrdal admits that in as much as impediments frequently prevent this from happening there will in practice be under-employment of available labour. Mellor considers that size of farm constitutes an important determining factor and notes the practical impossibility of transfer of family labour from over-manned to under-manned enterprises.[10] Eckaus has pointed out that an increase in input of labour generally needs to be accompanied by some increased input of capital which the cultivator simply has not got.[11] Owing to the great variety of local circumstances in the agriculture of developing countries each of these several theses may be substantiated in particular environments.

In order to establish some definitions which might secure general acceptance the International Conference of Labour Statisticians already at its ninth meeting in 1957 discussed the concepts of 'open under-employment' and 'disguised under-employment'. The former could be said to exist where the amount of work performed per annum was below normal for whatever reason, such as insufficient land. This under-employment could be either chronic or seasonal. It could co-exist with a labour

[5] R. Nurkse, *Problems of Capital Formation in Underdeveloped Countries*, Oxford, 1953, p. 33. See also: 'Excess Population and Capital Construction', in *Leading Issues in Developing Economics*, G. M. Meier (Ed.), New York, 1964, pp. 74–7.

[6] H. Leibenstein, 'The Theory of Underemployment in Backward Economies', *The Journal of Political Economy*, Chicago, April 1957, pp. 91–103.

[7] N. Georgescu-Roegen, 'Economic Theory and Agrarian Economics', *Oxford Economic Papers*, February 1960, pp. 1–40.

[8] T. W. Schultz, 'The Role of Government in Economic Growth', in *The State of Social Sciences*, Univ. of Chicago Press, 1956, p. 375.

[9] J. Viner, 'Some Reflections on the Concept of Disguised Unemployment', in *Leading Issues in Economic Development, op. cit.*, pp. 79–83. G. Myrdal, *Asian Drama*, *op. cit.*, pp. 2052–3.

[10] J. W. Mellor, *The Economics of Agricultural Development*, Cornell University Press, Ithaca, 1966, p. 167.

[11] R. S. Eckaus, 'The Factor Proportions Problem in Underdeveloped Areas', *American Economic Review*, September 1955, pp. 540 ff. See also, H. S. Ellis, 'A note on Unemployment in Underdeveloped Countries', *Zeitschrift für Nationalökonomie*, Vienna, 21 January 1966, pp. 64–8; S. Wellisz, 'Dual Economies, Disguised Unemployment and the Unlimited Supply of Labour', *Economica*, **35**, 137, February 1968, pp. 22–51; W. C. Robinson, 'Types of Disguised Rural Unemployment and some Policy Implications', *Oxford Economic Papers*, **21**, 3, November 1969; J. S. Uppal, 'Work Habits and Disguised Unemployment in Underdeveloped Countries': Theoretical Analysis, *Oxford Economic Papers, loc. cit.*

shortage at peak, e.g. harvest, periods. Its seasonal duration might be prolonged for natural causes, for example through late arrival of the rains; it might be seriously aggravated in cases where home-made products were being replaced by factory-made goods as a result of villages becoming drawn into the market economy. The concept of 'disguised under-employment' is difficult to distinguish from that of low-productivity employment, yielding an abnormally low income; and this concept of abnormally low labour productivity has been much emphasised in the recent literature.

Using these analytical tools a number of sample surveys have been undertaken with a view to trying to measure the extent of under-employment in particular countries. For instance, in Senegal 'open under-employment' was estimated to amount to 30 per cent of the agricultural labour force, in Kenya at between 500,000 and 700,000 man years, in Morocco at 150 days per year per person active in agriculture and in Madagascar at 12 to 80 per cent of the agricultural labour force according to region.[12] On the tea and rubber plantations in Ceylon the volume of open under-employment has been roughly estimated as equivalent to 10 per cent of the employed labour force.[13] As to labour productivity, the estimates indicate that in many developing countries the productivity of agricultural labour is less than half the national average, in Venezuela it is said to be only 22 per cent.[14] A number of earlier inquiries generally confirm these findings.[15]

Not merely is there much under-employment but it would appear to be increasing. Over the past few decades the amount of agricultural land under cultivation in the developing countries has been increasing less rapidly than the rural population, and since production techniques have hardly changed (at least until the Green Revolution which only began in the mid-sixties and only in certain places), this suggests that the amount of work performed on the land has increased less than the number of persons available for work. In other words, if historical series were available they would probably show a decline in the number of hours worked per person per year.

12 *The World Employment Programme, op. cit.*

13 *Matching Employment Opportunities and Expectations, A Programme of Action for Ceylon; Report, op. cit.,* p. 30.

14 *The World Employment Programme,* 1971, *op. cit.,* p. 44.

15 Studies made in Argentina, Barbados, Central African Republic, Ceylon, Greece, Guyana, India, Indonesia, Israel, Jamaica, Malaysia, Panama, Pakistan, Philippines, Puerto Rico, Senegal, South Korea, Syria, Thailand, Trinidad and Tobago and the U.A.R. were described in ILO, *Employment and Economic Growth, op. cit.,* pp. 24–31. See also N. Islam, 'Concepts and Measurement of Unemployment and Underemployment in Developing Economies', *International Labour Review,* March 1964, pp. 240–56. Also A. K. Mitra, 'Underemployment in Agriculture and its Measurement', *Asian Economic Review* (Hyderabad), **10**, 1, November 1967, pp. 51–7, which considers the case of India. Further discussion of the definitions can be found in ILO, *Employment and Economic Growth, op. cit.,* pp. 30–7; and also in *Measurement of Underemployment, Concepts and Methods,* Report IV, 11th International Conference of Labour Statisticians, ILO, Geneva, 1966 (roneoed), pp. 9–26.

Certainly if one utilises the criterion of disguised under-employment, defined above as abnormally low productivity, this productivity has been declining. When productivity is measured in terms of direct food calories produced, i.e. excluding the further transformation of feed crops into animal products, Bairoch has calculated that in a group of twenty-three developing countries agricultural labour's average productivity fell from 5·92 to 5·60 (million calories per male worker per annum) between 1909–13 and 1960–4; the fall was especially marked in Africa (6·88 to 4·71) and in Asia, excluding China (5·14 to 4·35). He quotes a figure of 4·9 as the minimum productivity level below which there is endemic danger of famine. He reckons that in the developed countries the figure was about 5·0 before they started their agricultural revolution, and that productivity today is about 60 in France and 180 in the United States measured in the same manner.[16]

What emerges strongly from these observations is the importance of raising the level of output. Nothing useful would be gained by urging under-employed farm people to work longer hours on the land if there were no increase in output as a consequence. By contrast, one could welcome a technical innovation which increased the volume of output without requiring any greater labour input – though in practice this would rarely occur – because the standard of living of the farm population would be improved. The key to the situation lies in introducing modern technologies into traditional agriculture so as to expand the volume of output, augment labour productivity, raise farm incomes and at the same time increase the amount of agricultural employment.

Agricultural Modernisation

To say that agricultural modernisation provides the key to rural development is to take refuge in a phrase. The transformation of traditional farming is itself an immensely complex process comprising a number of interlocking and interrelated problems which have existed for centuries holding the farm people prisoners in a vicious circle of stagnation and hopelessness. Outsiders who are able to compare their circumstances with those of farmers in developed countries can readily identify the deficiencies: the lack of modern technical inputs, notably seeds, water supplies, fertilizers and productive livestock; the lack of capital, even in minimal amounts, the widespread ignorance, illiteracy and lack of know-how; the systems of land tenure such that little if any of the benefit from improvements in output accrue to the cultivator; the lack of a well-organised market, either because the cultivators still live in what is largely a subsistence economy or because the marketing arrangements discriminate against the producer who, for lack of credit, is so often obliged to sell his crops just after the harvest when prices are at their lowest and whose only outlet is through a series of middlemen; finally the lack of institutional arrangements which would ameliorate some of these deficiencies –

16 P. Bairoch, *op. cit.*, pp. 34–66.

schools, extension services, credit banks, marketing co-operatives and so forth. Historically considered the traditional framework was adapted to maintaining the stability of society, not to facilitating progress, but today the farm people of developing countries are beginning to want progress and a chance to participate in the prosperity which they know exist already elsewhere.

If the vicious circle can be broken at just one point this may be enough to set in train a succession of modernisation processes. After all, the agriculture of the developed countries had also been gripped by the forces of stagnation over long centuries until some 200 years ago when in Western Europe the introduction of root crops into the traditional three-year crop rotation broke the vicious circle by suddenly increasing the productivity of the land and making it possible to hold larger numbers of livestock through the winter. Perhaps the introduction in the nineteen-sixties of the new Mexican varieties of wheat and Philippine varieties of rice first in India and Pakistan and later elsewhere may be destined to provide the initial breakthrough which the agriculture of the developing countries needs.

Not that the transformation of merely one facet of traditional farming will suffice. Just as in battle a breakthrough at one point in the line brings victory only if it is followed up and exploited to the full, so an agricultural breakthrough in matters of technology can achieve modernisation only if it is followed up closely by action on the other fronts – agrarian reform, marketing facilities and the rest. On these various topics a vast literature exists and is being added to by new studies every year. It would lie outside the scope of this book to comment on all the various issues involved; the interested reader can obtain appropriate bibliographies through FAO and through national libraries. Because the present book has employment as its concern it has seemed more useful to concentrate attention on a few vital matters especially relevant to employment creation in agriculture, namely: the intensification and diversification of production, the bringing of new land into cultivation and programmes of agrarian reform. These four will form the subject matter of the remainder of this chapter. Together with the modernisation of rural institutions (to be dealt with in Chapter 8) and the promotion of industries in rural areas already discussed, these will constitute the broad attack on rural poverty and underemployment, and should, by gradually augmenting the purchasing power of the rural masses, provide a firm economic base on which industrialisation and general economic and social development can be built.[17]

More Output from Existing Farms

Almost all the changes required to bring about an increase in the quantity and quality of the agricultural output involve a larger volume and greater

[17] For a summary of relevant Japanese experience see: K. Ohkawa and H. Rosovsky, 'The Role of Agriculture in Modern Japanese Economic Development', *Economic Development and Cultural Change*, October 1960, pp. 43–67.

diversity of inputs which in turn require the creation of a network of facilities so that the cultivator can have access to these materials and tools. This implies a series of economic measures enabling the farmer to purchase the additional inputs and making it worth his while; also new institutional arrangements giving him physical access to the new inputs and providing for storage and disposal of the additional output. But first it is convenient to consider the purely technical aspects of the innovations.

SOURCES OF INCREASED OUTPUT

Much of the cultivated land in developing countries needs improvement if it is to carry better crops and livestock. The nature of the measures will vary from district to district. In some the most urgent task will be to put a stop to erosion by wind or water through programmes of terracing, of contour ploughing, of planting windbreaks, of leaving strips of fallow, ploughing in stubbles and other crop residues, for example. In others attention will be concentrated on modification of cultivation practices: the design of plough, the depth of ploughing, adoption of frequent weeding and hoeing, adapting the traditional crop rotation more scientific-ally to the local ecology. In some crops, notably rice, the introduction of improved practices will depend on more exact water control which in turn implies modern techniques of irrigation (see below).

In traditional farming the cultivator provides his own seed by saving a portion of the last crop, but today his yields can be significantly higher if he purchases selected and certified seed which has been appropriately treated with fungicides and other protective preparations. In a number of countries the so-called 'high-yielding varieties' of wheat and rice are now being widely distributed. In addition the plant breeders have produced greatly improved varieties of maize, cotton, and to a lesser extent millets, sorghums and other basic crops. Although the breakthrough in varieties has been little short of dramatic during the past decade, much remains to be done in adapting these breeding techniques to climates and soils where the present high-yielding varieties do not prosper and to extending them to crops other than cereals, notably to oilseeds. The successful varieties must also secure consumer acceptance, which was not the case with some of the first of the new rice varieties developed in the Philippines.

The new varieties will produce to the limit of their potential only if they are adequately nourished with water and chemicals. The importance now being attached to irrigation is reflected in the national plans of many developing countries which allocate substantial financial resources to the construction of dams and reservoirs, to the drilling of wells, to the building of canals and field irrigation works and to the provision of land drainage. Provided that the irrigation projects are well prepared, costed and executed there can be no doubt of their benefit. In the late nineteen-sixties there were over 27 million hectares of irrigated land in India, over 12 million hectares in Pakistan and another 10 million in the rest of South-East Asia; nearly 10 million in Latin America; 12 million hectares in the Near East; but in African countries not very much irrigation except in the Sudan and

Madagascar.[18] Nevertheless much remains to be done. For instance, in the Far East region although 65 per cent of the area under wheat was irrigated in 1969/70, only 20 per cent of the rice area had irrigation.[19] It has been calculated that in India, Ceylon and Thailand only 5 per cent of the available river water is used for irrigation, and in Burma only 1 per cent.[20] The proportion of groundwater supplies which are being utilised is entirely unknown. A more important constraint than the quantity of water in most cases is the economic cost of bringing it to the farm land.

An increase in crop production depends also on the availability of plant nutrients which in many parts of the world have never hitherto been applied to crops, even the animal manure being used as fuel. Yet an important change has begun to occur. According to FAO estimates the consumption of chemical fertilisers in the developing countries over the period 1949–51 to 1966–8 increased from 1·4 to 10·2 kg (NPK nutrient content) per hectare of arable land. (The latter figure compares to an average of 68·5 kg in the developed countries at the same date.)[21] A number of developing countries have established fertiliser factories and several governments grant subsidies to encourage fertiliser consumption.

The use of chemicals to combat the many pests and diseases of crops is also becoming better appreciated, though more gradually. Pesticides and fungicides need in particular to be associated with some of the more sensitive of the new high-yielding varieties, but they are also generally beneficial. Uganda's Development Plan for 1966–71 provided subsidies for use of insecticides and set up teams for crop dusting in the cotton areas where large increases in yields have resulted.

Another method of getting more produce out of the land is by changing the cropping programme. This may be achieved in several ways. For example, some of the new rice varieties mature more rapidly than the old ones so that under conditions of controlled irrigation it becomes possible during the year to take two crops instead of one, or under favourable circumstances three instead of two. In some districts it has become possible for the cultivators to switch from a low-value to a high-value crop, either because irrigation water became available or because communications with an urban market were opened making feasible the delivery of perishables such as vegetables and fruits. In other countries a more balanced crop rotation has permitted the elimination of the former fallow season so that a cash crop can be grown every year, as for instance in Tunisia.[22] In countries which have no winter, very intensive programmes of diversified cropping are being successfully operated. In the Philippines the Rural Reconstruction Movement has introduced rotations which give five or six

18 FAO, *Production Yearbook, 1971*, Table 2.
19 FAO, *The State of Food and Agriculture 1971, op. cit.*, p. 87.
20 H. Oswald, *The Earth Can Feed Us*, Allen & Unwin, London, 1966, p. 70.
21 FAO, *The State of Food and Agriculture 1970*, Rome, 1970, p. 141.
22 A. Makhlouf, 'Nouveau Dualisme de l'Agriculture Tunisienne: Co-operatives Agricoles de Production et Grandes Exploitations Privées', *Revue Tunisienne de Sciences Sociales*, No. 9, March 1967, pp. 27–56.

crops per year including rice, manioc, maize, tobacco, oilseeds and a number of different vegetables. These efforts are supported by systematic experiments at the International Rice Research Institute at Los Baños.[23] The advantages of multiple cropping are not merely that the labour force is utilised more evenly throughout the year but also that the cultivator has something to sell almost continuously, thus reducing his credit problems. But on the other hand it presupposes that the cultivator has acquired considerable know-how or else is in constant touch with an extension agent, and it also requires a sophisticated marketing organisation and outlets.

A final, and for the future promising, aspect of diversification is the expansion of livestock production which until now has been held back in many developing countries by the insufficiency of feeding stuffs. Now that several of these countries can look forward to self-sufficiency in basic food grains in the reasonably near future it will become possible to devote more of the land to the cultivation of feed crops thus providing the materials for a livestock industry. In particular eggs, poultry meat and (in countries where this is acceptable) pigmeat offer to farmers the opportunity for a rapid increase in cash incomes without major new investment outlays but, as with fruit and vegetables, these products become feasible only where transport and distribution facilities exist or are being installed.

In concluding this brief review of some of the factors in agricultural modernisation which can increase the output from farms one point needs to be emphasised, namely the interrelationship between many of the factors. Crops will not respond much to the application of fertiliser unless they also receive sufficient water; the performance of high-yielding varieties will be disappointing unless they have water, fertiliser and some protection against diseases and pests; diversification, especially in the form of multiple cropping, depends not only on these various inputs being available and applied but also on cultivation methods and farmer know-how; expansion of animal production requires that some land be diverted from cash crops to the growing of feedingstuffs, which becomes possible for low-income farmers only when cash receipts per hectare have been raised. Success will therefore depend on the skilful combination of the modernising factors.

RESULTS ON PRODUCTIVITY AND EMPLOYMENT

Over the last few years solid evidence has been accumulating which shows the impact of technology on the agricultural practices and output of the developing countries. In the Far East region in 1969/70 some 40 per cent of the total wheat area was planted to high-yielding varieties. In India and Pakistan the average per-hectare yield, which for decades had stood at around 8 quintals (0·8 of a metric ton), has in the past three years

[23] R. Bradfield, 'Opportunities for Increasing Food Production in Tropical Regions by Intensive Multiple Cropping' no date (roneoed paper).

averaged around 12 quintals. The progress in rice in the Far East has been slower largely because, as noted above, only one-fifth of the rice area enjoys controlled irrigation. Thus only 11 per cent of the region's rice land is in high-yielding varieties and consequently in most of the countries the average yields have so far increased by only 10–15 per cent. However, in Ceylon the average paddy yield per hectare has risen since the nineteen-fifties from 19 to over 24 quintals per hectare.[24]

Among countries of the Near East the United Arab Republic has made the greatest strides. In 1971 more than three-quarters of this country's wheat area was sown to Giza 155, other dwarf varieties were being tested for resistance to rust and to lodging so that by 1974 the entire wheat area should be under high-yielding varieties. In Afghanistan the bottleneck of fertiliser shortage is being overcome by the building of factories and in Turkey the damage from rust by the introduction of less susceptible varieties. In the Africa region in the Maghreb countries and in Madagascar the existence of irrigation has made possible the increased use of fertiliser and high-yielding varieties of grains, but in other African countries, apart from the hybrid maize programmes in Kenya and Zambia, the absence of irrigation and of facilities for breeding and testing new varieties has impeded nationwide progress. Yet encouraging results have been obtained on individual projects. In Mali, for instance, the French Textile Fibre Development Company was able to obtain an increase of 50 per cent in yields of lint cotton on its lands;[25] in Upper Volta the Institute for Oilseeds and Vegetable Oil Research increased the yields of groundnuts from 500 to 1500 kg per hectare.[26]

In Latin America among the six largest countries only Brazil and Mexico have achieved a rapid growth in agricultural output, the former mainly by extending the cultivated area and the latter by augmenting per-hectare yields through use of the new varieties. In twenty years Mexico's average yield of paddy rice has risen from 20 to over 28 quintals and of wheat from around 10 to nearly 30 quintals. About 90 per cent of public investment in agriculture has been devoted to irrigation, and over the last fifteen years fertiliser consumption has tripled in Mexico. As an indication of the influence of water supplies in Mexico it has been calculated that during the years 1952–60 the annual rate of growth of per-hectare yields differed as between irrigated and non-irrigated lands as follows: for rice 0·58 and 0·50 per cent, for wheat 4·91 and 3·80 per cent and for sugarcane 1·91 and 0·45 per cent.[27] Not merely in Mexico but in other places such as the Punjab and Madras provinces of India it has been noted that periods of rapid growth in agricultural output coincide

[24] FAO, *Production Yearbook 1971*, Rome, 1972; FAO, *The State of Food and Agriculture 1971*, Rome *1971*.

[25] J. C. de Wilde, *Experiences with Agricultural Development in Tropical Africa*, Johns Hopkins Press, Baltimore, 1967, Vol. II, pp. 327–8.

[26] *Le Développement Rural dans les Pays d'Afrique Noire d'Expression Française*, SEDES, Paris, 1965, Vol. IV, pp. 1–76.

[27] J. Tamayo, *El Problema Fundamental de la Agricultura Mexicana*, Mexico, 1964, pp. 165–7.

with periods of intense activity in the construction of irrigation schemes.[28] None the less it would be inaccurate to correlate the increases in output solely with the introduction of irrigation; in the words of FAO 'it is extremely difficult to ascribe the yield increases to any specific component of the new technological package. As a rough measure (in the case of rice in the Far East) it may be estimated that about 45 per cent of the total additional yield can be attributed to intensified irrigation . . . 25 per cent to fertiliser use, 15–25 per cent to the genetic potential of the new high-yielding varieties (almost half of which can be achieved by local improved varieties) and a further 3 per cent to the genetic purity of the seed used.'[29] Elsewhere and for other crops the factor proportions would be different.

The significant conclusion which emerges is that in an increasing number of developing countries in widely differing regions of the world agricultural output is increasing rapidly wherever an appropriate technological package has been applied. This fact is of capital importance for the problem of low-productivity employment. Although the farm population is still growing – at between $1\frac{1}{2}$ and $2\frac{1}{2}$ per cent in most developing countries – the agricultural output is expanding substantially faster than that *in the districts where modernisation has been accomplished*, which means that at long last the output per head is rising and consequently incomes too (unless producer prices decline relatively – see below). In other words, agricultural modernisation *can* provide a remedy to low productivity and to disguised underemployment.

There remains the question of open under-employment, whether the new methods of farming absorb a larger volume of manpower. Of course it can be argued that the amount of income which a farm family receives is more important than the number of hours worked to obtain that income; indeed, the individual family might be quite happy to earn the additional income with no extra effort. However, all the evidence indicates a requirement of additional man hours per hectare where the new techniques are practised, and also seasonally a more even spread of labour input through the year. The 'new agriculture' may not be able to absorb all the agricultural unemployment and under-employment; that will depend in each locality on the extent of the diversification, on the labour requirements of the new commodities being produced and on the number of persons needing to work; but at least it makes a substantial contribution.

For instance, in the Philippines the Rural Reconstruction Movement operating in 118 districts (*barrios*) was able through the introduction of new crops and new cultivation practices to reduce the number of days' unemployment per district from 4,434 to 3,056.[30] Experience in India

[28] K. N. Raj, 'Some Questions Concerning Growth, Transformation and Planning in Agriculture in Developing Countries', *Journal of Development Planning*, United Nations, New York, No. 1.

[29] FAO, *The State of Food and Agriculture 1971*, op. cit., p. 87.

[30] A. Lorenzo, 'Employment Effects of Rural and Community Development in the Philippines', *op. cit.*, pp. 419–44.

has shown that the introduction of irrigation and related improvements to such basic crops as wheat, millet, cotton and chickpeas, required 2·4 times as much labour per hectare as previously. When to these crops were added rice and sugarcane, neither formerly possible, the labour requirement was 3·6 times than under dry farming.[31] A sample survey in the State of Madras showed a labour requirement of 24·5 days per acre per year with dry farming and 99·2 days with irrigation.[32] In certain instances the employment increase was such as to create a local labour shortage.[33] Similarly in the Philippines the per-hectare labour requirements for cultivating the new rice varieties IR8 and IR20 were 50 per cent greater than for cultivating the local 'Intan' variety by traditional methods.[34] Altogether, reviewing the data from a number of countries, Brown has concluded that the new varieties of the various grain crops require 10–60 per cent more labour per hectare than the traditional ones.[35]

More employment may also be created by switching to labour-intensive crops. This was the experience in Kenya in the Nyeri district when coffee, tea, pyrethrum and pineapples were introduced.[36] It can be increased through the introduction of an *additional* crop, either by double-cropping or by inter-planting with a tree crop. Thus in Madagascar a study revealed that whereas the local rice required 143 man-days per hectare per year the addition of the export variety (vary tsipala) required a further 143 days of which only a few overlapped in December and January with the local crop; alternatively the addition of cotton meant 180 to 220 more days' work per hectare with little seasonal overlapping when combined with the local rice.[37] Likewise in the Philippines the Coconut Administration by persuading cultivators to combine either rice or maize or pineapples with their coconuts was able to augment employment and still more substantially incomes. Examples could be multiplied. It is, of course, essential in programmes of diversification to ensure that the new combination of crops reduces rather than aggravates the seasonal peaks of labour requirements when there may be no additional hands available despite serious under-employment at other seasons.

The results may not in all circumstances be so favourable. There have

[31] Government of India, *Ministry of Food and Agriculture, Studies in the Economics of Farm Management, Delhi, 1957–62*, cited by M. Paglin, in 'Surplus Agricultural Labour and Development: Facts and Theories', *American Economic Review*, **65**, 4, September 1965, pp. 815–34.

[32] *Studies in the Economics of Farm Management, loc. cit.*, 1956–7, p. 73.

[33] O. P. Anand, 'Some Aspects of Optimum Benefits from Utilisation of Irrigation Potential of Chambal Valley Project', *Indian Journal of Agricultural Economics*, October–December 1960, No .15, pp. 19–32.

[34] Data assembled by the Rice and Corn Co-ordinating Council of the Philippines.

[35] L. R. Brown, *Seeds of Change (The Green Revolution and Development in the 1970s)*, Praeger, New York, 1970, pp. 103–4.

[36] J. D. MacArthur, *Some Thoughts on Future Trends in Farm Employment in Kenya*, Conference on Education, Employment and Rural Development, Univ. College, Nairobi, 1966 (roneoed).

[37] R. Gendarme, *L'économie de Magadascar*, Institut des hautes études de Tananarive, Ed. Cujas, Paris, 1960, pp. 157–62.

been instances of countries excessively dependent on the export of a single commodity where the Government decided that the national interest required a diversification into other products for which the local demand was increasing, but these other products were less labour-intensive than the export crops. Examples are the attempts in certain parts of South Asia to replace tea by rice and rubber by oil palms. In Brazil considerable areas of marginal coffee land were turned over to cattle production having a much smaller labour requirement. Such programmes need to be accompanied by efforts to stimulate industry in the affected districts and/or to facilitate the migration of surplus agricultural workers to other regions.

The employment-creating effects of agricultural modernisation will not be confined to the farm sector alone. Mention has been made of the increased volume of material inputs that have to be included in the technological package – more fertilizers, more pesticides, more irrigation canal construction and maintenance, more and better tools and machinery. Although some of the countries still have to import some of these materials, an increasing proportion of them is being manufactured locally, thereby creating jobs. Favourable effects will also occur after the production process – in storage, transport, processing and marketing of the larger volume of production. To cite a single instance: according to a USAID report the number of bakers in India increased by 80 per cent during the nineteen-sixties largely as a result of the increased output of wheat. In other branches of food processing and packaging the increase may be even more important. Beyond all this the increase in the purchasing power of the farm population has to be taken into consideration. Since the vast majority of these people are in the lower-income groups, their needs for consumption goods are oriented mainly towards clothes, furniture and a more varied diet, in short towards goods which can be produced within the country. The effect should therefore be to create additional employment in the industries concerned and only to a small extent an additional demand for imports. It can be seen from the above that the multiplier effects of agriculture modernisation can be expected to extend throughout the national economy.

PROBLEMS

It would be unfair to transmit the impression that here is a panacea ready to hand for solving the rural employment problem, and that all that is necessary is to spread the Green Revolution throughout all the developing countries. In fact as with any major innovations which demand a reorientation of the purposes of a traditionalist society the task of modernising agriculture gives rise to numerous problems of economic and social engineering and faces planners and legislators with difficult choices as between particular objectives of policy. Naturally, since experience with the Green Revolution is relatively recent – its application outside the two countries of origin, Mexico and the Philippines, is little more than a decade old – many mistakes have been made, some disequilibria unnecessarily generated, and only gradually are the important options making themselves apparent.

One problem arises from the tendency of the Green Revolution to exacerbate income differences among the farm population. Because the high-yielding varieties and the other components of the Green Revolution are adapted only to districts having certain ecological conditions, the farmers in those districts come to enjoy advantages over farmers elsewhere which are more pronounced than before the innovations became possible. Moreover, within the favoured districts the new technologies tend to be adopted first if not by the biggest landowners at least by the larger farmers who generally have somewhat better education and have access to some of the resources needed for the new practices. It is their incomes which are the first to benefit. Disadvantaged are the cultivators too ignorant and too poor to acquire the additional inputs. Disadvantaged also are the tenant cultivators whose leases frequently stipulate that any increase in the harvest accrues mainly or entirely to the landowner. Governments can palliate these effects by, for instance, amending tenancy legislation to secure to tenant cultivators the value of improvements and by orienting extension assistance especially to smallscale farmers. In some countries the situation created by the Green Revolution emphasises the urgency of far-reaching agrarian reform measures. It has nevertheless to be recognised that in the process of economic development not every citizen can increase his prosperity at exactly the same pace; some will move ahead first and faster, others will catch up later. The task facing governments is not so much to hold back the enterprising as to seek to prevent unacceptable extremes of inequality of wealth and income and in every feasible manner to enlarge the opportunities of the least advantaged groups.

Consider next the issue of mechanisation. Until not many years ago the agricultural advisers from industrial countries recommended the use of tractors and other farm machinery to which they were accustomed. Not merely could the machines perform more efficiently, e.g. plough and seed more evenly, waste less in threshing, etc., but they were eagerly sought by farmers who could afford them because they lightened the physical toil of work in the fields. Yet mechanisation also had disadvantages. In inexperienced hands the machines frequently broke down and the parts needed to repair them might be hundreds of miles away or not in the country at all. But much worse, by diminishing the number of hours required for any individual farm operation, mechanisation in most instances aggravated the existing under-employment. It was, however, for technical and economic rather than for employment reasons that the earlier ambitious schemes for large-scale mechanised production had to be abandoned or modified. One example was the collapse of the East African groundnuts scheme of the British Government's Overseas Food Corporation; another was the experiences of the General Tropical Oilseeds Company in Senegal which already in 1952 abandoned its full-scale mechanisation of groundnut production, continued on a semi-mechanised basis for another decade and finally from 1963 went over entirely to animal-drawn equipment. Similar setbacks were recorded in Nigeria and elsewhere. Greater success has been achieved where less ambitious equipment was introduced and where the organising agency used the peasant farmers to undertake the actual cultivation, as in Mali where the French Textile Fibre Development Company hire out basic equipment to peasant cultivators of cotton, resuming possession of it at the expiration of the contracts unless the peasants then wished to purchase it.

A certain degree of mechanisation of family farms is often advocated as a means of overcoming the labour shortage which occurs at peak moments of sowing and harvesting, or to prepare heavy soils which just prior to the rains may be too compacted to plough by hand. Much depends on the pre-existing cultivation methods in the particular locality; it may be quite sufficient to introduce animal-drawn equipment to replace the entirely manual cultivation. Sometimes the breaking of one bottleneck merely creates another one, as was the experience in Northern Nigeria where the introduction of tractor ploughing enabled each farmer to cultivate as much as 24 acres but then he could not possibly weed 24 acres until that process also was mechanised.[38] Machinery may have its justification in helping a man to farm a larger area where land is available (see discussion of land settlement below), but in the majority of regions the peasant has no opportunity to enlarge his holding and in such circumstances mechanisation generally has the effect of reducing labour requirements in terms of man hours. Recent sample surveys in Ceylon and India showed that full mechanisation reduced the man hour requirements per hectare by from 12 to 27 per cent.[39] This economy may be beneficial if the labour released can be profitably utilised elsewhere, as can be the case where the cultivator is changing over to a system of multiple cropping, but too often there is no occupational alternative and the result is merely an increase in idleness. One is forced to conclude that in effecting the transition from traditional to modern farming the introduction of machinery is neither wholly good nor wholly bad; the balance of advantage will depend upon local circumstances which must be closely studied in order to elucidate what degree of mechanisation will be the most advantageous economically and socially.[40]

Another issue or rather series of issues connected with the Green Revolution is the need to create the supporting facilities and services. It

[38] K. D. S. Baldwin, *The Niger Agricultural Project*, Cambridge, Harvard Univ. Press, 1957, p. 134.

[39] *Evolution Technologique de l'Agriculture et Emploi dans les pays en Voie de Développement*, Studies of the OECD Development Centre, No. 4, Paris, 1971, pp. 90–102.

[40] For further material on this topic the following may be consulted: *Le Développement Rural dans les Pays d'Afrique Noire d'Expression Française, op. cit.*, Vol. III, pp. 1–49; H. Béguin, 'Espoirs, Bilan et Leçons d'un Paysannat au Congo', *Tiers Monde*, Paris, **6**, 24, October–December 1965, pp. 891–913; ILO, *Memorandum on the Integrated Rural Development Scheme: Nigeria, Period March 1964–5* (roneoed), D.27, July 1965; E. S. Clayton 'Mechanisation and Agricultural Employment in East Africa', *International Labour Review*, April 1972; I. Inukai, 'Farm Mechanisation, Output and Labour Input: a Case Study in Thailand', *Essays on Employment*, W. Galenson (Ed.), ILO, Geneva, 1971, pp. 71–92.

would be outside the scope of this book to dwell on the provision of equipment repair shops, a distribution mechanism for seeds, fertilisers and other material inputs, storage depots, improved road access to market centres, transport services, extension agents, farmer training, credit institutions, and so forth. In numerous cases the technical innovation has been less than successful on account of the absence of one or more of these infrastructural supports. By the same token, where these aspects have been taken care of the impact of the innovations may be considerably enhanced. (Some of the institutional stimuli are discussed further in Chapter 8.)

A more delicate issue whose ramifications can be only touched on here is that of price policies with regard to agricultural products. A first and uncontroversial objective is to eliminate, or at least reduce, the seasonal price fluctuations during the year either by advancing credit to the cultivators so that they do not have to sell immediately after harvest when prices are at their lowest, or by establishing an agency which purchases from the producers at a fixed price. An objective more difficult to realise is that of price stability over a period of two or more years, because this requires not only the creation of storage facilities which involve considerable investment but also rather sophisticated judgements as to the future evolution of supply and demand. For instance, if the price of a certain commodity be maintained at what turns out to be an excessively high level, stocks will accumulate, the marketing agency will face a financial crisis and ultimately the price may have to be abruptly reduced. This was the experience of some of the Marketing Boards in West Africa. (In the case of export products the operation of price policies at the international level is referred to in Chapter 8.) An argument against excessive price stabilisation over the years can be advanced, namely the desire of the farmer to obtain a higher price per unit of output when, for climatic or other reasons, his harvest is small. In other words, the argument proposes a goal of stability of incomes rather than of price.

This leads to the more difficult question of price policy when the output of a basic commodity, e.g. a food grain, is augmenting rapidly and the choice appears to lie between maintaining the price through a quantitive limitation of production or reducing the price which may stimulate consumption in other uses, e.g. for livestock feeding, but which may force marginal producers to abandon. One constructive approach to this particular problem is the initiation of crop diversification programmes in which price policy may be used to encourage producers to switch to other commodities for which demand is expanding, providing that the extension and other services are simultaneously helping the cultivators to reorient. An illustration may be found in Brazil where the Coffee Institute was obliged, because of the export situation, to reduce coffee prices and producers were encouraged to turn to maize, cotton and other crops. By contrast there have been instances, as with rice paddy in Ceylon, where the maintenance of a high price has not only discouraged the cultivation of other crops but has failed to stimulate a larger output of rice, the cultivators being satisfied with their current levels of income.

It is sometimes suggested that the simplest way to raise the over-all level of farm income would be for the State to guarantee a high level of prices for all the important farm products. Adoption of such a policy would, it is true, increase the purchasing power of the farm population but the consequences would depend upon how the policy were financed. If the higher prices were paid simply by the creation of new money, the result would be inflation whereupon workers in other sectors of the economy would demand higher wages to compensate for the inflated cost of living, and a vicious spiral would begin. In theory the higher prices to agricultural producers could be financed entirely by taxes, particularly of a kind which transfer purchasing power from the non-agricultural to the agricultural sector, a procedure which need not be inflationary. This can be, and has been, done in industrialised countries where the farm population has become a small proportion of the whole and where the other sectors are sufficiently numerous and prosperous to bear heavy taxation. Such a situation is not found in most developing countries; hence the artificial support of agricultural prices pursued on a larger scale generally has inflationary consequences. (By contrast one of the classic techniques for raising capital for development is to keep down the level of consumption of the farming population – which can be likened to extracting forced savings from them – by keeping producer prices low relative to other prices). Clearly, therefore, there is no short cut to improving farm incomes by manipulation of prices; the improvement has to be achieved through increases in real output which should not, however, be diluted by allowing prices to fall.

Some economists have advocated and a few governments have experimented with the use of fiscal policies to encourage intensification of agricultural production,[41] the idea being to tax the potential rather than the actual production capacity of agricultural land. Practical obstacles are that not many countries have cadastral surveys and there are problems of assessing land's production potential. None the less in Morocco the fiscal reform of 1961 sought to define the revenue-producing potential of farm land and of flocks and herds.[42] Those who advocate such taxes would appear to believe that low productivity results from lack of motivation to produce more rather than from lack of resources and know-how. Such cases may be mostly confined to underutilised land on large estates, to which further reference is made in the discussion of agrarian reform (see below).

A different group of problems centres on the difficulties in securing acceptance of the innovations. In traditional farming systems the cultivators will resist techniques which contradict the local practices hallowed

[41] N. Kaldor, 'The Role of Taxation in Economic Development', in *Fiscal Policy for Economic Growth in Latin America*, Baltimore, 1965, pp. 70 ff; also K. C. Abercrombie, 'Fiscal Policy and Agricultural Employment in Developing Countries', in *Fiscal Measures for Employment Promotion in Developing Countries, op. cit.*, pp. 271–3.
[42] A. Tiano, *Le Maghreb entre les Myths*, Paris, 1967, p. 544.

by custom. Without considering here anything other than the employment aspect, they will frequently resist innovations which require that they themselves or other members of their families should work longer hours in the fields. When village people turn to industrial employment and take jobs in factories they are obliged to conform to the discipline and work hours of the firm, but in family farming no equivalent constraints exist and often, because of negative past experience, the cultivator does not in his mind associate extra effort with higher income. Much tact and patience and an approach tailored to local circumstances will be needed to break down these psychological obstacles. For example, in Tanzania in Sukumaland it was found that rather than undertake the laborious work of carting animal manure to the fields and spreading it there, the cultivators preferred to take an additional piece of land leaving the manure unused. In regions, e.g. parts of Tunisia, where animals were hitherto used only for work it proved difficult to convince the peasants of their potential as sources of income.[43] Part of the opposition was due to the realisation that this innovation would involve devoting more man hours to the care and feeding of the animals.

In spite of the many real problems relating to employment and to income improvement which arise in the course of agricultural modernisation, one thing seems certain, namely that a sufficient beginning has been made in the application of the new technologies to hold out the hope, which did not previously exist, that the long era of stagnant agricultural production in the developing countries can be replaced by an era of expanding output, enabling farm incomes to rise, labour productivity to increase and a larger volume of agricultural employment to be generated. In the course of engineering the widespread application of the Green Revolution and all that goes with it difficult problems present themselves both economic and social in character, problems to which by no means all the solutions have been found. These are currently the subject of much study and experimentation, and while it is important that they be dealt with in a way which defuses rather than aggravates social tensions in the rural community, yet they are not of such a nature as to block permanently the progress toward better living conditions for the farm people.

Land Settlement

The scope for expanding output from existing farms is now recognised to be large, but this in itself is not a sufficient objective. Already in most developing countries an important proportion of the farms are too small, even if cultivated in the most intensive manner possible, to provide incomes deemed adequate by the modest local standards; and inasmuch as the rural population continues to grow many of the larger farms will become

---

43 The opposite situation is described in Madagascar by J. C. Devèze, 'Essais de Prise en Charge des Attitudes Psychosociologiques des Paysans, Lors d'une Opération de Développement Rural à Madagascar', *Economie Rurale*, Paris, No. 88, 1971, pp. 121–6.

too small either because of subdivision among the sons or because a whole clan of families tries to live off what the holding can produce. As the number of families increases so does the demand for more farms. This demand can be met in two ways, either by colonising and cultivating hitherto unoccupied land or by taking over and parcelling out existing large properties. In the present section the first of these options will be discussed.

In a number of developing countries large areas of land exist which could not be occupied for permanent settlement until new technological capabilities became available: for example, dry savannah regions where irrigation is feasible, e.g. in sub-Saharan Africa, or tropical forest areas which can now be cheaply cleared by heavy equipment, e.g. the Oriente of the Andean countries. These lands when brought into cultivation may be as productive as the older areas of settlement, if not more so. On the other hand, there are some countries, notably in the monsoon areas of the world, where virtually all the potentially fertile land has long been settled and where that which remains unoccupied is so poor as to be more suitable for afforestation than for farming. In both cases, though for different reasons, programmes of colonisation are likely to encounter formidable difficulties and need to be particularly carefully prepared. It is hardly surprising that among the various attempts in recent years the failures outnumber the successes. Without going at length into the technical and economic issues it may throw light on the employment potential of land settlement schemes to refer briefly to a few of the decisive factors.

The first requirement naturally is an in-depth study of the area selected for settlement, its agricultural potential, the costs of preparing it for settlement, the linking of it to markets and the provision of minimum public and social services. Too often a district has been selected because it was an empty spot on the map without regard to whether it could be made economically viable. The next basic decision concerns the character of the settlement: is it to be a government-directed operation from the start or is it to be a voluntary scheme in which the Government does no more than make land available to applicants, perhaps building an access road, no more. When the choice is for a government-operated scheme it can comprise either a spartan or a very elaborate provision of facilities, the latter entailing a large amount of non-reimbursable expenditure. Another choice lies between allowing unrestricted acquisition of land and setting limits to the size of holdings; in the latter case the optimum size may depend upon the degree of mechanisation envisaged and upon the level of income which the settlers may aim at earning. There is always a temptation to fix on a size enabling a large number of families to be accommodated but which is too low for economic viability. Another aspect which it is essential to clarify in advance is the legal title to the new lands and to provide the settlers with documents indicating un-equivocally their status whether of tenancy or of outright ownership.

As regards the settlers themselves these will in most cases come either from a non-agricultural background or from a part of the country where the environment and methods of farming are different; in both cases the colonists will need a period of technical training to be followed by some supervision from extension advisers during the first years of settlement. Almost all of them will lack sufficient capital to equip their new farms and to bridge the initial gap between expenditure and the commencement of a flow of income. In some schemes the basic equipment, buildings, machinery and even livestock, has been provided by the Government as an outright grant; in others it is provided in the form of loan capital through commercial banks or some government financing agency at specially favourable rates of interest. Too often the mistake has been made of burdening the new farms with an excessive load of investment and an indebtedness from which the settlers are subsequently unable to free themselves. Finally, the settlement will need a variety of ancillary services including storage, packing, transport, marketing and in some instances processing of the produce, as well as on the social side some facilities for recreation and sport. For certain of these activities the settlers may acquire greater strength if they form and work through a co-operative; for others they may establish a community development programme if dynamic leadership can be found.[44]

Perhaps the most daunting aspect of settlement schemes, and the one which limits their capacity to create new employment, is their cost. The actual figure in any particular case will depend on a number of factors: how elaborately the settlement is equipped, whether it is a 'peripheral' settlement adjacent to an existing community or a 'nuclear' one located far away, whether the holdings are large or small, whether irrigation or other major works have to be constructed, whether the production plans envisage monoculture or diversified farming, the latter usually demanding heavier initial investment. To cite but three examples, one from Asia, one from Africa and one from Latin America: Fisk describes a project of the Federal Land Development Authority in Malaysia in which 100 families were settled at a cost of $6,400 per family, while a report on tropical Africa quotes figures ranging from £1,300 to £2,500 per family in the English-speaking countries of that region; by contrast a project on the Alto Beni in Bolivia cost as little as $700 in 1963 ($1200 at 1971 prices) per family of five persons, partly because it was located on the Altoplano near existing settlements and benefiting from existing infrastructural facilities.[45]

[44] For observations on these various matters see W. A. Lewis, 'Thoughts on Land Settlement', *Journal of Agricultural Economics*, 11, 1, Agricultural Economics Society, Reading, June 1954; also *The Community Development Approach to Land Settlement*, Publication No. 66.IV.5. United Nations, New York, 1967.

[45] E. K. Fisk, 'The Mobility of Rural Labour and the Settlement of New Land in Underdeveloped Countries', *Journal of Farm Economics*, Menasha, 43, 4, November 1961, pp. 761–78. ILO, *Report on the Meeting of the ILO Advisory Working Group on Rural Employment Problems in Tropical Africa* (English-speaking Countries), Lagos, 1–10 November 1965, Doc. D. 11 (2) 1966 (roneoed). J. Rada Monje, *Estudio de Costos de la Colonización*, U.S. Aid Mission to Bolivia, La Paz, 1963, pp. 91–3.

The high cost of settlement projects has obliged a number of governments to modify and reduce the scope of their settlement programmes. For example, the 'villagisation' programme in Tanzania which had been designed to relocate 1 million persons during the period of the 1964–9 Plan was cut back in 1966 in favour of strengthening the extension advisory service to existing settlements. Likewise the Brazilian plan for the colonisation of the north-east had to be severely reduced because of the expense. The Kenyan Government invested heavily in establishing settlers on the lands formerly farmed by Europeans and experienced difficulties in collecting interest and repayment on the loans which it had advanced.

In practice many governments have faced a hard choice between establishing an adequately equipped settlement at a cost which excluded any possibility of economic viability or alternatively operating a voluntary scheme with investment overheads kept so low that within a year or two the scheme would probably collapse for lack of social infrastructure. Thus, for instance, in Ecuador, after a review of the various settlement programmes being operated, it was recommended to discontinue the extremely costly projects being operated by the Social Assistance Administration where the capital – output ratio was calculated at 4·91, to give more support to the much simpler 'voluntary' settlement schemes having a capital – output ratio of 0·83, and to expand activities on the virgin lands in the Oriente (capital–output ratio of 1·52).[46]

Of course a simple calculation of capital–output ratios tends to ignore the indirect benefits which may accrue to the nation from such colonisation schemes – the exploitation of otherwise untapped natural resources, the relief of overcrowding in congested districts, an improved balance of payments through expansion of exports, an essential counterpart to the decentralisation of industry and the creation of new poles of economic growth, and so forth. Taking the long view, the pluses may well outweigh the minuses in very many cases, but governments are constrained in practice by the financial resources currently at their disposal and it is this which has almost everywhere kept the settlement programmes relatively modest in scope.

Consequently the employment effects have not been remarkable when viewed in the perspective of the rate of growth of the farm population. For example in Nigeria where the number of young persons leaving school each year exceeds 700,000 the number of persons settled during the past decade does not reach five figures. Even in such a small country as Guatemala the number of persons given new land over the years 1954 to 1962 represented only 7 per cent of the increase in the agricultural population during that period; instead of the 6,000 families actually settled the need was said to be for the settlement of 240,000 families.[47] Likewise in the Philippines the National Resettlement and Rehabilitation Administration

[46] *Informe al Gobierno del Ecuador sobre Reforma agraria y Colonización*, ILO/TAO Ecuador/R. 9, ILO, Geneva, 1966.
[47] S. L. Barraclough and A. L. Domike, 'Agrarian Structure in Seven Latin American Countries', *Land Economics*, **42**, 4, November 1966, pp. 391–424.

was able to settle only 30,000 families over a period of nine years, representing 6 per cent of the increase in the rural population.[48] In Ceylon the ten-year Plan for 1959–68 envisaged the settlement of 100,000 families but because of the many difficulties encountered the programme was only partially realised. In Ghana where 80,000 families had to be relocated because of the submersion of their lands under the artificial lake of the Volta project, after sixteen villages (out of fifty-two planned) had been established at great expense it was decided to abandon mechanised bush clearance and to undertake the remainder by less costly manual methods. In Mali the activities of the 'Office du Niger' extending over a period of thirty years succeeded in establishing only 38,000 settlers on 50,000 hectare of irrigated land, there being many who abandoned and went away. Even in the United Arab Republic where as a result of the Aswan high dam a major extension of the cultivated area from 5·6 to 6·9 million feddan was achieved over the period 1952 to 1970 and although in the latter year there were 160,000 persons working on the new lands, yet so great had been the growth in population that the amount of arable land per person (in farming) was no higher than at the beginning. Of course without the dam and the land settlement the man–land ratio would have deteriorated instead of being stabilised, but the future outlook is sombre with little possibility of further extension of the farm area and with agricultural population still increasing.

In India during the first three Five-Year Plans (1951–66) about 1 million families consisting of Pakistan refugees, landless labourers and Harijans were settled on some 4·6 million hectares. In Israel one-fifth of all immigrants have been absorbed in land settlement projects and yet the productivity of the agricultural labour force has constantly increased, despite the scarcity of land.[49] Brazil has had successful settlement projects, e.g. the Itaguai scheme;[50] also Madagascar in its western and middle-western districts and Senegal in the river delta. Other encouraging examples could also be cited.

Settlement schemes of a rather particular character derive in some countries from Youth Service programmes. There are some governments which have mobilised young people and as part of, or as alternative to, their military service have set them to work on land clearance and land improvement projects. Subsequently colonies of young people have been established on the reclaimed lands, e.g. in several African countries. The chances of success are greater if the young colonists themselves come from an agricultural rather than an urban background, but even so because of their lack of experience as independent cultivators they need more supervision than other settlers and particularly the support of some

[48] A. Lorenzo, 'Employment Effects of Rural and Community Development in the Philippines', op. cit., pp. 423–4.

[49] E. Kanovsky, The Economy of the Israeli Kibbutz, Harvard Middle Eastern Monographs No. 13, Cambridge, Mass., 1966, p. 131.

[50] Inter-American Committee for Agricultural Development, Posse e Uso da Terra e Desenvolvimento Sócio-econômico do Setor Agricola-Brazil, Washington D.C., 1966, pp. 575–83.

agency to take care of marketing their products. It has been found efficacious to charge the local district administration with responsibility for the welfare of these young colonists, supported by the technical services of the agricultural and other appropriate ministries.

In the early stages technical and administrative leadership is a prerequisite. Partly it will be supplied from outside but partly also through selection and training from among the colonists themselves, as has been the practice for instance in Madagascar and the Ivory Coast. The leadership of the settlements has to decide, among other things, on the vexed question of the distribution of the project's income as between debt service, investment in community facilities and satisfaction of the colonists' current needs. The main body of young settlers will also have to be given training either prior to entering the project or in the course of their farming activities or both. In numerous instances this training is oriented not only to modern farming practices but also to the learning of rural crafts as a means of generating supplementary income – for example the training provided by the Civic Service in Madagascar. In addition to training, the Young Pioneers, as in Dahomey, may be given a grant in kind such as seed, fertilizer, insecticide, some animals and furnishing for their new homes as well as a small sum in cash to tide them over until their first harvest. Experience has indicated that the establishment of youth settlements is even more costly than ordinary ones in terms of finance and supervision.

It is not easy to formulate an objective judgement on the usefulness of land settlement schemes; so much depends upon the form which a particular scheme takes and on the wider development strategies of the country in question. Moreover, most of the existing schemes have been initiated comparatively recently and it is recognised that the cost/benefit picture will become clear only after the lapse of some years. However, it is pertinent from the employment-generation point of view to compare the cost of such schemes with the cost of creating an equivalent volume of employment in manufacturing industry or by augmenting the volume of production on existing farms. In the majority of cases the two other options mentioned will be less costly in terms of commitment of current financial resources. But to say that is not to provide the definitive answer, because it has to be remembered that the total number of farm families remorselessly increasing and that each family passionately desires its own piece of land. To satisfy this endemic land hunger is an obligation which governments feel a responsibility to meet as far as they can; and while part of the demand may be met by settlement projects, part may also be dealt with through measures of agrarian reform to which we now turn.

Agrarian Reform

Creation of employment is normally only one among many considerations in the promotion of agrarian reform programmes. A principal objective is to achieve a greater degree of equality in the distribution of land – the

153

major natural resource available to the rural population. Within the framework of this governing objective two other preoccupations can be distinguished: first, the creation of agricultural holdings approximating more closely to the optimum size, and second, steps to improve the prevailing forms of land tenure.[51]

Concern at the maldistribution of agricultural land is especially pronounced in countries characterised by large estates on the one hand and mini-farms plus a mass of landless labourers on the other. It has been estimated in Latin America that 90 per cent of the land is in the hands of 10 per cent of the landowners. In Colombia, for example, 64 per cent of the holdings are not large enough to maintain a family.[52] In some regions of Asia the inequalities in land ownership are almost as great. But there are here two distinct issues: one is the fact that in democratic societies an excessively unequal distribution of land ownership is socially unacceptable, while the other is to seek to arrive at a size distribution of holdings which maximises the efficiency of agricultural production. In countries where many of the large estates are underutilised and the mini-farms too small for subsistence the two issues can be treated as one, but as soon as an agrarian reform programme is launched and also in countries where the contrasts are less stark, the policy choices as to size of farm present themselves.[53]

Large farm enterprises possessing, as they generally do, superior management and command of resources are more likely to keep up to date in the adoption of technologies and to have flexible responses to changing production methods and changing market situations. They can exploit the economies of scale, particularly in spreading the overhead costs over a large volume of output, this being the more marked when they are oriented to monoculture. Because of their (generally) more extensive methods of cultivation the districts in which they are located require less investment in public services – roads, schools, clinics, etc. – than densely populated areas of small farms. In some types of farming, notably in plantation crops, they have been the technological pioneers, identifying the most profitable new practices which later the smallholders imitated.

The advantages of small farms have been the subject of study by numerous authors.[54] There is general agreement that within any type of

[51] *Agrarian Reform and Employment*, ILO, Geneva, 1971. D. Warriner, *Land Reform in Principle and Practice*, Oxford, 1969.

[52] *Progress in Agrarian Reform, Fourth Report*, United Nations, New York, p. 173.

[53] E. Flores, *International Labour Review*, July 1965, pp. 22–37; see also E. O. Heady, 'Optional Sizes of Farms Under Varying Tenure Forms, including Renting, Ownership, State and Collective Structures', *American Journal of Agricultural Economics*, **53**, 1, February 1971, pp. 17–25; also K. L. Bachman and R. P. Christensen, 'The Economics of Farm Size' in *Agricultural Development and Economic Growth*, H. M. Southworth and B. F. Johnston (Eds.), Cornell Univ. Press, Ithaca, 1967, pp. 234–57.

[54] The following is a selection of sources dealing with this topic: For Indonesia: D. Penny and M. Zulkifli, 'Estates and Smallholdings: an Economic Comparison', *Journal of Farm Economics*, Menasha, **45**, 4, December 1963, pp. 1017–21. For India:

farming system a strong inverse correlation is found between size of farm and output per hectare. This is due partly to the difference in quality between hired labour and family labour, the latter having more at stake takes more trouble; partly also to closer supervision by the head of a famlly. Indeed on mini-farms the only way of obtaining a minimum livelihood is to extract the maximum from the insufficient land available to the cultivator. But as to labour productivity the evidence is more confused; quite often the small farms will register a lower productivity than larger farms because on the former there is more under-employment.[55] Small farms tend to have inferior technology through lack of know-how and of access to material inputs and capital. On a wider front they exercise a beneficial social influence in dampening down the rural exodus, migration to the towns being generally less pronounced in countries where small farms predominate, e.g. Ceylon, than in countries of large estates, e.g. Chile and Colombia.

This listing of the advantages and disadvantages of large and small farms does not add up to anything in the nature of a definitive recommendation, for the good reason that the priorities among objectives will vary between countries and between regions within a country. Strictly from the point of view of maximising employment there can be little doubt that a regime of small farms provides more jobs per 100 hectares of farm land than a regime of large estates, but where the small farms are 'mini' the additional employment will be bought at the price of disguised under-employment and a low standard of living.

Apart from the question of farm size, the other preoccupation of agrarian reform programmes is with the amelioration of land tenure. In many developing countries sharecropping, various systems of leasing and other forms of customary tenure all tend to be weighted more in favour

R. Krishna, 'Land Reform and Development in Southern Asia', in *Land Tenure, Industrialisation and Social Stability*, W. Froelich (Ed.), Milwaukee, Marquette Univ. Press, 1961; also M. Paglin, 'Surplus Agricultural Labour and Development: Facts and Theories', *American Economic Review*, **55**, 4, September 1965, pp. 815–34; also A. M. Khusro, 'Returns to Scale in Indian Agriculture', *Indian Journal of Agricultural Economics*, **19**, October–December 1964, pp. 51–80; also A. K. Sen, 'An Aspect of Indian Agriculture', *The Economic Weekly*, annual number, February 1962; also C. H. Hanumatha Rao, 'Alternative Explanations of the Inverse Relationship between Farm Size and Output per Acre in India', *The Indian Economic Review*, 1, 2, October 1966, pp. 1–12. For Brazil and Uruguay see H. Giberti, 'Uso Racional de los Factores Directos de la Produción Agraria', *Desarrollo Económico*, Buenos Aires, **6**, 21, April–June 1966, pp. 17–56. See also S. L. Barraclough and A. L. Domike, 'Agrarian Structure in Seven Latin American Countries', *op. cit.*, p. 402. For Colombia see also: Comité Interamericano de Desarrollo Agrícola, *Tenencia de la Tierra y Desarrollo Socio-económico del Sector Agrícola, Colombia*, Panamerican Union, Washington D.C., 1966, Chapter III, pp. 137–76; and *The Colombia Report, op. cit.*, For Kenya see W. Barber, 'Some Questions about Labour Force Analysis in Agrarian Economies with particular reference to Kenya', *East African Economic Review*, Nairobi, **2**, 1, June 1966, pp. 23–37; and, more generally: J. W. Mellor, *The Economics of Agricultural Development, op. cit.*, p. 168.

[55] When land is scarce and labour plentiful it is of course, much more important to increase the productivity of land than of labour.

of the landlord than of the tenant or cultivator. The latter receives in many instances an inadequate share of the output, he has no right to reimbursement for any improvements he might make to the land or buildings (and consequently he makes none), and he can be evicted at unreasonably short notice. Sometimes even where the cultivator believes he is the owner of the land his legal title is unclear.[56] In Jordan, for example, a solution to the problem of land titles was followed by a marked improvement in cultivation practices. In Mexico and in India in certain districts the granting of greater security of tenure was a signal for the cultivators to switch to more remunerative crops. Where attempts are being made to persuade tribal people to change over from shifting cultivation to permanent settlement the provision of clear legal instruments, whether of tenancy or of ownership, is often found to be the most essential element in the programme. Therefore, the rationalisation of tenure arrangements, by stimulating the adoption of modern methods and by augmenting the volume and value of output per hectare can have a very positive influence on labour productivity and employment.

There are five distinct types of programme which may be considered as coming under the general rubric of 'agrarian reform'. The first is the taking over of all or parts of the large estates and distributing the land among individual cultivators or to co-operatives. This was done in Mexico after the revolution and in Japan after the Second World War where, as a result, the proportion of the farm land cultivated by peasant owners rose from 54 to 92 per cent. A similar intention was spelt out in the Iranian legislation of 1962 which set the landowners a time limit to dispose by sale or lease of land in excess of 30 to 200 hectares according to region.[57] In most cases the peasant demand for additional land is so intense that governments have to take steps to prevent excessive fragmentation by decreeing a minimum size of holding: examples being Bolivia, Panama and Pakistan, the last having two minima, one for subsistence holdings and a higher one for economic holdings.

Land redistribution through the expropriation of large properties is an expensive exercise. Not only is there the cost of compensation (except in times of revolution) to the former landowners, though this may take the form of issuance of long-term bonds, but the costs of establishing the new farmers and analogous to those incurred in the land settlement schemes described above. In Colombia the Land Reform Institute (INCORA) was spending 20,000 pesos ($1,150 at the 1969 exchange rate) per family exclusive of any expenditure on irrigation or public services.[58] Other countries have had similar experiences. Partly for this reason some governments instead of proceeding to expropriation have adopted fiscal

[56] *The Landless Farmer in Latin America*, New Series 47, ILO, Geneva, 1957; see also ILO: *Agrarian Reform, with Particular Reference to Employment and Social Aspects*, International Labour Conference, 49th Session, Geneva, 1965, Report VI, p. 41; also United Nations, *Progress in Agrarian reform, Fourth Report*.

[57] A. Ajdari, 'Les Conditions de la Réforme Agraire en Iran', *Développement et Civilisations*, Paris, No. 22, June 1965, pp. 37–46.

[58] *The Colombia Report, op. cit.*, p. 75.

measures to encourage large landowners to dispose of part of their properties. Thus in Argentina and Chile special taxes were imposed on 'absentee' landowners; in Colombia and Venezuela there is a tax on all unutilised land; elsewhere a tax graduated according to the size of property. The effectiveness of these measures does not appear as yet to have been established.

The second of the five approaches to agrarian reform consists in regrouping the scattered parcels of land comprising a farm and in enlarging such farms by addition or amalgamation – in short, 'land consolidation programmes'.[59] Circumstances do, of course, exist where some fragmentation is justified, e.g. where the farmer has one plot on the hill and another in the valley, one irrigated and another on non-irrigable land; but in general consolidation promotes higher per hectare output by enabling a cultivator to adopt modern practices without waiting for his neighbours to agree to do likewise. But the employment effect of a programme confined to the regrouping of strips is likely to be negative; it merely reduces the number of man hours needed. The programme acquires its justification when it comprises also the *enlargement* of the farm so as to occupy the family more fully at the same time as increasing the revenue.

The third approach consists in systematising landlord–tenant relationships along the lines described above. It should also include arrangements for eliminating the middlemen who interpose themselves between landowner and tenant cultivator, taking part of the proceeds – for instance the zamindari in India and the jagirdar in Pakistan.

Fourth comes the rationalisation of customary tenures and the joint cultivation of tribal property. In some cases the lands are parcelled out into individually owned holdings; in others, as in parts of Senegal, the government takes over the land, making it available on lease to cultivators or to co-operatives. The bringing of nomads into permanent settlement is an element of this programme.

A fifth possibility in agrarian reform is to establish production co-operatives. These may be set up in districts where small farms predominate by persuading the peasants to pool their resources and cultivate their land in common; or they may be set up in connection with expropriation schemes, the land being distributed only nominally to the peasant cultivators but in practice being vested in the co-operative or collective farms. The advantage claimed for this approach is that it can achieve economies of scale in the purchase of inputs, in cultivation and in marketing, which are impossible in a regime of small farms. This advantage may be outweighed by absence of incentive to work hard and well, especially in cases where pressure has been put upon the peasants to join the cooperative.

As to the pace of agrarian reform, there are some who advocate carrying it through swiftly on a nationwide basis, especially where there are glaring inequalities in land ownership. Delay may enable large landowners to

[59] *Progress in Land Reform, Fourth Report, loc. cit.* 'Back to the Land: the Campaign Against Unemployment in Dahomey', *International Labour Review*, January 1966, pp. 29–49 and particularly pp. 41–3.

defeat the intentions of legislators by, for example, transferring title to parts of their estates to relatives. Others recommend a gradual implementation of the programme on two grounds: first, the inevitably heavy expenses which governments must incur in settling the new cultivators on their lands, and, second, the likelihood that in the reformed districts there will initially be a decline in the volume of agricultural production. As to this latter there have been disquieting experiences. Thus in Bolivia after the reform undertaken in 1953 it was ten years before the national agricultural output recovered to its former level, and then the recovery was due to the opening up of virgin land in the Santa Cruz and Beni regions because in the districts of the agrarian reform the level of production was still stagnating, the cultivators having received no training and lacking credit. Similarly, in Ecuador the *Huasipungeros*, the estate workers who hitherto had been paid partly in cash and partly by being allowed the personal use of plots of land, were transformed into owner cultivators by the agrarian reform law of 1964, but immediately their incomes diminished since they no longer benefited from the seeds, fertilizers and tools formerly provided by the estate owners. Meanwhile the latter, faced with a labour shortage, turned to mechanisation which augmented the rural unemployment. Output declined because the new farms were insufficient in size and insufficiently equipped due to lack of advance planning.[60] In Iraq, following the land reform of 1958, the production of cereals is reported to have declined by 50 per cent, and it was not until 1963 that the authorities began to provide the cultivators with valid land titles and to create co-operatives which might compensate to some extent for the peasants' lack of training and experience. In Mexico where the reform was begun as long ago as 1915, that part of the land which was assigned to *ejidos*, co-operatives having rather limited functions, is in general the worst farmed and least productive, and the *ejidarios* have not shared with the other farmers (full owners) in the dynamic expansion of Mexican agriculture. The evidence suggests that the dislocation in production may be temporary or more permanent depending upon the extent to which the responsible authorities take steps to provide the supporting services and facilities without which the new farms cannot become viable.

On the other hand in cases where the reform programme was well prepared and well implemented encouraging successes have been recorded. Perhaps the most publicised case has been that of Japan where the post-war land reform occasioned only a minor interruption to the growth of output and where over the subsequent twenty years agricultural production has doubled. (This has been accompanied by a massive transfer of manpower to other sectors so that during the same period the farm population almost halved.)[61] In the 'million acres' programme in Kenya in the settle-

[60] *Informe al Gobierno del Ecuador sobre Reforma agraria y Colonización, op. cit.*, pp. 41–54.

[61] T. Misawa, 'Agrarian Reform, Employment and Rural Incomes in Japan', in *Agrarian Reform and Employment, op. cit.*, pp. 143–64. P. M. Raup, 'Land Reform and Agricultural Development', in *Agricultural Development and Economic Growth, op. cit.*, pp. 267–314.

ment areas of the highlands the value of output is reported to have increased by 150 per cent; in one district, Mweiga, output increased by 221·8 per cent while the volume of employment doubled.[62] Likewise in the United Arab Republic the results of the reform have been in general satisfactory. Most of the former tenants and sharecroppers transformed into owner-cultivators have substantially increased their incomes, and when surveyed after ten years only 5 per cent were less well-off while a further 5–10 per cent had become unemployed (due to lack of hired worker jobs). However, the new owner-occupiers were not able to devote an adequate proportion of their incomes to investment in improvements.[63] Indeed, one of the problems which merits attention in formulating reform schemes is the likelihood of some unemployment arising among those former estate workers who have not received grants of land and among peasants' younger sons who can no longer hope to inherit part of the family farm because subdivision below a minimum size has become illegal.[64]

The income and employment effects of the creation of production co-operatives or collectives are as yet unclear, the experiences being contradictory. Thus the collective farms established in Algeria have encountered many difficulties while the large co-operatives created in Tunisia have been abandoned. However, in the Comilla district of East Pakistan the Agricultural Institute successfully organised the grouping of peasants for joint cultivations by tractor. In Nigeria it is believed that collective organisation will augment the productivity of small farms.[65] The agrarian reform project of Choapa in Chile seems to have succeded in raising the incomes of the participants, due in large part to the facilities provided by the Agrarian Reform Corporation (CORA).[66] African experience indicates that production co-operatives succeed more particularly in the cultivation of tree crops.

Reviewing as a whole the experience to date which developing countries have had with agrarian reform programmes, both those involving the creation of new farms and those concerned with improvements in the tenure system, they can certainly achieve an important increment in agricultural output and employment (after some temporary dislocation) provided that the schemes be carefully prepared and that an adequate supporting organisation, social as well as economic, is made available for the people affected. Failure to arrange such institutional support, or false economies in its extent, can condemn the schemes to continuing

[62] E. S. Clayton, 'Agrarian Reform, Agricultural Planning and Employment in Kenya' in *Agrarian Reform and Employment, op. cit.*, pp. 119–42.

[63] G. S. Saab, *The Egyptian Agrarian Reform* 1952–62, Oxford Univ. Press, 1967.

[64] J. C. de Wilde, *Experiences with Agricultural Development in Tropical Africa, op. cit.*, Vol. I, pp. 135–48, and Vol. II, pp. 3–83.

[65] H. A. Oluwasanmi, *Agriculture and Nigerian Economic Development*, Ibadan, Oxford Univ. Press 1966, p. 188.

[66] R. I. Durán, 'Asentamientos de Choapa: Cambios en la Tenencia de la Triera y en los Ingresos de los Campesinos', *Economia*, Santiago de Chile, No. 93, January–April 1967, pp. 3–13.

backwardness and in some cases to disintegration. The increased output is translated into higher incomes for the participants compared with their former living standards. As to the effects on the actual volume of employment, these may be favourable where as a result of the land redistribution a more intensive cropping programme is adopted and more livestock are kept, but this may be partially offset by the loss of employment on estates. Again, the introduction of supporting services for the new farmers – e.g. the farm requisites purchasing co-operative, the packing house, the marketing agency, the credit office, the training courses and so on – these will all provide additional employment in the locality though not agricultural in character. In other words, agrarian reform achieves its principal purposes of diminishing social and economic inequalities in the agricultural sector, but its income and employment benefits depend on the extent to which it achieves a technological modernisation of the farming systems with the consequences described in the first part of this chapter.

Chapter 8

General Stimuli to Employment

Chapters 3–7 have been devoted to a review of the problems of employment creation in large- and small-scale industry, in construction and public works and in agriculture – the many obstacles and the many opportunities. But at several points in the discussion some of the difficulties of a more general character were deliberately deferred in order not to break the immediate narrative. In the present chapter these deferred issues will be considered because, as will become clear, unless action be taken in regard to them simultaneously with the action directed to specific matters in manufacturing and in farming, the success of the latter will be jeopardised. In engineering a country's economic development it is not possible to modernise one part of the assembly line while leaving other parts in the horse-and-buggy age.

These more general topics can be grouped into three broad categories. In the first category come all those supporting measures so frequently referred to in Chapter 7 without which agriculture cannot be modernised – the training, the marketing organisation, the access to credit. In the second come the mobilisation and planned orientation of investment funds from both domestic and foreign sources without which the development of agriculture, manufacturing and of public works programmes cannot proceed. In the third come the measures designed to expand the markets, both domestic and export, for manufactures and for primary products, for it is a truism to observe that the larger the volume of output that can be sold the larger the number of jobs created. In each and all of these areas of policy there is, as will be seen, important scope for private initiative; nevertheless, a major share of the responsibility for action lies with governments and other public and semi-public bodies.

Action in these areas can have three positive influences on the volume of employment. First, it creates jobs in the facilities themselves – the staff of the training courses, of the savings banks, of the marketing boards and so on. Second, by enabling the output of agriculture and of manufacturing industry to expand more rapidly it stimulates their demand for manpower. Third, and this is the aspect to which perhaps greater attention than hitherto should be given, it can in each sector deliberately encourage an orientation to the more labour-intensive commodities and to the more labour-intensive techniques of producing them. It is this last consideration which has prompted the inclusion of these topics for brief review in the present report; otherwise it would have sufficed to refer the reader to the voluminous literature which on all of them already exists. This chapter (and the next) are reminders that problems of employment promotion are an inseparable part of problems of general development.

Supports for Modern Farming

EDUCATION AND TRAINING

As was stressed in Chapter 7 the introduction of modern technologies into farming, whether through the Green Revolution or by other means, presupposes and requires a transformation in the custom-bound attitudes of farm people and also making available to them the know-how needed in their new tasks. This implies programmes for the children in village schools, for the adults already working on farms and for the training of those who are going to do the teaching and extension.

In many developing countries agriculture features as a curriculum subject in all primary schools and instruction includes work in the school garden or on a near-by farm.[1] President Nyerere of Tanzania has said: 'the school community should consist of people who are both teachers and farmers, and pupils and farmers', thus indicating the emphasis he wished to place on the practical orientation of the teaching. In some countries an effort is made to reach those who, for one reason or another, never pass through the primary school system, as for example in Upper Volta where in 1961 a special service of rural education was inaugurated for these young persons.[2] A later age group, namely those who have just left primary school, is dealt with in Tunisia through an ILO/UNICEF project, in the Kenyan Youth Centres[3] and in the short courses for young farmers aged seventeen to twenty-five in Chile.[4] For adults the so-called 'basic education' programmes of UNESCO, although designed primarily as a vehicle for the spread of literacy, also include simple agronomic information. Lastly there is the continuing work of the extension agents who, dealing with cultivators in groups or individually, try to direct their attention to the possibilities of bettering their condition – improved methods of cultivation of traditional crops to achieve larger quantity and higher quality, hints on marketing, the introduction of new crops and of livestock, information . as to obtaining seeds and fertiliser.[5] The ILO

[1] V. L. Griffiths, *The Problem of Rural Education*, UNESCO, International Institute for Educational Planning, Fundamentals of Educational Planning, No. 7, Doc. IIEP.68/II.7/A, Paris, 1968.

[2] *Education Rurale en Haute-Volta*, Société d'Etudes pour le Développement Economique et Social (SEDES), Paris, July 1966.

[3] G. W. Griffin, 'The Development of Youth Centres in Kenya', *International Labour Review*, July 1963, pp. 58–73.

[4] 'Youth and Work in Latin America, II: Youth Employment Prospects', *International Labour Review*, 90, 2, August 1964, pp. 150–79 and *ibid.*, pp. 171–205.

[5] S. M. Makings, *Agricultural Problems of Developing Countries in Africa*, Oxford Univ. Press, Lusaka, Nairobi, Addis Ababa, 1967, pp. 62–77. J. C. de Wilde, *Agricultural Development in Tropical Africa, op. cit.*, Vol. I, pp. 157–97.

co-operates with the governments of Colombia and Mali in such training programmes.

Generally speaking rather little has as yet been undertaken for the female half of the farm population. A few notable exceptions are the special courses for women within the adult education framework in India, Iran, Khmer Republic and Thailand, the women's clubs in the community development projects in Uganda and the courses under the auspices of the Civic Service in the Ivory Coast, the Young Pioneers in Malawi and the Youth Service in Zambia.

Secondary agricultural education has primarily the objective of preparing teachers for village schools, training course instructors and extension assistants; and it is vigorously utilised for this purpose in for example China, the Philippines and Morocco where the 1965–7 plan envisaged that 18 per cent of all secondary school pupils should take agricultural courses. For higher education many of the new universities in the developing countries have agricultural faculties, while those who have specialised can pursue post-graduate work in institutions of world renown such as the International Research Institute of Tropical Agriculture in Nigeria or the International Rice Research Institute in the Philippines.

One of the faults which the agricultural education authorities are still trying to correct in a number of developing countries is the overly theoretical content of the formal courses with their chemistry, physics and biology crowding out advice on practical husbandry. Another is the insufficient integration with over-all national agricultural policy so that individual instructors may be recommending more widespread cultivation of a crop whose output the Government is trying to curtail. Only in a few countries does the extension service keep in mind the desirability of using agricultural modernisation to maximise employment, e.g. putting little emphasis on mechanisation and much on double-cropping and on livestock products. Lastly, the agricultural staff – teachers, extension advisers, research workers – is hopelessly inadequate in almost all the countries. To cite just one example: in Madagascar it is reckoned that the agricultural staff should double every five years to keep up with the rural needs.[6] It is unfortunately still quite usual for a single agricultural officer to be responsible for a district containing several thousand cultivators. But the enlargement of these services presents a heavy salary bill to governments whose financial resources are already strained.

COMMUNITY DEVELOPMENT

This is an important reason why attempts are made to make available funds go further by enlisting the participation of the villagers themselves – a 'do-it-yourself' form of development; but another reason is that community development projects absorb, at least temporarily, under-employed manpower, at the same time creating a sense of involvement in the outcome of the project. It is often enough for one organiser from outside the village

[6] Commissariat général au Plan, Tananarive: *Plan Quinquennal* 1964–8, pp. 48–50 and 177.

to be present while the rest of the leadership and all the workers are provided from among local people. The most usual types of project are well known: land clearance, well-digging, draining schemes, local roads, building of houses, schools and dispensaries, sports fields, community halls, storage depots and packing sheds, and so forth. In societies unfamiliar with joint activities the necessary enthusiasm will be generated only where the project brings tangible and personal benefit to the participants themselves – improving *their* land, *their* homes; by contrast where there exists some tradition of social activity the projects can be oriented successfully toward improvements which benefit the village as a whole.[7]

Community development programmes have proved valuable as an adjunct to land settlement schemes, e.g. in Malaysia and Nigeria, creating a sense of co-operation and identity among the new settlers.[8] They may also be used as part of or as a supplement to public works programmes, taking over responsibility for those aspects of a task which require less specialised knowledge and equipment, e.g. the ditch-digging part of an irrigation scheme. More generally, they offer a means of accomplishing certain local improvements which would have to wait a long time if requested through routine channels and financed from public funds.

Similar programmes entitled 'animation rurale' are operated in the francophone countries of Africa, the major distinction being that these are administered as an integral part of the local government services and contain generally a larger 'official' element.[9]

Doubts have been expressed in some quarters as to how beneficial the effects of these programmes really are. Myrdal in his *Asian Drama* has pointed out that in India the projects chosen usually benefit the better-off members of the village – the most influential. Others fear that attention and effort may be diverted to embellishments and away from the more urgent matters of expanding food production and building new industrial activities. In other words the programmes should aim to create permanent, not merely temporary, additions to employment and revenue.[10] That each village programme should establish such employment and income goals was one of the recommendations of an ILO mission in the Philippines which advised on their Community Development and Rural Reconstruction activities.[11]

[7] H. de Decker, *Nation et Développement Communautaire en Guinée au Sénégal, op. cit.*, pp. 21–35.

[8] United Nations, Economic and Social Council, 42nd Session, *Report of the World Conference on Agrarian Reform*, Doc. E/4298, 1966, p. 124.

[9] Y. Goussault, 'Rural "Animation" and Popular Participation in French Speaking Black Africa', *International Labour Review*, June 1968, pp. 525–50; also, J. Serreau, *Le Développement à la Base au Dahomey et au Sénégal*, Paris, Librairie générale de Droit et de Jurisprudence, 1966, pp. 107–58; V. Ch. Diarassouba, *L'Évolution des Structures Agricoles du Sénégal, op. cit.*, pp. 187–97.

[10] See *Policy Issues Concerning the Future Evolution of Community Development*, Administrative Co-ordinating Committee of the United Nations, ACC/WGRCD/XV/ Working Paper No. 2, (Geneva, 10–15 July 1968).

[11] ILO Research Project, *The Impact on Employment of Community Development Programmes in the Philippines*, Draft Final Report, Vol. 2, pp. 401–9.

There are two further issues involved here. One is the attitude of professionals who prefer to see a school house built properly by the Works Department instead of clumsily by villagers, and the other is the belief held by planners and officials that villagers are poor judges of what is really their long-term interest. Certainly when economic growth and development have reached a more advanced stage the scope for programmes of this kind will diminish, but as long as there is in every direction more to be done than the governments and their staffs can possibly accomplish, the mobilisation of voluntary effort at the local level can make a real contribution to employment creation and at the same time improve the living conditions of the people.

MARKETING

One of the considerations which deters a traditional cultivator from making an effort to expand his output, and still more from trying a diversification to other products, is how to find an effective market outlet. There are still millions in agriculture who have no roads and no transport connecting them to markets and who in consequence farm almost entirely on a subsistence basis. There are other millions who, although access to market is possible, find themselves entirely in the hands of middlemen, either because the distances are too great or because they have no means of transport of their own. There are those who live within walking distance of a population centre and who attempt to evade the middlemen by carrying their produce to town and selling it at curbside markets; but the quantities which any particular peasant has to offer on any one day are pathetically small, and in the case of perishables the wastage is enormous.[12]

These basic shortcomings cannot be remedied overnight, yet in various ways step by step progress can be accomplished. For instance, a significant improvement occurs already when a municipality builds a covered market with display, washing-down and drainage facilities and with cool rooms where perishables can be held overnight. The provision of a bus service, if necessary subsidised, between outlying villages and the town makes the market accessible to a much larger number of cultivators, freeing them from their utter dependence on middlemen. At a higher level of sophistication, where the peasants are already market-conscious and local leaders are available, it may be possible to form a village marketing co-operative through which, at the least, the sales to the middlemen are conducted under supervision or which grades, packs and transports the produce to urban selling points itself. In districts where a food processing plant has been established the local farmers may be producing under contract for the plant, though too frequently they ignore their contractual obligation if at a certain season they can obtain a higher price by sale for direct

12 J. W. Mellor, *The Economics of Agricultural Development, op. cit.*, pp. 328–44; J. C. Abbott, 'The Development of Marketing Institutions', in Southworth and Johnston, *op. cit.*, pp. 364–402; also J. C. Abbott, 'The Role of Marketing in the Growth of Agricultural Production and Trade in Less Developed Countries', *Monthly Bulletin of Agricultural Economics and Statistics*, FAO, Rome, September 1960; also S. M. Makings, *Agricultural Problems of Developing Countries in Africa, op. cit.*, pp. 101–31.

consumption, which is one reason why such plants often fail. In some countries in order to regulate the market for a basic foodstuff or for a major export commodity the government establishes a marketing agency which offers to purchase from the producer at a fixed year-round price; but to make this price effective the agency needs to have staff at a great number of buying points throughout the growing areas and needs storage accommodation sufficient to hold the large quantities of the commodity which will be offered immediately after harvest when the farmers are short of cash; otherwise the farmers will still have to resort to middlemen. In Honduras, for example, the peasants can sell their cereals to a nationwide network of silos established by the National Development Bank; in South Korea the Government provides crop loans at low rates of interest on cereals deposited by the farmers after the harvest in approved warehouses. The Marketing Board or Agency in some instances is empowered to deal in all types of agricultural produce, as is the case in Senegal where the Board not only handles the export of groundnuts but also the import of such basic foods as rice, millet and maize; likewise in Burma there is a single agency. By contrast in Kenya and elsewhere in East Africa separate Boards have been established for each major commodity: for coffee, tea, pyrethrum, cotton, maize, meat and live animals, dairy produce.[13] In countries where the Boards do not have a statutory monopoly for the purchase of the commodities concerned they find difficulty in competing with the traditional private system whereby itinerant traders pass from farm to farm offering cash for small unweighed quantities so that the grower does not know what price per kilogramme he is receiving but he is saved the trouble of carrying it himself to the Board's depot. The Board cannot offer an equivalent service on account of the expense involved. A different problem arises in respect of export commodities where, more usually, the Board does have a monopoly. Wishing for the growers' sake to smooth out the violent price fluctuations which occur on international markets, the Board will attempt to maintain a steady price from season to season only to find that in face of persisting price weakness on world markets it has accumulated enormous stocks which it finally has to to liquidate at a loss. (This matter will be referred to again in the discussion of export markets below.) Despite the many real difficulties there is a whole range of improvements which governments, and also producers themselves, can introduce which will have beneficial effects on farmers' incomes.

FARM CREDIT

In all developing countries the millions of cultivators who live near the starvation line are sooner or later forced to live on the food they have not yet produced, in other words they are large users of credit. They have always depended on the traditional moneylenders of the local community. On their unmodernised holdings they are a bad credit risk; most will never

[13] J. C. de Wilde, *Agricultural Development in Tropical Africa*, op. cit., Vol. II, pp. 24–32.

be able to repay the principal while many default on their interest payments which is one reason why village moneylenders seldom become very rich in spite of charging exorbitant rates of interest. Since the typical cultivator has already borrowed up to the hilt to meet current consumption needs, he finds it impossible to obtain further credit when offered a technical innovation which requires additional capital. Nor has he yet, save in a few exceptional cases, reached the stage of development of, for example, Western European peasants toward the end of the nineteenth century who had sufficient substance to be able to establish their own co-operative credit societies. In many instances he is unable to distinguish conceptually between a loan and a subsidy.

A considerable number of governments have instituted systems of farm credit either directly or through the intermediary of a semi-public institution, primarily with the purpose of breaking the nexus of high interest rates but also with the objective of encouraging agricultural modernisation. The credit is needed most acutely by small-scale cultivators in the lowest income groups, not by the larger farmers who are catered for by the commercial banks; yet these cultivators are usually the least creditworthy. For this reason many governments prefer to operate the so-called 'supervised credit schemes' whereby the granting of credit is tied to implementation of a farming plan recommended and supervised by the local extension agent which ensures, as far as that is possible, that the credit is devoted to production-improvement purposes.[14]

In many countries the attempt has been made to combine an official governmental system of credit at national and regional level with organisation of a co-operative character at local level, thus seeking to achieve professional management at the same time as enlisting the participants' knowledge of local conditions. This is the formula adopted in Tanzania where the National Development Credit Agency, set up in 1964, lends both direct to individuals and also to local co-operatives, but 95 per cent of its loans go through the co-operatives. It has encountered administrative problems; however, the number of borrowers rose from 5,000 in the first year to 100,000 in 1968.[15] In India in 1966 the number of members of agricultural credit co-operatives already exceeded 26 million. In some African countries credit has been provided in kind in the form of seeds, fertilisers, tools, work animals, and the interest and repayment collected in kind from the crops produced – a system which prevents the diversion of the credit to non-productive uses.[16] In some cases credit has been made

[14] H. Belshaw, *Agricultural Credit in Economically Underdeveloped Countries*, FAO Agricultural Studies, No. 46, Rome, 1959; P. Kohn, 'The Role of Agricultural Credit in Economic Development', *Agricultural Planning Studies* 1963, FAO, 1964; G. Leduc, 'Le Rôle du Crédit dans la planification du Développement Agricole', *Penant*, No. 701, April–June 1964, La Documentation africaine, Paris, pp. 153–66.

[15] H. H. Binhammer, *Institutional Arrangements for Supplying Credit and Finance to the Rural Sector of the Economy in Tanzania*, Economic Research Bureau, Univ. College, Dar es Salaam, Doc. 68.17 (roneoed).

[16] R. Baudouin, 'Le Crédit Agricole en Afrique Sub-saharienne', *Tiers-Monde*, Paris, 7, 27, September 1966, pp. 619–28.

167

available in lieu of part of the wages to those who have volunteered to work on local irrigation and drainage schemes. Credit is also frequently linked with land settlement and agrarian reform programmes. Further examples of successful supervised credit schemes are the *Associacao de Credito e Assistencia Rural* in Brazil and the *Expanded Agricultural Credit Programme* in Ceylon, the latter being provided partly in kind and linked to the rice expansion programme.[17] There can be little doubt that credit will have to play an important role in making the techniques of the Green Revolution available to the small-scale cultivators and not just to the larger ones.

CO-OPERATIVES

It would be beyond the scope of the present report to review the whole library of literature which exists on the subject of agricultural co-operation,[18] from traditional forms of communal work as found among the Kpelle in Liberia,[19] the kibboutzim of Israel, the credit and marketing co-operatives of the European type on to the co-operative collectives of the socialist countries. In some countries these co-operatives have first been introduced on a wide scale in connection with agrarian reform programmes, e.g. in Iraq, Iran, Syria, Tunisia and the U.A.R.;[20] sometimes in connection with land settlement schemes as in Kenya and Nigeria.[21] Broadly speaking the African co-operatives are primarily engaged in marketing activities while those of the Near East and Far East are specially concerned with farm credit.

In numerous instances the local co-operative has become multipurpose in character, assuming responsibility not merely for credit and for marketing of produce but also for the purchase of farm requisites, the organisation of cultural and recreational activities, for extension, home economics instruction, food processing and so forth. Examples of successful multi-purpose co-operatives can be found in the U.A.R., in Tunisia at Cap Bon, at Cotia in Brazil, Cogua in Colombia, the Victoria Co-operative in Costa Rica and the John. XXIII Co-operative in Veraguas in Panama.[22] In India the Khadi weaving co-operatives have extended into many other functions thus becoming multi-purpose.

[17] H. S. Wanasinghe, 'Link-up between Co-operative Credit, Production and Marketing in Ceylon', in International Co-operative Alliance, *Agricultural Co-operative Credit in South-East Asia*, Asia Publishing House, Bombay, 1967, pp. 100–11.

[18] ILO, *The Role of Cooperatives in the Economic and Social Development of Developing Countries*, International Labour Conference, 49th Session, Report VII (1), 1965.

[19] H. D. Seibel, 'Traditional Co-operatives among the Kpelle in Liberia', in D. Oberndörfer, *Africana Collecta*, Bertelsmann Universitätsverlag, Freiburg in Breisgau, 1968, pp. 115–28.

[20] J. von Muralt, 'Rural Institutions and Planned Changes in the Middle East and North Africa,' in UNRISD, *A Review of Rural Co-operation in Developing Areas, op. cit.*

[21] E. H. Whetman, *Co-operation, Land Reform and Land Settlement*, The Plunkett Foundation for Co-operatives Studies, London, 1968, pp. 56–9.

[22] Th. F. Carroll, 'Peasant Co-operation in Latin America', in UNRISD, *op. cit.*, pp. 1–94.

The limiting case is where the individual surrenders all his land, save a garden plot, and most of his animals to a comprehensive production co-operative – likewise called a collective – which then operates as a single large farm. Outside the socialist countries there has not been much experience with this form of organisation, and most of it has been negative.

Undoubtedly a successful co-operative has a favourable influence on farm incomes and on employment. It achieves economies of a scale which is not available to the members acting as individuals, it enables them to obtain farm credit on more advantageous terms, generally it has stronger bargaining power *vis-a-vis* sellers of materials and buyers of farm produce, it can find market outlets for new products and thus facilitate diversification, it can either itself or in collaboration with a commercial enterprise undertake the processing of certain products, it can be the intermediary for working with the national education and extension authorities in the organisation of training courses and demonstrations. In these and many other ways it can be the motivating force for progress in the village.

INTEGRATION

One of the main dangers in initiating these programmes of supporting institutions for rural development is the proliferation of local bodies each under the auspices of a different ministry and each with responsibilities partially overlapping those of others. Apart from the unnecessary administrative expense, the farmers lose interest when they are constantly being referred from one office to another. Since most of the problems concerning the modernisation of agriculture and the promotion of rural employment have social as well as economic aspects and necessitate a multi-disciplinary approach, it has become widely accepted that what is needed is a single authority at local level which integrates all the services and activities, and a number of governments are moving toward, the establishment of bodies which approximate to this pattern.

Many examples can be cited. There are the rural expansion centres in Senegal (CER) composed of representatives of all the services operating in the locality;[23] the regional action centres for rural development (CARDER) in Dahomey; the 'combined units' started already in 1954 in the U.A.R.;[24] the basic democracies councils in Pakistan and the panchayati raj in India;[25] the popular communal assemblies in Algeria,[26] the work of the National Institute of Agricultural Technology in the Argentine, or in

[23] R. Descloîtres, J. C. Reverdy and R. Volante, *L'Administration Locale du Développement Rurale au Sénégal*, Centre Africain des sciences humaines appliquées, Aix-en-Provence, 1964; E. Costa, 'Problèmes et Politiques de l'Emploi au Sénégal', *op. cit.*, pp. 494–5; V. Ch. Diarassouba, *L'Évolution des Structures Agricoles du Sénégal – Destructuration et Restructuration de l'Economie Rurale*, Editions Cujas, Paris, 1968.

[24] United Arab Republic, Institute of National Planning, *Research Report on Employment Problems in Rural Areas, Report E on Impact of National Development Projects*, December 1965, pp. 94–122.

[25] A. T. R. Rhaman, 'Rural Institutions in India and Pakistan', *Asian Survey*, Berkeley, 8, 9, September 1968, pp. 792–805.

[26] R. Descloîtres and R. Cornet, *Commune et Société Rurale en Algérie*, Centre africain des sciences humaines appliquées, Aix-en-Provence, November 1968.

Guatemala the Ministry of Agriculture's Service for the Economic Development of the Indians, in Mexico the Ministry of Education's brigades for literacy, the well-being of the Indians and agricultural improvement, and generally in Latin America the many community development programmes.[27] The role of the Party in one-party countries is exemplified in the case of Guinea, where it plays a major part in promoting rural development.[28] France has pursued the integration principle in francophone African countries through the Society for Technical Assistance and Co-operation (SATEC) and the Bureau for the Development of Agricultural Production (BDPA).[29] One instance of ILO's work in this field is the project for raising the level of agricultural production and employment in the Ifo, Otta and Ilaro districts of Western Nigeria.[30]

Finally, perhaps the largest single attempt at the integrated approach is the Andean Indian Project involving all the Andean countries from Argentina to Venezuela under the auspices of the United Nations, ILO, FAO, WHO and UNESCO.[31] In each of these instances the attempt has been made to integrate all the approaches, the technological, educational, economic, social, societal and cultural, and to concentrate on raising rural levels of living through agricultural modernisation and the stimulation of additional remunerative employment.

Investment for Industrial Development

In Chapters 3 and 5 frequent references were made to the penury of financial resources which in almost all developing countries holds up the expansion of industry and consequentially of employment. In those chapters various avenues were explored for utilising the *available investment resources* as constructively as possible for the generation of jobs, but obviously the more the resources themselves can be augmented and wisely used the greater the possible volume of employment. It is therefore pertinent to examine briefly the ways in which the volume of investment funds might be stimulated.

Rich people, and by the same token rich countries, find no difficulty in saving a relatively high proportion of their income, but the situation is quite different in the developing countries where the masses live on the

---

[27] See 'Popular Participation and Principles of Community Development in Relation to the Acceleration of Economic and Social Development', *Economic Bulletin for Latin America*, United Nations, 9, 2, November 1964; also 'Integral Local Development Programmes in Latin America', *op. cit.*, 13, 2, 1968.

[28] H. de Decker, *Nation et Développement Communautaire en Guinée et au Sénégal*, Mouton, Paris, La Haye, 1967, pp. 45–216.

[29] G. Gosselin, *Développement et Tradition dans les Sociétés Rurales*, Etudes et documents, New Series, No. 76, ILO, Geneva, 1970.

[30] P. Mueller and K. H. Zevering, 'Employment Promotion Through Rural Development: a Pilot Project in Western Nigeria', *International Labour Review*, August 1969, pp. 111–30.

[31] C. d'Ugard, 'Experience in the Andean Region', *Community Development Theory and Practice, Round Table*, Inter-American Development Bank, April 1966, pp. 99–122.

margin of subsistence. For these people, after satisfying their basic physical needs, there is little left over to save. That is why in the developed countries gross savings represent about 22 per cent of GDP (in the years 1966–8) compared with 15 per cent as the average for the developing countries.[32] Indeed, when one recalls that in 1970 average per caput GDP was $219 in the developing countries compared with $2,838 in the developed countries (in both cases excluding the centrally planned economies), a saving rate of 15 per cent must be regarded as a considerable achievement. Table 8.1

Table 8.1   *Gross Domestic Fixed Capital Formation as Percentage of GDP*

Country	Period	Average percentage over period
Bolivia	1962–8	17·0
Gabon	1966–8	29·2
Iraq	1965–8	15·5
Ivory Coast	1960–8	16·6
Peru	1967–78	20·6
Thailand	1967–8	29·3
Tunisia	1965–8	22·6
Zambia	1966–8	21·6

Source: United Nations, *op. cit.*, Table 27, p. 72.

gives the figures for selected countries. It would appear that during the nineteen-sixties the proportion of GDP devoted to fixed capital formation was rising in Africa and, with some important exceptions, in Asia but it fell slightly in Latin America. In the great majority of developing countries the national development plans at the end of the sixties provided for devoting to investment between 20 and 40 per cent, according to country, of the incremental growth of GDP,[33] which reveals a stern determination to sacrifice present advantage for future benefits.

Investment funds may be generated in three separate ways. They can arise from voluntary savings on the part of individuals and of enterprises; they can be derived from forced savings either via taxation or via the influence of permitted inflation; they can also be obtained from foreign countries through private or public channels. Virtually every developing country utilises all these techniques in some combination or other in the effort to accelerate development, but for the purposes of description it will be convenient to examine each of the three separately.

[32] United Nations, *World Economic Survey 1969–70*, New York, 1971, p. 69.
[33] United Nations, 'Targets Indicated in Recent Development Plans: a Statistical Compendium', *Journal of Development Planning*, No. 1, 1970, Table I and II, giving marginal rates of gross national savings by countries.

VOLUNTARY SAVINGS

In the present context voluntary savings are treated as roughly synonymous with 'private saving'[34] and, as table 8.2 indicates, it is private saving which in many countries accounts for the greater part, in some instances the totality, of national saving. The relative importance of individual as distinct from corporate saving differs from country to country; generally it tends to be greater in countries where large corporations – mining or other – are not predominant. The techniques used for the encouragement of savings vary according to which section of the community is being addressed. Thus, to attract individual savers it is desirable to have a

Table 8.2   *Net Domestic Savings as Percentage of GNP 1966–8; Selected Countries*

Country	Total savings	Public savings	Private savings Total	Individual	Corporate
Colombia	8·4	5·0	3·4	0·8	2·5
Costa Rica	8·8	0·8	8·0	7·6	0·3
Mauritius	10·9	−0·4	11·4	2·4	9·0
Malaysia (West)	13·6	3·5	10·1	9·9	0·3
Panama	9·6	2·2	7·4	0·3	7·1
Peru	11·6	−0·3	11·9	3·3	8·5
Philippines	10·1	0·3	9·8	7·1	2·7
Thailand	16·8	1·0	15·7	14·1	1·6
Tunisia	8·0	3·7	4·3	0·9	3·4
Venezuela	11·3	6·6	4·6	3·2	1·3

Source: United Nations, *World Economic Survey, 1969–70*, New York, 1971, Table 37, p. 96.

diversity of institutions, such as commercial banks, national banks, co-operative banks, mutual savings associations and so forth, and a multiplicity of selling points or branches. It is also desirable to offer generous rates of interest, as is done, for example, in Mexico, India, Pakistan and the Philippines. In South Korea the raising of the rate of interest in 1965 from 15 to 30 per cent attracted a considerable volume of deposits to the banks. The periodic issue of premium bonds on savings certificates drawn by lot may be a further stimulant, as also the various national lotteries.

Individual savings can also be encouraged by means of tax exemptions. In numerous countries interest is tax-free on certain classes of government bonds; life insurance premiums are generally deductible for tax computations. A negative approach to the same goal is to tax especially heavily luxury consumption goods which by definition are purchased by the well-to-do who may thus be stimulated to spend less and save more.

[34] This is not strictly accurate; e.g. investment of profits by State-run industries is both voluntary and public in character.

The encouragement of corporate savings is achieved primarily by using fiscal techniques. For instance, corporation taxes may be remitted on that portion of the profit which is reinvested; or specially favourable depreciation allowances may be granted in order to foster the ploughing back of profits. However, certain governments go further and have enacted statutory dividend limitation while some, in the case of foreign firms, set limits to the proportion of profits which may be remitted abroad. In this category of stimulants fall also the measures concerning the granting of import licences for new or replacement equipment.

The effectiveness of these several techniques for calling forth more savings from individuals and from enterprises depends in considerable part upon governments' over-all economic policies. Thus the further a government pushes, for social or ideological reasons, in the direction of income equality the lower will be the average propensity to save; and there are many governments which seek to impede the payment of exceptionally high salaries or the gaining of individual profits through such activities as real estate speculation. Unfortunately it does not follow that the opposite policy of permitting wide income differentials will bring forth savings unless measures are simultaneously taken for restraining luxury consumption, along the lines mentioned above. Corporate saving can likewise be jeopardised by policies designed to restrict the profit-earning capacity of private enterprise. There are cases where firms making good profits are required by the Government to reduce their selling prices, and others where they are obliged to take on additional (and unwanted) staff as a contribution to the unemployment problem. Such policies will have an adverse effect on the total volume of savings unless the reduction in corporate saving is compensated by increased savings in the public sector.

FORCED SAVINGS

Conforming to the earlier definition of voluntary savings, forced savings are here equated with public savings though these are in practice accomplished in a variety of ways.[35] The classical theory of public finance expects governments to cover current expenditure from current revenue and to finance capital expenditure under normal circumstances either by floating loans or by achieving a budget surplus. In developing countries the circumstances are seldom normal and few governments are either able or willing to follow these precepts to the letter.[36] Yet there have

[35] When a government makes a bond issue this is neither forced nor public saving; the subscriptions are voluntary and come from the private sector. Similarly, a government may choose to allocate to the private sector by means of loans to firms part of the funds it has raised via forced savings.

[36] R. Nurkse, *Problems of Capital Formation in Underdeveloped Countries*, Oxford, Blackwell, 1953, p. 150; see also Koichi Emi, 'Epargne et Investissement par le Budget de l'Etat', *Les Problèmes Fiscaux et Monétaires dans les Pays en Voie de Développement*, Third Rehovoth Conference, Dunod, Paris 1967, pp. 137 *et seq.*, and in the same Conference Report, N. Kaldor, 'Les Prélèvements Fiscaux dans les Pays en Voie de Développement', p. 208.

been notable examples of development through forced savings over a prolonged period. One was the case of Japan where in the last part of the nineteenth century the Government by means of heavy land taxes was able to appropriate to itself the benefits of rising agricultural productivity, using these resources for the building up of manufacturing industry. Another was that of the Soviet Union where by means of obligatory deliveries from the collective farms of produce at artificially low prices the Government was able in effect to extract from the farm population a massive volume of savings and use it for industrial development which in turn generated employment in the non-agricultural sectors. It is possible that at some point in the years ahead the Government of a country where the Green Revolution has taken firm root could divert at least part of the consequential increase in agricultural productivity via taxation to the financing of industrial development, as the Japanese did; but it must be counted as unlikely because today the social climate has become so different. In most developing countries the public demand for governmental services, schools, hospitals, water and electricity supplies, and so on, has become so insistent that the revenue raised is never sufficient to meet the needs which can with justice be classed as urgent; hence the chance of budget surpluses is remote. Or again, it is difficult for a government to attract savings by issuing bonds because people with money to invest can find far more lucrative opportunities in, for example, real estate where fortunes can be made from the giddy growth of land values in expanding cities. It must be concluded therefore that the mobilisation of savings through orthodox fiscal devices is not a policy which can be pursued extensively in most developing countries.

There remains the other alternative of savings generated through inflation, either accidental or deliberate. The financing of developmental activities by the simple expedient of creating new money is a temptation to which all governments have yielded at one time or another; and aside from the supply of money, other indirect routes lead to the same result. Not many writers use the model of Kahn and Keynes of the nineteen-thirties to suggest that unemployment in developing countries can be cured by the creation of purchasing power, because it is recognised that their model applied to the special circumstances of industrial countries in the grip of an economic depression, in particular it assumed the existence of under-utilised resources – skills, plant and infrastructural facilities. As Perroux has pointed out,[37] the case of developing countries usually bears little resemblance to that. Their economies are not like a motor car equipped with an engine in full working order which merely needs some petrol in the tank to get it started again. In these countries the engine, indeed the whole car, has still to be built: they do not have unused capacity (except in the special sense and for the special reasons discussed in Chapter 3); they lack a pool of skilled labour available for work; the Keynsian multiplier cannot operate because of the absence of organised markets

[37] F. Perroux, *Les Techniques Quantitatives de la Planification*, Paris, Presses Univ. de France, 1965.

for goods, capital and labour and the lack of economic integration between the various regions within a country; bottlenecks abound everywhere.

Under such circumstances a policy of deficit financing and its accompanying inflation does little good, so it is argued, and causes much harm. It particularly penalises the masses of farm people and others who are on the fringe of the market economy and whose incomes do not respond except with a major time lag to the rising level of the cost of living. It also penalises the large numbers of persons working in the public service and other institutions where wages and salaries are adjusted only at widely separated intervals, not to mention the pensioners and other recipients of fixed incomes. In general it results in a transfer of purchasing power from the lower to the upper income groups and in consequence can be expected to provoke luxury spending and social unrest. Many developing countries have been through analogous experiences.[38]

However, there are others who incline to the view that considering all the circumstances of developing countries, a policy of inflation, deliberate but controlled, can contribute handsomely to capital formation and productive investment. The most spectacular example of this policy is provided by Brazil where inflation has been running at 20 per cent per annum. To neutralise the usual evils of inflation the Brazilian authorities have resorted to five levers of control: strict limitation of the budgetary deficit, price regulation, wage restraint, a 'crawling peg' rate of exchange and the process of 'monetary correction'.[39] This last constitutes the key to the system. Every year the paper value of capital, rent, pensions, savings, loans, bonds and securities, and fixed assets is revalued in accordance with the price index; and the paper capital gain resulting from this is tax-free. Thus the value of the saver's capital is protected, investment is not discouraged, depreciation occurs at realistic rates, industrial employment expands rapidly.[40] Such a package of policies may not be exportable without considerable modification to countries with a different political and social framework, but for Brazil where in the early nineteen-sixties much higher rates of inflation prevailed the system appears to generate rapid investment whilst distributing consciously rather than haphazardly the social burden.

FOREIGN CAPITAL

In addition to the investment resources mobilised via voluntary and forced savings, all developing countries obtain capital from abroad partly in the form of private investment and partly as official loans and grants.

[38] F. Perroux, 'Trois Outils d'Analyse pour l'Etude du Sous-développement', *Cahiers de l'Institut de Science Economique Appliquée*, Série F, No. 1, Paris, ISEA, 1955, pp. 30 *et seq*. See also: A. Peacock and G. K. Shaw, *Fiscal Policy and Employment in Less Developed Countries*, Part I, Paris, OECD Development Centre, July 1970.

[39] M. H. Simonsen, *Inflacão: Gradualismo e Tratamento de Choque*, Apec, Rio de Janeiro, 1970.

[40] 'Brazil: the Moving Frontier', *Economist*, London, 2 September 1972.

For some of these countries foreign capital represents a rather minor element in the total annual fixed capital formation, but in other cases it may account for almost all of it.

Clearly, any action which increased the flow of these funds would also, provided they were prudently used, create additional employment. The role of financial assistance has been recognised in the International Development Strategy adopted by the United Nations which specified that each developed country should endeavour to reach by 1972 or at latest by 1975 a target of net transfer of resources equivalent to 1 per cent of its GNP; and within this target official development assistance should reach a minimum net amount of 0·7 per cent. In the year 1970 the net flow of resources from countries members of the Development Assistance Committee of the OECD represented 0·78 per cent of their combined GNP and their official development assistance 0·34 per cent.[41] This indicates that while private investment was somewhat above target the official element was less than half the hoped for volume. In absolute terms the 1970 net total reached $15·5 billion, or $5 billion less than if the 1 per cent target has been reached.

The fulfilment of these targets would therefore provide developing countries with a great deal more in the way of capital resources for economic development and for employment creation in the years ahead. One of the means by which the flow of development finance can be augmented is by linking its provision with the International Monetary Fund's allocation of Special Drawing Rights to developing countries.

The distinction between *gross* and *net* flow of funds has become important in the present decade because for many developing countries the reverse flow of funds, comprising the servicing and repayment of debts already incurred, has grown so large that it almost, in a few cases entirely, swallows up the inward flow of new foreign capital. It has indeed been said that the nineteen-seventies will be the Decade of Debt Development. This difficulty is reaching such proportions that not only will considerable debt rescheduling have to be programmed but also careful scrutiny will be required regarding the terms of new lending, with the objective of increasing in every way possible the proportion of soft loans.

INVESTMENT POLICIES AND EMPLOYMENT
Attention has so far been devoted solely to the mobilisation of domestic savings and to the flow of foreign capital, but equally important are the uses to which such funds are put. The first task is to overcome the suspicions of those masses who for centuries have known nothing but economic insecurity, and whose suspicions are expressed in a strong propensity to hoard. After all, until quite recently the farm people of industrialised countries kept their savings 'under the mattress'. Equally unproductive is the propensity to invest in precious stones, gold and silver

41 OECD, *Development Assistance, 1971 Review*, Report by Edwin M. Martin, Chairman of the Development Assistance Committee, December 1971, pp. 33 and 36.

ornaments and other objects of durable value. In many countries a high proportion of savings is channelled into the acquisition of land – by peasants to provide security for their children and by town dwellers as a convenient and usually rewarding speculation; the result can be measured in the rapid rise in land values often to heights having little relation to the land's income-yielding potential. Few governments of developing countries have yet found effective ways of checking this diversion of savings toward unproductive activities.

By contrast most of these governments do seek to orient that part of savings which is available for investment by specifying certain industries wherein new investment will enjoy fiscal benefits, generally those industries which can contribute to import substitution or to an expansion of exports.[42] But the further question arises, namely whether governments could not do more to orient investment to labour-intensive branches of industry or, within an industry, to firms utilising labour-intensive techniques. These objectives may be furthered by the use of one or more of the following three policy instruments: discrimination in lending policy, fiscal concessions and/or subsidies.

As regards lending policy a number of governments have established special banks or credit agencies for the purpose of channelling investment funds to cottage industries and to smallscale enterprises in general where there is a presumption of labour intensity. Not only does this give such firms preferential access to the capital market, but frequently the interest rate and other loan conditions are geared to be more favourable to the smaller than to the larger firms. Similar benefits may be extended to firms which undertake to obtain their raw materials or semi-processed goods from local rather than from foreign sources.

Fiscal measures can be used in various ways to stimulate employment. For instance, a tax may be levied on the import of eqnipment which could be produced locally; alternatively, tax exemptions may be extended to entrepreneurs producing capital goods in substitution for imports. Exemptions in the form of accelerated depreciation, reduced rates of profits tax, and so on, may be granted to firms undertaking a stipulated investment and providing a stipulated volume of employment. Thus, in Senegal such favours are available to firms creating at least forty new and permanent jobs (twenty outside the Cap-Vert province) and investing at least 40 million CFA francs (20 million ex Cap-Vert) irrespective of branch of industry.[43] Experience with incentives of this type has been mixed. In several cases the concessions have been generous to the point of causing considerable loss of revenue to the Government without at the same time achieving anything very tangible in employment of viable new businesses.

[42] 'Tax Incentives for Investment in Developing Countries', *Staff Papers*, International Monetary Fund, July 1967; 'Tax Incentives in Latin America', *Economic Bulletin for Latin America*, March 1964; see also: ILO, *Fiscal Measures for Employment Promotion in Developing Countries, op. cit.*, 1972.

[43] E. Costa, 'Employment Problems and Policies in Senegal', *International Labour Review*, May 1967, p. 430.

Such cases have been noted in Costa Rica, Guatemala, Mexico, Panama and Jamaica.[44]

A different approach is that of cash subsidies based on the numbers employed but not tied to the hiring of extra staff. In Puerto Rico in 1963 a Special Incentive Scheme along these lines was introduced. Firms whose staff consisted of two-thirds or more of male workers received an additional $100 subsidy per worker. These grants could be used for any purpose beneficial to the staff, e.g. for training, housing, transport, etc. Similar experiments have been tried in other parts of the Caribbean.

Table 8.3   *Cash Subsidies to Firms in Puerto Rico*

Zone	Up to 30 workers $ per firm	30–100 workers $ per worker	Over 100 workers $ per worker
1	30,000	430	400
2	20,000	210	190
3	15,000	150	140
4	10,000	105	95
5	7,000	90	75

Source: ILO, *op. cit.*, p. 197.

In respect to foreign firms where the investment capital comes from abroad the approach may have to be rather different. The extractive industries are by nature capital-intensive, utilising for the most part specialised equipment only obtainable from foreign sources. In as much as this characteristic has to be accepted, the governments of the developing countries concerned often prefer to ask the foreign firms to create additional employment by constructing roads, schools, clinics and other facilities which the Government itself cannot yet afford. In manufacturing industries, especially when foreign firms are requesting permission to establish themselves in the country, they can be oriented towards labour-intensive techniques by application of the same incentives mentioned in the preceding paragraphs as well as those listed in Chapter 3. But where the new products are destined for export care must be taken not to impose conditions on manufacturers which would jeopardise the cost competitiveness of the products in foreign markets.

In respect to official assistance received from foreign governments or through multilateral agencies some of the conditions frequently attached to such loans would appear to call for modification. For instance, aid has

[44] ILO, *Fiscal Measures for Employment Promotion in Developing Countries, op cit.*, Also in G. Lent, 'Tax Incentives for Investment in Developing Countries', *Staff Papers*, IMF, July 1967. Also in P. L. Chen-Young, 'A Study of Tax Incentives in Jamaica', *National Tax Journal*, September 1967.

in many cases been tied to the financing of the import components of approved projects, a condition which puts an artificial premium on capital-intensive schemes and on procurement from abroad. Thus the Report of the Commission on International Development recommended that 'aid-givers' remove regulations which limit or prevent contributions to the local costs of projects, and make a greater effort to encourage local procurement wherever economically justified.[45] More generally, the untying of aid could make a major contribution by freeing recipients from the compulsion to purchase equipment at prices often higher than those prevailing elsewhere and from having to utilise more capital-intensive equipment than they need. Some progress in untying aid has already been made but much remains to be done.[46]

Much can be accomplished by the borrowing governments themselves in choosing the projects for which they seek foreign financial assistance. Thus when foreign funds are sought to support the setting-up of an industrial development agency, the directives of this body should be oriented less towards prestige projects than to the encouragement of the smaller firms characterised by labour-intensive organisation. Foreign funds can suitably be requested also for public works projects which by their nature employ much labour – road building, drinking water supplies, the smaller irrigation projects, for example. If the responsible authorities accustomed themselves to calculating by means of 'shadow', or opportunity cost, prices as recommended in earlier chapters, the advantages of such an orientation of investment funds would become apparent.

From this brief review it may be concluded that the investment policies which the governments of developing countries pursue can have a massive influence on the evolution of employment. In several directions there is scope, without in any way prejudicing the over-all objectives of economic growth, for using the partial control over investment resources and the total control over fiscal measures which governments possess to orient new enterprises and the expansion of existing enterprises toward employment promotion. Such a policy need not be pushed to the extreme of creating jobs which are purely nominal and introduce all the debilitating consequences of semi-idleness; it can on the contrary promote a selective expansion of those industries and techniques within industries which are the most appropriate to the country's stage of economic development.

Expansion of Markets

The creation of additional productive employment can take place only to the extent that ways and means can be found to expand the market demand for the commodities produced. More food must be eaten, more raw materials bought by manufacturers, more finished goods purchased

[45] *Partners in Development, op. cit.*, p. 177; see also H. Singer, 'International Policies and their Effect on Employment', *loc. cit.*

[46] For discussion of this problem and for a possible approach towards generalised untying of aid, see OECD, *Development Assistance, 1970 Review, op. cit.*, pp. 52–7.

by consumers, more services required from teachers, doctors, house-builders, and so on. Part of this market expansion can occur locally, i.e. within the frontiers of the developing country concerned, while part will be sought in foreign markets. In the one case the factors governing the evolution of demand are different from those operating in the other case, and it is convenient to discuss the two markets separately.

THE DOMESTIC MARKET

Consider first the volume of private, as distinct from public, consumption expenditure. The expansion of this type of consumption in any individual country depends upon the rate of growth of purchasing power in the hands of the public, while the *character* of the expenditure depends on how the purchasing power is distributed; a country where much of it is in the hands of relatively few rich people will have a consumption pattern different from that in a country with a more egalitarian distribution. Looking ahead, what is decisive is the rate of growth of numbers of persons in each principal income group.

Governments can to some degree influence both the components of this situation. They can stimulate purchasing power in general by allowing wages and salaries to rise more rapidly than the over-all rate of growth in labour productivity, in other words by permitting some degree of wage-push inflation – a policy whose pros and cons have just been disscused. They can make the distribution of purchasing power more egalitarian by increasing taxes on the rich and by raising the wages of the lowest paid workers through minimum wage legislation or by other means. Whatever their policies in these directions may be, the national planning authorities have to take the likely consequences into account in making forward estimates of the evolution of demand for particular commodities and groups of commodities. Since a large quantity of data exists concerning the income-elasticity of demand for various classes of consumption goods, even in developing countries, the elaboration of such projections should not present too much difficulty; yet until now only a minority of developing countries have constructed forward-looking evaluations of domestic demand for each of the main food categories, for clothing, housing, furnishings, radios, bicycles, motor-cycles, and so forth. These projections of demand, however rough in the first instance, and with experience their accuracy will be improved, provide the evidence essential for determining the choice between for example alternative manufacturing investments and the most appropriate size of the new plant. They likewise will indicate the scope for agricultural diversification and which new foodstuffs are likely to be demanded in the years ahead. In formulating such projections regard must be had not merely to calculations based on assumed income-elasticities of demand but also to the presence of absence of infrastructural facilities enabling that demand to manifest itself; for instance, there may be in the cities a numerically important income group with a potentially strong demand for liquid milk, but this demand will not become effective until the necessary transport and storage facilities have been provided for keeping the milk cool and bringing it to the towns from the producing areas.

Forward estimates also need to be formulated concerning the volume and character of public consumption, i.e. the rate of expansion of the government's requirements for doctors, school teachers, public works personnel. The governing factor here is not the national needs which will be enormous for many years to come, but rather the quantity of revenue which the Government expects to be able to raise to finance its various programmes. As noted in the discussion of public works activities in Chapter 5, even in the poorest countries there exist some opportunities for additional revenue raising and hence for generating further employment in these public service activities.

The most discouraging feature which emerges in the majority of these projection exercises is the small size of the market for any individual article of consumption. This is due partly to the low level of *per caput* income among the masses and partly to the fact that most of the developing countries are small in population. Thus within the national boundaries there is often insufficient demand to justify erecting, say, a cement plant, a sewing-machine factory, a plate-glass works, not to mention a steel mill or an automatic assembly. This has been one of the main considerations behind the move in many regions of the world to establish some form of Common Markets between groups of developing countries. Through the progressive abolition of tariffs over a period of years between group members it is hoped to provide a larger effective market for manufacturers leading to a specialisation in each member country on those products for which it is best suited. The international trade aspects of these groupings will be considered further below.

THE FOREIGN MARKET

One of the most publicised among the many difficult problems of economic growth is that of trying to expand the exports of the developing countries to developed ones, an endeavour which in recent years has had mainly disappointing results. Especially in countries where export business represents, or could represent, an important proportion of the national economic activity, the volume of exports which can be achieved obviously has major influence on the volume of employment. Export expansion will not only increase the number of jobs in the particular branch of activity concerned, it will also have significant indirect effects. For example, it will stimulate an expansion of demand for materials used in connection with the export commodity, e.g. for fertilisers, grading machines, packaging materials, warehouses, and so on, most of which can be produced within the country and thus provide additional employment. In a number of cases the export product will also call into existence manufacturing facilities using this product as their raw material: for example, the transformation of coffee beans into instant coffee, the crushing of oilseeds into oil and oilcake, the manufacture of cotton and wool into finished textiles. Here too new employment will be created as exports expand. And there is a further effect – the so-called 'multiplier'; the wages paid out and the profits earned in all these additional activities add to the purchasing power of the people and thereby generate a volume of demand for the goods and services substantially larger than when these people were unemployed or partially employed; if the necessary materials, tools and machines are available this can lead to substantially increased employment.

Export expansion is therefore of extreme relevance to employment promotion. However, a detailed examination of this topic would lead into a consideration of the manifold problems of international trade concerning which an extensive literature already exists. For further information in this field the reader can be referred, *inter alia*, to the Report of the Third United Nations Conference on Trade and Development (Santiago, 1972), to the reports of the sessions of UNCTAD's Trade and Development Board and to the various special studies published by its secretariat. In the remaining pages of this chapter only the highlights of the developing countries' export problems and of the issues involved in trying to resolve them can be recapitulated.

Declining Share in World Trade

During the nineteen-fifties and nineteen-sixties the exports of the developing countries taken as a whole were increasing but much less rapidly than those of the industrial countries so that their share in world exports declined steadily from 27 per cent in 1953 to 17·6 per cent in 1970.[47] This decline was associated with a change in the commodity composition of world trade. Thus, during the nineteen-sixties the trade in manufactures, which accounts for three-quarters of the exports of the industrial countries, increased by 124 per cent whereas trade in primary products, which account for three-quarters of the exports of the developing countries, rose by only 57 per cent. Moreover, the terms of trade have for most of the post-war period been moving against the developing countries. The index of unit prices of exports of agricultural products fell during the latter part of the fifties, was stationary at a low level during most of the sixties and has recovered only somewhat since 1969. The unit price index for minerals fared a little better but experienced extreme fluctuations, while the index of prices of manufactures continued rising throughout.

The developing countries have met this situation by using their best endeavours to increase the share of manufactures in their exports, which has risen from 16 per cent in 1963 to 24 per cent in 1969; but so far only a relatively small number of developing countries have been able to participate in this diversification of exports.

In each of the main commodity groups there are special market features which largely explain why the developing countries' exports expand so slowly. In respect to tropical agricultural products, such as coffee, cocoa, tea and bananas, *per caput* consumption appears to be close to its ceiling in most of the developed market economy countries; though there remains room for expansion in the socialist countries (see below). In temperate

[47] GATT, *International Trade 1966* and *International Trade 1970*, Geneva.

farm products the exporters in the developed countries can generally outsell those of developing countries both in quality and price. Agricultural raw materials face intense competition from synthetics: synthetic rubber, man-made fibres, plastics (versus leather). Some minerals have done well, for instance bauxite; others such as tin have been losing ground. Agricultural products processed in developing countries encounter stiff tariff and non-tariff barriers in developed countries' markets. The same applies to almost all manufactures. For a long time it was too readily assumed that developing countries, because of their inexhaustible supply of labour, would of course have a competitive advantage in the export of labour-intensive products. As pointed out in Chapter 3 this is not necessarily so; although hourly wages are generally lower in developing than in developed countries, relative labour productivity in many manufacturing processes is even lower in the former, which makes for high unit costs and poor competitive capacity. The situation varies from product to product and from country to country. Dividing manufactures arbitrarily into two categories, labour-intensive and capital-intensive, it would appear that the developing countries as a whole have maintained their *share* of world exports about equally well in both categories.[48] What is significant is that the rate of growth of *world* trade in labour-intensive manufactures has been slower over the last decades than the rate of growth of capital-intensive exports. The same observation applies to primary products where exports of fuel and minerals (capital-intensive) have been expanding faster than exports of agricultural products (in the main labour-intensive). This phenomenon is largely explained by factors on the demand side, namely that demand is in general stronger for the raw materials and products of the 'new industries' which tend to use capital-intensive techniques; it is more sluggish especially in the developed countries for food and for the products of the traditional industries. This must be reckoned as a built-in disappointment for the export prospects of the developing countries.

Indeed, unless substantial changes in trade policies occur the future outlook is disquieting. Projecting from present trends the FAO sees a continuing decline in the developing countries' share in world exports of food and agricultural raw materials, while the OECD sees a decline not only in these but also in ores and minerals. Even in petroleum, where hitherto a limited number of developing countries have done well, the outlook is for a more rapid increase in the developed countries' own supplies, e.g. from Alaska and from the North Sea. Since the developing countries' rate of increase in exports of manufactures, welcome though it be, is unlikely to be sufficient to offset the poor growth rate in primary products, a continuing decline in their share of world exports as a whole may continue. This is the more unfortunate when it is remembered that their

[48] Non-ferrous metals, iron and steel, chemicals, engineering products and road motor vehicles are classed as capital-intensive. Textiles, clothing, leather, footwear, furniture, travel goods, glass, wood and cork manufactures and 'other' are classed as labour-intensive.

populations are growing faster than those of the developed countries and that their unemployment and under-employment are more severe.

The question therefore arises: what measures might be taken to arrest and if possible reverse this trend? Can room be found for a greater volume of these countries' exports in world markets, or must they become more inward-looking and plan their economic growth on the basis of a greater degree of self-sufficiency? Answers to these questions can be considered from three points of view: better marketing, increased market access and a larger market share.

Marketing
A very real difficulty for manufacturers and other producers in developing countries is to establish satisfactory market outlets and selling arrangements in developed countries. Of course no problem arises in the case of staple primary products which are sold through the commodity exchanges in North America and Europe; nor does one arise for items produced by a subsidiary of a foreign company which are sold abroad through the parent organisation. The people who face difficulties are the small-scale and medium-scale manufacturers who have no foreign contacts, no information as to the tastes and styles abroad and who, initially at least, are producing in small quantities. Every entrepreneur in a developed country knows the difficulties, the expense and the risk involved in trying to build up a market in another developed country, yet he has access to a network of sophisticated marketing agencies; how much harder must it be for the inexperienced entrepreneur in a small developing country.

It is usually necessary for the producer or manufacturer to establish a relationship with a firm in the importing country to whom the produce is sold under contract. This firm may be a wholesale distributor or the owner of a chain of retail stores or a manufacturer buying semi-processed goods for final finishing. For example, bananas had been grown on a small scale for many years in the smaller Caribbean islands, but it was only when in the early fifties a foreign firm was willing to take the responsibility of shipping and selling that banana cultivation expanded and became a major export. Similarly, in certain Central and South American countries the products of artisan industry had no more than a limited local market until the arrival of North American chain store enterprises offering firm contracts for large quantities of items of prescribed design and quality. Such firms command marketing know-how and can develop the needed sales outlets.

While some manufacturers individually take the initiative in working out relationships with firms in foreign markets, others may require assistance from their governments, while farmers may need to band together in producers' associations in order to be able to negotiate on level terms with the foreign buyer. Where the export product is of national importance the Government may have to concern itself with ensuring that the terms of sales contracts are fair.

In many countries there are individual growers or manufacturers who believe they have have an opportunity to produce profitably a commodity not hitherto exported, but they have no means of ascertaining the extent of demand abroad or how to arrange transport and selling. Some governments maintain commercial attachés at their embassies abroad charged with responsibilities in this field, but in many cases they lack the training or the time, or both, to follow through in developing new markets. Marketing advice can be obtained through the UN Trade and Information Centre in Geneva which is prepared to put sellers and buyers in touch with one another and which will, on request, undertake market surveys. Much more work of this kind will be required in the coming years if the obstacles in the sphere of marketing developing countries' exports are to be overcome.

Market Access
Even the most efficient marketing organisation cannot do much to expand export sales as long as the developed countries continue to maintain their formidable array of trade barriers, which protect their own producers (or deprive their own consumers) by denying free access to their markets. Here one must distinguish between the practices of the market economies and the centrally planned economies, and in each case between primary products and manufactures.

Considering first the trade restraints imposed on primary products, a calculation has been made showing the proportion of imports subject to restraints of one kind or another (see table 8.4). At this period in the mid-sixties, and the situation is probably no better today, over 60 per cent of the developed countries' imports of primary products were subject to restraints. Duties applied to one-third of their imports, fiscal charges to 43 per cent and quantitative controls to about one-quarter. Some of these restraints take the form of internal taxes imposed for revenue purposes: for instance, in most industrial countries petrol and tobacco are subject to such taxation and it is difficult to estimate how much larger the consumption would be if these were removed. But for most of the temperate agricultural commodities the restraints take the form of tariffs and quantitative controls both having the object of protecting domestic producers. Supported by this protection the farmers of the developed countries have over the past two decades made greater technological progress than ever before, and have increased their output faster than the increase in consumer demand, with the result that the selfsufficiency ratios of these countries have steadily risen.[49] According to the FAO projections this trend will continue throughout the nineteen-seventies.

As is well known, the Kennedy Round of tariff reductions accomplished little in the field of primary products, nor have the subsequent efforts in the GATT, in UNCTAD and in bilateral discussions proved any more fruitful. In each of the developed countries agriculture is going through a major transformation with large numbers of farm people leaving the land and an

[49] FAO, *Agricultural Adjustment in Developed Countries*, Doc. ERC. 72/3, Rome, 1972, pp. 125–8.

increasing proportion of small farms becoming economically unviable. In such circumstances governments are reluctant to open their doors more widely to foreign agricultural produce which would diminish the prices and/or the volume of sales of domestically produced foodstuffs. Yet in as much as some measure of trade liberalisation is generally recognised as desirable, the problem reduces itself to finding practicable procedures for gradually augmenting market access. Certain interesting precedents exist:

Table 8.4   *Proportion of Imports Subject to Restraints*

	All types*	Quantitative restraints
	per cent	
Food and tobacco: weighted average	56	33
Sugar	100	82
Other basic foods	75	47
Vegetable oils	78	28
Fruit and vegetables	64	41
Oilseeds and feed	41	18
Beverages, spices and tobacco	38	17
Industrial raw materials: weighted average		
Metals and minerals	21	3
Fibres, hides and rubber	10	2
Other agricultural raw materials	66	28
Petroleum and products	100	38
Total products listed: weighted average	61	26

Source: Gertrud Lovasy, *Effects of Reducing Barriers to Trade in Primary Products in Developing Countries' Exports*, IBRD, August 1966 (unpublished); cited in IMF and IBRD, *The Problem of Stabilisation of Prices of Primary Products: A Joint Staff Study (Part I)*, Washington D.C., 1969, p. 28. For detailed statistical data on tariffs and non-tariff barriers affecting imports of specific primary commodities into major industrial countries and *ad valorem* tariff equivalent of variable levies in the EEC, see UNCTAD secretariat study: 'Programme for the Liberalisation and Expansion of Trade in Commodities of Interest to Developing Countries' in *United Nations Conference on Trade and Development: Second Session*, New Delhi, Vol. II: and also *Commodity Problems and Policies*, New York, 1968, pp. 85–97.

*'All types' includes tariffs, fiscal charges and quantitative restrictions.

for instance, the United States Sugar Act which reserved a proportion of the U.S. market for foreign suppliers, or the policy of the Swedish Government which aims at stablising the agricultural self-sufficiency ratio at around 80 per cent. For some commodities a stage-by-stage reduction in import duties or excise taxes might be envisaged as something to which farmers could reasonably adjust.[50] The same principle would need to be applied to synthetics: to quote the language of the International Development Strategy (paragrah 29), 'where natural products are able to satisfy present and anticipated world market requirements, in the context of

[50] For further discussion of this problem see FAO, *op. cit.*, pp. 182–3.

national policies no special encouragement will be given to the creation and utilisation of new production, particularly in the advanced countries, of directly competing synthetics'.

As regards manufactures and semi-manufactures, important reductions in tariff barriers were accomplished in the Kennedy Round and subsequently; a further round of negotiations is expected to commence in 1973. A substantial number of industrial countries now accord special preferences to a range of manufactures originating in developing countries. However, many important items are excluded from this regime, particularly the majority of processed agricultural and forestry products; and since most of these countries' import duties escalate according to the stage of fabrication of the commodity, in practice the developing countries are obliged to sell raw materials rather than processing them prior to export – witness the case of oilseeds. Reduction of barriers against processed agricultural products could add significantly to the export earnings of developing countries. Or again, it happens that the effective rates of duty imposed by industrial countries are higher on the types of manufactures which developing countries export than on those exported by developed countries.[51] A similar discriminatory effect may be noted in the incidence of quantitative restrictions. An UNCTAD study showed that in 1967 'imports of items subject to quantitative restrictions into the countries imposing the restrictions were 10·4 per cent of their total imports of manufactures and semi-manufactures from developing countries but only 3·4 per cent of their total import of manufactures and semi-manufactures from developed market economy countries';[52] the items chiefly affected being textiles, clothing and other processed agricultural products. A welcome initiative has been the commitment of the Commission of the European Community to liberalise textile imports by conceding a 5 per cent per annum reduction in quota restrictions over a period of five years.

Turning to the markets of the socialist countries where the volume of imports is regulated by state purchasing policies rather than by tariffs, most of the trade is conducted through the machinery of bilateral agreements. A recent UNCTAD analysis focused mainly on developments in 1969 showed that the exports of developing countries to this group of countries were composed of more than 80 per cent of food and raw materials. Only a small percentage, 16 per cent, represents manufactured goods (SITC 5–8) the predominant items being textile yarn and fabrics, copper, tin, and clothing and footwear.[53] When these processed products are imported it is

[51] United Nations, *The Kennedy Round: Estimated Effects on Tariff Barriers*, Part Two: 'The Structure of Protection of Protection in Industrial Countries and its Effects on the Exports of Processed Goods from Developing Countries', B. A. Balassa, New York, 1968.

[52] UNCTAD, *An Analysis of Existing Quantitative and other Import Restrictions in Selected Developed Market Economy Countries on Products of Export Interest to the Developing Countries*, Doc. TD/B.C2/83, 13 November 1969, p. 34.

[53] *UNCTAD Review of International Trade and Development*, 1971 'Part One: Recent Trends in Trade and Development, Annex', Table and paragraphs 26 to 27, Doc. TD/B/369/Add. 1, 9 August 1971.

frequently as payment in kind for assistance (from socialist countries) in the establishment of manufacturing plant.

There have been some significant changes in the commodity composition of this trade since 1960. Thus the share of manufactured goods rose from 7·9 per cent in 1960 to 15·8 per cent in 1969. Also, the share of food, beverages and tobacco increased from 28·6 per cent in 1960 to over 40 per cent in the second part of the decade, accompanied by a fall in the share of crude materials. The rise in the share of food products reflected largely the increased importance of sugar since 1960, for which Cuba was the main supplier.

In respect to tropical products which interest many developing countries the consumption in socialist countries remains low (see table 8.5). In 1970

Table 8.5 *Consumption of Selected Commodities in Western Europe and Socialist Countries*

	Western Europe 1964–6	Soviet Union and Eastern Europe 1964–6	1970
	Kilograms per person per annum		
Coffee	3·5	0·2	0·4
Cocoa	1·6	0·4	0·5
Tea	0·8	0·2	0·2
Bananas	6·7	0·2	0·3

Source: FAO, *Agricultural Adjustment in Developed Countries*, Doc. ERC 72/3, June 1972, p. 176.

coffee consumption was one-ninth of the West European level, banana consumption less than one twentieth, though as can be noted the consumption levels are increasing. It has been estimated that a more liberal import policy in the socialist countries in regard to these items as well as for sugar and citrus fruit might add some $2 billion to the export earnings of the developing countries.[54] The same study suggests that by liberalising market access the developed market economy countries could increase their agricultural imports also by $2 billion (at 1970 prices).

Market Shares

The act of opening the door to a larger volume of imports of primary products and manufactures into the developed countries, while an essential first step, begs the question of who is to benefit from the resulting increase in world trade. Under present circumstances the lion's share of any such increase must be expected to accrue to the developed exporting countries, except in regard to tropical products which they do not grow. In the first place, as has been noted above, these countries enjoy a comparative cost advantage in respect to most temperate agricultural products and some

[54] FAO, *op. cit.*, p. 185, para .716.

manufactures. Second the existing incidence of tariff and non-tariff barriers discriminates in favour of the exports of developed countries. The share of the developing countries in world exports has been falling, though this fall was at least temporarily arrested in 1971. If this trend is to be reversed, it will not be enough to open the markets of developed countries; deliberate action will have to be taken to improve the developing countries' market share. A number of approaches to this objective may be considered.

In respect to primary products, individual developed countries could reserve a portion of their market for developing countries' produce either by means of bilateral contracts or through a distribution of import quotas along the lines of the U.S. Sugar Act or by means of preferences such as the European Community accords to certain countries under the Yaoundé agreements. Alternatively, the same objective may be attained through the instrumentality of inter-governmental commodity arrangements. Whilst such arrangements, it is true, have usually been negotiated with a view to steadying the price of a particular commodity and avoiding the accumulation of surpluses, those arrangements which include export quota provisions do in fact secure to each exporting country its share in the world market; and the allocation of quotas could, if desired, be used to augment progressively the shares of developing countries. Admittedly, this objective is not at present generally accepted. On the contrary, the recent pressure for liberalisation of trade in agricultural products has been exerted primarily by developed exporting countries with the aim of expanding their own agricultural exports. A somewhat different method, applicable in the case of tropical products, would be for importing countries which levy fiscal charges on the import or consumption of these commodities to agree to refund all or part of the proceeds of these taxes to the producing countries. (Note: the extension of this principle to any temperate product would merely make an unnecessary present to the developed exporters.)[55]

In the field of manufactures and semi-manufactures reference has already been made to the scheme of preferential arrangements for developing countries' exports drawn up within the UNCTAD in 1970. Although the scheme accords less favourable treatment to processed agricultural products, several labour-intensive manufactures such as textiles have been put on exceptions lists and more generally the scheme applies solely to tariffs and does not provide for any reductions in non-tariff barriers, none the less it has been estimated that its effect will be to increase the developing countries' exports of manufactures and semi-manufactures from the recent $7 billion per annum to around $8 billion.[56]

A number of socialist countries have rallied in support of the principle

[55] United Nations, *The International Development Strategy in Action: the Role of UNCTAD*, Report by the Secretary-General of UNCTAD to the Third Session of the Conference, Doc. TD/99, 15 February 1972, pp. 31–7.

[56] H. B. Chenery and H. Hughes, 'The International Division of Labour: the Case of Industry', paper presented to the European Conference of the Society for International Development, The Hague, 24–7 October, 1971.

of preferences for developing countries. In 1970 at the Fourth Session of UNCTAD's Special Committee on Preferences five socialist countries (Bulgaria, Czechoslovakia, Hungary, Poland and the Soviet Union) made a Joint Declaration stating that in principle preferential treatment should be extended not only to manufactures and semi-manufactures but also to raw materials and processed agricultural products. Further, recognising that only some socialist countries operate a tariff system through which such preferences could be accorded, the Joint Declaration emphasised that each socialist country will implement these measures for preferential treatment in conformity with the modalities of its foreign trade system.[57]

It must be concluded that more progress has been made by the developed countries taken as a whole in respect to manufactures than in regard to primary products, particularly agricultural commodities. While any progress is welcome, it has to be recognised that primary products are, and for many years will remain, the preponderant part of the developed countries' exports, that agricultural products are usually labour-intensive and that it is the markets for these which seem to be the most difficult to expand.

There remains the question of expanding trade among the developing countries themselves. Considered in isolation such trade does not necessarily promote an *increase* in employment. Supposing that countries A and B, which hitherto have each grown their own rice and manufactured their own textiles, now decide that in future A will give up growing rice and will import its requirements from B, while B will give up making textiles and will import its requirements from A, there is no net addition to employment. If, however, this division of labour led to an increase in labour productivity in the two countries, as would probably be the case, then purchasing power would expand, consumer demand would rise and additional employment would be created. And because, as noted, the national market of so many developing countries is small, an expansion of markets by means of international division of labour can assume great importance.

This is the thinking which has inspired the creation during the last few years of numerous trade groupings or common markets. In Latin America there is the Latin American Free Trade Association (LAFTA) comprising 11 countries, the Andean customs union covering 5 countries, the Central American Common Market (CACM) also with 5 and the Caribbean Free Trade Association (CARIFTA). In Africa there is the East African Community (3 members), the West African Economic Community (7), the Central African Customs and Economic Union (4), the Organisation of Senegal Riparian States (4), the Common African, Malagasy and Mauritian Organisation (15) and the Council of the Entente States (5). The Middle East has the Arab Common Market comprising four countries. In Asia though certain regional and subregional groupings have been

---

[57] UNCTAD, *Report of the Special Committee on Preferences on the Second Part of its Fourth Session*, 21 September to 10 October 1970; Part 2, Chapter 1, § C, Doc. TD/B/329/Add. 3, pp. 3–6.

formed none has yet led to a free trade association or equivalent. So far the results of these efforts have been modest. Only in Latin America has intra-regional trade developed faster than the total trade of the countries of the region over the past decade; but most of the other groupings have been established too recently for important benefits to be recorded.

Mention should also be made of an effort between the developing countries of several continents to develop their trade exchanges within a common framework, namely the sixteen countries which in 1971 to the exchange of tariff and trade concesions of a multilateral character covering some 300 headings in the Brussels Tariff Nomenclature and amounting at that time to some U.S. $550 million of their exports. The Protocol includes accession procedures for other developing countries wishing to join.[58]

By exploiting all these various approaches to market expansion – in the developed market economy countries, in the socialist countries and among the developing countries themselves – much still remains to be accomplished in increasing the developing countries' exports. Such expansion, as has been seen, not merely generates employment in the export sector but also additional employment in those branches of activity favourably affected by the backward and forward linkage. Furthermore, increased exports earn additional foreign exchange which for many countries is the major bottleneck restricting the import of the capital goods on which the growth of industry and of industrial employment depends. For all these reasons more positive action on the part of the governments of developed countries to augment their imports of both primary products and manufactures from developing countries could make a real contribution to the solution of the employment problem in the latter.

[58] The sixteen countries are: Brazil, Chile, Egypt, Greece, India, Israel, Korea, Mexico, Pakistan, Peru, Philippines, Spain, Tunisia, Turkey, Uruguay and Yugoslavia.

Part Three

THE QUALITY AND QUANTITY OF LABOUR

Chapter 9

Introduction

Employment policy consists not solely in stimulating the demand for manpower but equally in exercising an influence on the quality and the quantity of labour available for employment both now and in the future. In many cases the volume of employment which can be offered depends to a large extent upon existence or absence of specific skills: a road-building programme may be held up for lack of surveyors, a house-building programme for lack of carpenters. Because bottlenecks of this nature are frequently experienced in developing countries the policies pursued in regard to education and training can be of capital importance in the strategy of job creation, the objective being to attain the proportion of skilled workers and the distribution of skills between occupations appropriate to the stage of the country's development. Governments may also influence the size (as distinct from the qualifications) of the labour force by their encouragement or otherwise of emigration and by their demographic policies.

Moreover, these two groups of policies – the qualitative and the quantitative – interact on one another. Thus, an extension of the period of education and/or of training has the effect of withholding part of the population from the labour market for the duration of the additional courses. It may also reduce the birth rate by postponing the average age of marriage and by arousing interest in family planning, an interest found more frequently among the better educated groups. In the reverse direction a reduction in the size of the labour force through emigration will affect its quality, positively if most of the emigrants are unskilled workers, negatively in the opposite case.

While these three elements of employment strategy – training, emigration and demographic policy – will be examined successively in Chapters 10 to 12, it should be borne in mind that all three of them need to be geared, far more deliberately than is at present the case in most developing countries, to the current and prospective employment needs. They should form integral components of manpower planning without which the whole process of industrialisation and economic growth may be jeopardised.

Chapter 10

Training Policies

The process of economic development is characterised by an ever greater subdivision of labour. This needs to be reflected in an increasing specialisation and complementarity in the qualifications possessed by the labour force, thus permitting the introduction of modern technologies in manufacturing and other economic activities. In the majority of developing countries the shortage of skills of various kind impedes the execution of development programmes, and from this it might appear reasonable to conclude that an increase in training facilities of all kinds would have an employment-promotion effect. In prac e the training programmes have to be more discriminating. A particular country may have a shortage of bricklayers and a surplus of lawyers, a shortage of foremen and a surplus of civil servants. One of the responsibilities of the authorities operating training programmes should therefore be to identify bottlenecks, the occupations in which qualified personnel is insufficient, and orient the programmes specifically to the elimination of those bottlenecks. Further, since the organisation of training facilities, including the preparation of instructors, may take a considerable time, it is essential to look ahead to the likely requirements for skilled manpower in five and ten years; and in this exercise the authorities will need to collaborate closely with the national planning agency, where such exists.[1]

The provision of vocational training may be considered from three points of view. First there are the traditional types of training programmes both prior to and in the course of employment. Second, there are the various temporary measures which may be taken to make good a lack of adequate training facilities. Third, attention should be directed to certain experimental innovations which in the circumstances of some countries may help to accelerate the creation of the required skills. In the present report the concern will be with the organisational aspects of these programmes rather than with their technical content.[2]

---

[1] On the subject of manpower planning, see OECD, The Mediterranean Regional Project, *Forecasting Educational Needs for Economic and Social Development*, by H. S. Parnes, Paris, 1962, also *Economic and Social Aspects of Educational Planning*, UNESCO, Paris, 1965; also, J. Mouly, 'Problèmes de la Planification de la Main-d'oeuvre', *Tiers-Monde*, Paris, No. 41, January–March 1970.

[2] In regard to the latter see: United Nations Economic and Social Council, *Training National Technical Personnel for the Accelerated Industrialisation of the Developing Countries*, Doc. E/3901/Rev.1, Geneva 1964; also ILO, *Human Resources for Industrial Development, op. cit.*

196

Traditional Systems and Methods of Training

PRE-EMPLOYMENT VOCATIONAL TRAINING

This type of training is made available chiefly through technical schools, vocational training centres and centres for accelerated training. The principal aim of institutions of this kind is to ensure that 'theoretical and practical training progress are in step with each other; they should continue the pupils' general education and provide the link between school life and the world of work; they should enable their trainees to acquire their practical skills systematically, unhampered by the requirements of industrial production'.[3]

Under the circumstances prevailing in many developing countries this aim is imperfectly achieved. In the first place a proportion of those who pass through technical schools and colleges do not proceed to take jobs in the occupations for which they have been trained but prefer to seek administrative work which in most countries enjoys a higher social status. This tendency is moreover encouraged by a widespread defect in the curricula of these schools which usually contain too much theory and insufficient orientation to practice. Furthermore, the training courses frequently turn out a surplus of certain skills and too few in others. For instance, in the francophone African countries the technical colleges produce workers well qualified in particular narrow specialisations whereas what the countries most urgently require are persons who have acquired a broad general competence as, for example, mechanics to staff maintenance and repair shops.[4] This can have the paradoxical result of creating unemployment in the category of trained persons. In India's Third Five-Year Plan it was estimated that among those who had passed through secondary education, either general or technical, over 1 million were unemployed. Surveys carried out in Ceylon, Malaysia and the Philippines have shown that the incidence of unemployment is higher in the more highly educated groups. In Ceylon, for instance, the proportion of persons 'never yet employed' in the 15–24 age group was 35 per cent over-all but 76 per cent among those with 'O' level qualification.[5]

The fact that general education and technical training are so poorly correlated with employment opportunities should give cause for serious concern since they are costly to provide, absorbing substantial amounts of scarce investment resources and scarce teaching staff. A number of governments recognise these shortcomings and are currently making efforts to change the character of the courses and to adapt them more effectively to national requirements; such is the case in Morocco, Tunisia, Korea, India, Malaysia, Pakistan, Thailand and (with the assistance of

[3] ILO, *op. cit.*, p. 84.

[4] E. Rossignol, 'La Formation Professionnelle dans les Pays en Voie de Développement', *Avenirs*, Paris, No. 168, November 1965.

[5] ILO, *Matching Employment Opportunities and Expectations: a Programme of Action for Ceylon, op. cit.*, Table 10, p. 33. This may reflect largely the fact that people with secondary education include a high proportion whose families can afford to support them while they seek 'acceptable' jobs.

197

UNESCO and the Organisation of American States) in certain countries of Latin America, to mention but a few examples.

Some of the deficiencies of conventional training programmes have been overcome by means of establishing accelerated vocational training centres which cater mainly for adult trainees. Generally speaking, such facilities can be set up more rapidly, in as much as the teaching personnel can be found and trained quickly, and the content of the courses has a more practical bias and is better tailored to the background and experience of the participants. It is a system capable of turning unskilled into semi-skilled workers and of upgrading the existing levels of skill among large numbers of persons who already have some experience of industry or other regular employment. It is however, also a costly programme and can be justified only in circumstances where the demand for workers in these several categories is expanding fast. By contrast, where industrialisation is proceeding rather slowly the products of these accelerated training courses tend to be preferred by employers and are used to replace unskilled labourers, thus merely shifting the unemployment to the latter group.[6]

IN-PLANT TRAINING

This type of training can be offered to the worker either at the beginning of his industrial career or at a later stage in order to improve his degree of skill. Its essential characteristic is that the worker learns his skill through personal contact with an already skilled worker and while actually performing his job. In its more sophisticated version it becomes the classical apprenticeship arrangement governed by a contract between master and apprentice, which specifies that the practical learning is supplemented by a certain amount of theoretical instruction. Apprenticeship in the older European sense of the term is infrequently found in developing countries whereas the more informal arrangements of in-plant training on the American model are widespread.

These offer numerous advantages especially in countries where the governments cannot afford an adequate programme of the more formal training centres. On-the-job training dispenses with the need for full-time instructors, the skills being taught by personnel within the firm. It ensures employment for the trainee in the firm where he works and it takes care to impart skills for which a current demand really exists. For example, in Saudi Arabia the Arabian Oil Company has succeeded in rapidly transforming bedouins into skilled workers and foremen.[7] Other multi-national corporations have operated similar programmes with satisfactory results. However, the great majority of firms in developing countries, either because of their small size, or their lack of resources, or their attitudes, are unable or unwilling to offer training facilities of this kind. In such situations it is open to governments to provide employers with incentives in the form

6 For an examination of the practical problems see: *Algeria, National Institute for the Vocational Training of Adults*, Report prepared by the ILO as executive agency for UNDP, Geneva, 1970.

7 E. Gannagé, *Institutions et Développement*, Collection *Tiers-Monde*, 1966, p. 25.

of subsidies or of assistance in kind; in Tunisia pressure is brought to bear on the large firms to provide in-plant training, while the smaller firms are organised in groups for this purpose.

In Latin America in particular, over the past two decades, several countries have established nationwide programmes of apprenticeship. The salient characteristics of the enabling legislation are threefold. First, the organisms established are tripartite in that they are directed by representatives of government, workers and employers, acting jointly. Second, by providing for alternation of periods of work and periods of attending training courses they open the opportunities of training to young persons who could not afford, even with bursaries, to attend full-time at a vocational training centre. Third, they oblige employers to accept a certain quota of apprentices and to pay them both while at work and while attending the courses.

In the beginning the facilities were provided chiefly for industrial workers – the National Service of Industrial Apprenticeship in Brazil (SENAI), the National Commission for Apprenticeship and Vocational Training in the Argentine subsequently attached to the National Council for Technical Education (CONET), the National Service for Apprenticeship and Industrial Labour in Peru (SENATI), the National Apprenticeship Institute in Costa Rica (INA). Later the same principles were extended to the field of commerce, for example the National Service of Commercial Apprenticeship in Brazil (SENAC). In Colombia the National Apprenticeship Service (SENA) from its inception covered industry, commerce and also agriculture, as was the case likewise with the National Institute for Educational Co-operation (INCE) in Venezuela. The training courses are oriented partly to the provision of specialised skills, partly to turning out much-needed repair and maintenance staff for workshops and partly to preparation for middle-level management posts.[8]

As to the financing of these programmes, it was assumed that they would expand *pari passu* with the development of the national economies and would indeed contribute to this growth. It was therefore decided in most of these countries to levy a tax of 1 per cent on the wages and salaries bill of the enterprises concerned (2 per cent in the case of Colombia) and from the proceeds of these taxes the training centres were created. Employers who provided within their own firms' officially approved courses could have part or the whole of the tax reimbursed. In some of the countries

[8] M.A. Horowitz and M. Zymelman, *Valoración del Programa Intensivo de Preparación de Mano Obra Industrial del Ministerio de Educación y Cultura del Brazil*, CINTERFOR, Montevideo, 1967 (roneoed); Directoria do Ensino Industrial, *Evaluación de Programas de Formación Profesional*, CINTERFOR, Montevideo, 1969, Doc. RT 040; for Colombia see: Servicio Nacional de Aprendizaje, *Evaluación de la Formación Profesional*, Bogotà, 1969; for comparison of eight Latin American countries see: Argentina, Consejo Nacional de Educación Técnica, *Análisis de Formación Profesional en Empresas*, CINTERFOR, Montivideo, Informes, No. 18; see also *Seventh Conference of American States Members of ILO, Buenos Aires*, 1961, Report III, ILO, Geneva 1961, pp. 33–7; see further: *Seminario Sobre Bases para una Política de Formación Profesional para América Latina*, Vina del Mar, Chile, 28–30 November 1966, CINTERFOR, Montevideo, 1967.

a further contribution was raised from an additional tax on firms employing more than 500 persons.

Special arrangements have been found necessary in order to meet the needs for managers at all levels. In numerous countries management training centres and/or productivity centres have been established, frequently with the assistance of the ILO and the UNDP. Such centres now exist in all regions, especially in Latin America and in Asia.[9] Such management training has already had very positive results, as in encouraging a fuller utilisation of equipment through introduction of shift work as well as increasing labour productivity through better organisation and utilisation of staff. But the productivity centres, with some exceptions, for lack of adequate local data and personnel and (particularly in Asia) for lack of sufficient independence from government, have yet to make useful contributions to labour management practices.

Supplementary Methods of Obtaining Trained Personnel

In countries, and there are many of them, where the presently existing training facilities are insufficient and where the lack of skills constitutes a serious impediment to economic progress, other devices have to be resorted to, if only during a transitional period. One of these is to permit or even encourage the import of foreign skills, either on a selective basis to man certain key posts or occupations, or more generally to give preference to skilled labour within the framework of a national immigration policy.

It is the common practice for foreign firms engaged in the extractive industries in developing countries to bring their own technical specialists and top managerial staff; similar arrangements characterise the subsidiaries of foreign companies in the fields of banking, commerce and some branches of manufacturing. Some developing countries' governments have a deliberate policy of using foreign personnel to foster national development, as for instance in the Ivory Coast, until such time as local nationals acquire the needed qualifications.[10]

Apart from these and certain other special instances, however, it cannot be said that immigration currently plays a significant role in augmenting the quantity of qualified manpower. Thus, in the early 1960s at a time when in Rio de Janeiro alone there were reported vacancies for 7,500 skilled workers, the Intergovernmental Committee for European Migration was able to send not more than 250 skilled workers to Brazil.[11]

[9] ILO, Sixth Asian Regional Conference, Tokyo, Sept. 1968, Report III, *Management and Personnel Policies and Practices*, ILO, Geneva, 1968, pp. 95–8, and *Eighth Conference of American States, op. cit.*, pp. 193–6.

[10] L. Roussel, 'Employment Problems and Policies in the Ivory Coast', *International Labour Review*, December 1971, p. 510.

[11] W. M. Besterman, *Immigration as a Means of Obtaining Needed Skills and Stimulating Economic and Social Advancement*, United Nations World Population Congress, Belgrade 1965, Doc. WPC/WP/277.

In some countries recent political history coupled with nationalistic policies inhibits the use of foreign specialists on any scale, as for example in African countries where the policies of 'Africanisation' set limits to the use of technicians of European stock. Yet even here there are exceptions: the Tunisian Government, after going through a nationalist phase, adopted in 1965 more liberal legislation concerning the use of foreigners,[12] while in Morocco temporary exceptions to the Moroccanisation policy are made deliberately in order to ensure the efficient operation of important industries.

The second device principally used for augmenting the supply of skills is to permit or assist nationals to go abroad to acquire their higher qualifications. Already in 1966 there were, according to a UNESCO report, no less than 200,000 nationals of developing countries studying abroad; today the figure is certainly much higher.[13] Some of these students make their own arrangements, some are sent under the auspices of bilateral agreements between governments or between institutions of higher learning, some are sponsored by multi-lateral assistance programmes.

In many specialised fields a period of study in a foreign country offers the only possibility of obtaining the necessary qualifications, yet certain dangers have to be recognised. The contents of the courses in the foreign country, designed as they are primarily for nationals of those advanced countries, may be to a greater or lesser extent ill-adapted to the circumstances which the student will find on returning to his own country where everything is different. One way of obviating this disadvantage is to establish institutions for higher levels of training within the developing regions where they may serve groups of countries. Thus under the auspices of the ILO two training centres in labour management have been established, one for francophone African countries at Yaoundé in Cameroon and the other for Latin American countries at Lima, Peru. The ILO likewise set up the Inter-American Centre for Research and Documentation in Vocational Training in Montevideo, Uruguay. The United Nations system assisted in establishing a Technical Research Institute (ICAITI) for the training of Latin American technicians and research workers. The Asian Productivity Centre organises vocational training courses in individual Asian countries. At world level the ILO already in 1965 with the co-operation of the Italian Government created in Turin an International Centre for Advanced Technical and Vocational Training.

In some instances the developing countries themselves combine together to create common institutions. Among the francophone countries of Africa mention may be made of the Agronomic Institute at Wakombo in the Central African Republic, the Animal Husbandry Institute at Fort Lamy, the School of Business Administration at Brazzaville and the Polytechnic at Libreville, all of these coming under the authority of the Foundation for Higher Education in Central Africa and offering training

[12] Noe Ladhari, 'L'Emploi de la Main-d'oeuvre Etrangère en Tunisie', *Revue Française du Travail*, April–June 1966, No. 2, pp. 29–40.
[13] *Study Abroad*, Vol. 18, UNESCO, Paris 1969, pp. 33–8.

in agriculture, animal husbandry administration and industry for citizens of the four countries of the sub-region.[14]

Another danger involved in sending students to study in advanced countries is that an important proportion of them fail to return to their countries of origin. They are tempted to settle down in the countries where they study partly because they find there is a wide choice of contacts among colleagues in the same profession whereas back at home they might have to work in some remote area deprived of intellectual stimulus. They are also tempted by the higher salaries and standards of living obtainable after qualification in the advanced country. Some governments seek to discourage this brain drain by granting scholarships to students on the condition that they return to serve in their home countries for a stated number of years; some bring pressure to bear on the families of those who do not return. Neither measure is wholly efficacious and a steady loss of trained personnel continues. The only certain solution is the long-term one of economic development whereby the exercise of a profession becomes as attractive in a developing country as elsewhere.

New Approaches to Vocational Training

All the methods used for the training of skilled workers, technicians and professional people have been evolved in the advanced countries and adapted over the years to their circumstances. Considering that they have been implanted virtually without change in the very different environment of the developing countries, it is surprising that they have had any success at all, and without doubt some favourable results have been achieved. Yet the opinion is widely held that the heavy investment which the establishment of training facilities requires ought to be yielding more substantial returns. The contrast between the social background of a trainee and the industrial milieu to which he is being recruited is far greater in a developing than in a developed country. More often than not he comes from a village where the only non-agricultural pursuits are a few local crafts and where he has never experienced the nexus of working by the clock for a fixed number of hours per day. Because the training programmes of the advanced countries contain little or nothing to prepare him for this abrupt transition, attempts have been made to re-think the kinds of preparation suitable for introducing him to the new world of organised industry.

In most developing countries there are still sections of the population which primary schooling does not reach at all; very many of those who begin a primary education do not complete it and only a fraction proceed any further. In Latin America it has been calculated that only 9·5 per cent of those who enrol in primary school complete the final year and only 1·5 per cent go on through secondary school.[15] In Africa less than 10 per cent

14 E. Rossignol, 'La Formation Professionnelle et Technique dans les Pays en Voie de Développement', *op. cit.* p. 25.

15 R. R. Lyons, *Problems and Strategies of Educational Planning; Lessons from Latin America*, International Institute for Educational Planning, UNESCO, Paris, 1965.

of those who complete a primary education continue to any secondary schooling either general or technical.[16] Generally, the proportion of skilled workers plus technicians constitutes less than 2 per cent of the labour force of developing countries. Furthermore, after leaving school many remain jobless for several years: in Africa in the urban areas the majority of the unemployed are adolescents. These facts suggest the need for something which bridges the gap between leaving school and taking a job or entering into formal vocational training, something which combines certain elements of general education with others which prepare the young person for his role in life.

To meet this need a variety of programmes are being tried out which are generally entitled 'prevocational training'. The purposes which they all have in common have been described thus:

'They should cater for girls and boys from twelve and up to approximately eighteen years of age, who are either still attending schools of general education, or who are not at school, having completed part or all of primary education, or having never attended school regularly if at all; they aim at imparting basic practical instruction and related technological knowledge by carrying out productive work, and at educating responsible citizens who are capable of contributing to the development of their community or country; they prepare for entry into full vocational training for a specific trade or other occupation, of which they may constitute the basic stage, or into employment; they are part of the curricula of primary or general secondary schools or are given outside the official systems of education and training'.[17]

Programmes of this type have been introduced in India, Mali, Tunisia and the United Arab Republic with financial aid from UNICEF and technical assistance from UNESCO and the ILO. They have not yet been adopted on any significant scale elsewhere.[18]

Another important type of initiative in this field has been the formulation of youth programmes which combine practical work with an element of training. Such programmes range from the relatively modest activities of local youth clubs, through services specially organised for unemployed adolescents, up to nationwide Youth Service such as the Young Pioneers and the Civic Services organised in some African countries. In some instances they cater for specially disadvantaged groups of young people, in others by contrast for those already qualified – e.g. in some Asian and Latin American countries. Some of these programmes are arranged as a

[16] A. Callaway, 'African School Leavers and their Employment Problem', *Community Development Journal*, Manchester, 3, July 1966, pp. 12–23.

[17] ILO, *Meeting of Experts on Programming Prevocational Training Schemes*, Geneva, 16–27 September, 1968, Report, Doc. MEPVT/1968/Rev., pp. 3–4.

[18] For some account of the problems encountered in the course of these experiments see: Report of *ILO's Study Group on Prevocational Training for countries in the African and Asian regions*, Tunis, 20 May–1 June 1968, ILO, Geneva, 1969, Doc. ILO/TAP/INT/R.16.

follow-up for school leavers; some are in connection with or in substitution for military service, where the youth can be put to work on schemes of national utility, e.g. in some countries of the Middle East, Asia, South America and the Antilles.[19]

The content of these programmes varies greatly from case to case. Some focus on training of a rather less formal character than regular vocational training; others specialise in training leaders for rural community development activities; others are connected with the settlement of young people from urban areas on new agricultural land; others are integrated into public works programmes of the kinds described in Chapter 6. What they have in common is the aim of removing the young from the demoralising efforts of street lounging, giving them positive and useful tasks to perform and at the same time preparing them at least to some extent for their future careers.

Conclusions

What clearly emerges from this brief review of the training programmes in developing countries is the sharp contrast between the vast mass of manpower with little formal education and no vocational training and, on the other hand, the great dearth of skilled or even semi-skilled workers. Only very slow progress toward satisfying this demand for training can be made, given the existing situation – the resources at the disposal of national authorities and the present ordering of priorities. The whole problem of the teaching of skills needs to be reconsidered and the attack on it reorganised from three angles – greater impact, more rapid procedures and greater economy of resources.

The attack on ignorance and lack of skills needs to be more massive and more widespread. In view of the inevitable leakages of trainees who never complete their courses and those who subsequently pass into occupations other than those for which they have been trained, as well as those who study abroad and do not return, the *effective* output of qualified people is even less than the *apparent* which argues for a major increase in the enrolment capacity of training courses. This in turn probably means having greater recourse than hitherto to unconventional methods of training since the traditional facilities are so costly and instructors so scarce. It also implies a radical dispersal of the facilities away from the major urban centres to the smaller provincial towns where a wide section of the population can have access to them – a policy which might, as a by-product, do something to stem the exodus to the large metropoli.

The new approach must also emphasise the element of *acceleration* in training. giving something useful to the many young people who cannot

19 'Special Manpower Mobilisation Schemes and Youth Programmes for Development Purposes', *International Labour Review*, January 1966, also 'Youth Services for Economic and Social Developments', *International Labour Review*, April 1967; see also Recommendation No. 136 concerning special youth employment and training schemes for development purposes adopted by the Fifty-fourth Session of the International Labour Conference, June 1970.

accustom themselves yet to long-drawn-out periods of instruction. This will involve ruthlessly eliminating the more theoretical components of the courses and concentrating on giving practical experience, on 'learning through doing'. Part-time training and part-time employment integrated together in schemes operated under tripartite auspices seems to be one successful way of cutting down the time involved in apprenticeship while also bringing home to the young worker the practical utility of what he is learning.

Thirdly, if the volume of training is to be massively increased the cost per trainee must be massively reduced. There are numerous ways of effecting economies without jeopardising the quality of the instruction provided. Some of these have been well enumerated in one of the United Nations' reports on the World Social Situation:

'reduction in the high rate of educational wastage in developing countries ... by better counselling and instruction, revised curriculum and improved techniques of testing; reduction in the length of training, with more intensive application to study during periods when schools are open; extension of training facilities, particularly at lower levels of education, by employing persons at lowered hiring standards, if this can be done on a pragmatic basis, by a stricter scrutiny of the formal qualifications really needed for the specific tasks envisaged; brief training programmes undertaken by educational institutions on an extension basis to augment the low supply of certain kinds of services in rural areas . . .; use of part-time teaching services of a number of persons professionally active in given fields; use of trainees to "train" others (a notable feature in many workers' educational schemes); use of machines and programmed methods of instruction . . .; greater utilisation of invested capital by running schools all year round or by offering evening courses; reduction of the proportion of educational costs devoted to buildings. . . .'[20]

To refer to just one of the items in the above list, the adoption of up-to-date teaching techniques with computerised learning programmes purveyed to students through individualised closed-circuit television enabling each to learn at his own pace, though expensive to install, would do much to by-pass the bottleneck of shortage of instructors. It is also an appropriate form of equipment for rich nations to make available through their aid programmes, whereas if they were to send teachers (as has been tried) these often have a wrong background.

Certainly more investigation is required into alternative techniques of instruction geared to the social patterns of the societies from which the trainees come. Too little is known as to what succeeds and what does not;[21] and success should be judged not by abstract academic standards

[20] United Nations, *World Social Situation*, New York, 1966, p. 54.

[21] P. Drouet, 'Economic Criteria Governing the Choice of Vocational Training Systems', *International Labour Review*, September 1968. J. Maton, 'Experience on the Job and Formal Training as Alternative Means of Skill Acquisition: an Empirical Study', *International Labour Review*, September 1969.

but by the ability to produce those skills for which local demand is strong. Moreover, there will be not one but several successful recipes tailored to the differing situations in the several regions of the developing world.

The attainment of these goals further requires much more consultation between the educational authorities and those responsible for national planning. The expansion of training facilities and their distribution between the principal occupations is a process which takes time, so that a period of years rather than of months elapses between the initial decision and the moment when qualified workers begin to emerge. For this reason the planners have an obligation to try to estimate the needs for skills in the various branches of the economy not in regard to tomorrow but in the context of employment oriented development plans covering five or ten years. Few governments yet give, within the framework of over-all planning, a sufficiently central place to the planning of human resources.[22]

All the above considerations add up to the clear need for most developing countries' governments to accord a considerably higher priority to education and training within the complex of their employment strategy. A higher priority rating would justify the allocation of a larger volume of resources to this work, it would prompt them to assign top-quality administrators and teachers to training programmes and would suggest the utility of including requests in this field more frequently in the lists which they draw up for bilateral and multilateral foreign assistance. In the process of catching up with the industrialised countries the developing peoples will be leaping over many intermediate stages of growth and will, within a decade or so, be operating the technologies of the future. Because this can already be foreseen, it is imperative to prepare now a generation capable of responding to the challenge.

[22] J. Mouly, 'Human Resources Planning as a Part of Economic Development Planning', *International Labour Review*, September, 1965, also: J. Mouly, 'Quelques Problèmes Techniques de Planification de la Main-d'oeuvre', *op. cit.* p. 58 ff.

Chapter 11

Migration and Emigration

Movements of population can significantly hamper or facilitate the task of trying to match the demand for employment with the available job opportunities. Within a particular country the flow of migration may be toward districts where industry and employment are expanding or it may be predominantly toward the larger cities where unemployment is already acute. Emigration may take the form primarily of reducing the numbers of unskilled persons seeking work or it may remove some of the best educated who can least be spared. The policies adopted by governments in respect to these various population movements should be considered as an integral element in employment strategy.

Internal Migration

THE FACTS
Aside from a numerically small amount of land settlement (see Chapter 7) where in most cases only a fraction of the settlers are persons transferred from urban areas, virtually all internal migration is from the rural areas to the cities, generally to the big cities. (This is sometimes accomplished in stages, people moving first from the countryside to newly-established towns, and later to big cities.) The data in table 11.1 indicate the striking contrast between the rate of growth of population in cities of over 20,000 inhabitants and the rate in the rural areas of developing countries. Part of the urban growth, of course, is contributed by the city people themselves; and though fertility rates are lower in cities than in rural districts, this diminution may occur only in the second generation of immigrants, the first generation maintaining almost the same rates as those prevailing in the country districts whence they came.[1] Yet an important proportion of the urban increment is provided by migration. Thus in Latin America in the period 1950 to 1960 this proportion was estimated to be 35 per cent in Chile, 38 per cent in Panama, over 40 per cent in Ecuador, Mexico and Nicaragua and 50 per cent in Brazil, Venezuela and the Dominican Republic.

What is most significant from an employment point of view is the rate of growth of the active population, defined here as those in the age groups

[1] D. Lambert, 'L'Urbanisation Accélérée en Amérique Latine et la Formation d'un Secteur Tertiaire Refuge', *Civilisations*, Brussels 1965, p. 485. See also P. O. Olusanya, 'Rural – Urban Fertility Differentials in Western Nigeria', *Population Studies*, London, **23**, 3, November 1969, pp. 363–78.

fifteen to sixty-five. Table 11.1 shows how for the developing countries as a whole the rate of growth of this 'active' or potentially active section was increasing faster than the increase in the growth rate of total population. Quite certainly its growth in the cities has been even more marked, though data are not available because the great majority of the migrants from the rural districts are young persons, chiefly males, of working age. (The male–female ratio is notably higher in the cities than in the rural areas of developing countries.) it is this extremely rapid expansion of the urban population of working age which particularly aggravates the unemployment problem in cities. And there is every sign that unless checked it will continue and indeed accelerate.

Table 11.1   *Average Annual Rates of Growth of Urban and Rural Population 1950–70 and Projections to 1980*

	1950–60	1960–70	1970–80 projected
Urban	4·0	4·3	4·3
Rural	1·8	2·1	2·2
Total population	2·3	2·7	2·8
Active population	1·5	2·1	2·5

Source: N. T. Wang, 'The Role of Public Investment in Employment Promotion', in *Fiscal Measures for Employment Promotion in Developing Countries, op. cit.*, Tables 1 and 3.

This rural exodus is incited by a number of 'push' factors which impel young people to get away from the rural districts. Because population increases while the cultivated area remains static, many of the young have no hope of obtaining a piece of land from which to earn a living; nor are there employment opportunities locally outside farming, and in such few jobs as there are the wages are low. Further, the housing is bad, water supply uncertain, school and health provision inadequate, sport and entertainment non-existent. Beyond this, many of the younger generation want to break away from the custom-bound atmosphere of their homes and the restrictions on social behaviour.[2]

These influences are complemented by numerous 'pull' factors – the apparent attractions of city life: the hope of a job, the higher level of wages, the bustling social life, the freedom from family censure, the bright lights. In spite of the urban unemployment most of the immigrants

[2] *Why Labour Leaves the Land – a Comparative Study*, ILO, Geneva, 1960, No. 59. See also, D. Warriner, 'Problems of Rural – Urban Migration: Some Suggestions for Investigation', *International Labour Review*, May 1970; also P. Bairoch, *Urban Unemployment*, ILO, Geneva, 1972, especially Chapter 2; see further, P. C. W. Gutkind, 'African Responses to Urban Wage Employment', *International Labour Review*, February 1968; and W. Elkan, 'Circular Migration and the Growth of Towns in East Africa', *International Labour Review*, December 1967.

succeed in finding at least temporary work within two or three months, and for some the temporary job leads to a more permanent one. Certainly urban wages are substantially higher in real terms, even allowing for the higher cost of living in cities,[3] as the table 11.2 indicates. Nor is this all. Over the past two decades the real incomes of wage earners seem to have been *increasing* faster than the national average increase in most developing countries. For instance, already during the nineteen-fifties in Latin America real wages were rising at 4–5 per cent per year while GNP *per caput* was increasing at only 1·5 per cent, in Africa real wages at 4 per cent but GNP *per caput* at only 1 per cent.[4] A similar trend can be noted in Asian countries.[5]

Table 11.2   *Differences between Urban and Rural Incomes*

		Average urban wage (when average rural income = 100)
Brazil	(1960)	over 300
Ceylon	(1963)	over 200
India	(1962)	250
Ivory Coast	(1965)	800
Pakistan (East)	(1963–4)	270
Phillippines	(1965)	250
Venezuela	(1962)	250
United Arab Republic	(1960)	400

Source: Several authors cited by D. Turnham, *The Employment Problem in Less-developed Countries: a Review of Evidence*, OECD, Paris, June 1970, p. 104.

In some countries these income differentials are inherent in declared government policy. Thus in the view of a *Meeting of a Tripartite Labour Conference of East Africa* held in Dar-es-Salaam in 1962 'it was felt in the long run it was better to have a smaller but satisfied and efficient labour force rather than a large, badly paid and frustrated labour force'. In a number of countries governments have introduced minimum wage legislation which tends to raise urban wage-earners' incomes.[6] In yet others it is government policy to favour their civil services with relatively high wage and salary scales which in some cases makes it difficult for

[3] And even allowing for the fact that many elements in rural incomes tend not to be counted or to be under-valued.
[4] H. A. Turner, *Wage Trends, Wage Policies and Collective Bargaining: the Problem for Underdeveloped Countries*, Cambridge, 1965, pp. 13–14.
[5] 'Conspectus of wage trends in developing countries: III. The Far East', in *Wage Policy Issues in Economic Development*, A. D. Smith (Ed.), London, Macmillan for the International Institute for Labour Studies, 1969, pp. 23 ff.
[6] See, for example, D. Chesworth, 'Statutory Minimum Wage Fixing in Tanganyika', *International Labour Review*, July 1967.

private enterprise to recruit staff and creates a pool of educated unemployed turning down other work in the hope of ultimately obtaining a government job.

Moreover, even though the existence of urban unemployment is generally known to the would-be migrant, he may also know that it is only in the cities that the volume of employment is increasing at all appreciably, a tendency inflated by the concentration of public and private investment in urban areas, and he hopes to be one of the lucky ones. It is expectation of earnings rather than any certainty which draws him to the town. In a city where the volume of employment is rapidly expanding, this may paradoxically create more than average local unemployment, because not merely will the back-flow to the country of disillusioned job-seekers be reduced but the rumour of new job opportunities will whip up a more rapid migration from the countryside.[7]

Nor should more general and personal factors be overlooked. Physical mobility, for example, plays a role: in countries, e.g. some in Latin America, where an extensive road network has been built and where government provides a cheap bus service to the villages, rural–urban visits between family units are facilitated and frequently lead to migration. Estrangements in the family, tribal or ethnic disputes, ideas and hopes implanted by priests or school teachers, glimpses of city life seen at the cinema – many non-economic influences are at work on the minds of village people and may quickly become decisive for those who are adventurous and have no ties.[8]

CORRECTIVE MEASURES

During the nineteen-seventies the urban population between the ages of fifteen and sixty-five years must be expected to grow at more than 3 per cent per annum, which is certainly faster than the expected growth rate for urban employment. It follows that in default of corrective action the volume of urban unemployment will also expand with all the dangerous consequences of social instability. On the employment creation side a number of possible policies have been described in Chapters 3–6, but measures are also possible and needed to check the over-rapid growth in the urban labour force.

Some writers have recommended a reduction in, or a freezing of, the

[7] J. R. Harris and M. P. Todaro, 'Migration, Unemployment and Development: A Two-Sector Analysis', *American Economic Review*, March 1965; also, C. R. Frank Jr. 'Urban Unemployment and Economic Growth in Africa', *Oxford Economic Papers*, 20, 2, July 1968; also, S. Wellisz, 'Dual Economies, Disguised Unemployment and the Unlimited Supply of Labour', *Economica*, 35, 137, February 1968, p. 43; also concerning the Caribbean, W. A. Lewis, 'Employment Policy in an Underdeveloped Area', *Social and Economic Studies*, Institute of Social and Economic Research, University College of the West Indies, Jamaica, 7, 3, September 1968.

[8] J. C. Caldwell, 'Determinants of Rural – Urban Migration in Ghana', *Population Studies* (London), 22, 3, 1968; see also, Gian S. Sahota, 'An Economic Analysis of International Migration in Brazil', *The Journal of Political Economy*, 76, 3, March–April 1968.

salaries in the upper echelons of business management and of the civil service and the professions,[9] but such a policy although possessing social advantages would not influence the wage levels of unskilled workers who constitute the vast majority of the migrants. A more widespread adoption of 'intermediate technology' as advocated in Chapter 3 would, by altering the proportion between skilled and unskilled workers in favour of the latter, increase the demand for those categories of which the supply is most plentiful. Governments can also take action in respect to rural–urban wage differentials, not of course by decreeing an absolute reduction in urban wages, but rather by seeking to set limits to increases:

'A programme aimed at restraining the growth of urban wage earnings would consist of individual measures or, under the umbrella of an incomes policy, a set of measures to influence the rate of increase of collectively negotiated wages in the private sector, government pay scales and minimum wage rates – the major institutional channels through which wage increases are obtained.'[10]

Without some restraint on wage increases the class of employed people becomes more and more privileged and isolated, as has been the experience, perhaps inevitably, in the extractive industries. With some restraint the total volume of employment could be higher than otherwise and the benefits of receiving regular earnings could be more widely spread.

It is sometimes suggested that an equally valid way of checking the rural exodus is to orient investment and technological development more in favour of the rural areas and the rural population. The opportunities for augmenting rural employment, it is true, are not negligible and several of them have been discussed in Chapters 6 and 7. However, when one considers the sheer size of the rural population and the vast number of square kilometres which it inhabits one may doubt whether the maximum resources which any government could mobilise for the modernisation of farming and the village economy could have sufficient impact in the short run greatly to diminish the relative unattractiveness of rural life. None the less, measures have been taken in some developing countries as, for instance, in Jamaica where the Government in its 1963–8 Plan made provision for special mortgages to finance the rehousing of the poorest people in rural areas, or in the Congo (Brazzaville) where the civic service helps erect cultural centres and supplies an ambulant cinema.[11] Some other governments attempt to canalise the urban inflow away from the metropolitan area and towards the secondary centres of economic growth.

[9] R. G. Hollister, 'Manpower Problems and Policies in Sub-Saharan Africa', *International Labour Review*, May 1969, pp. 577–96.

[10] P. H. Thormann, 'The Rural-Urban Income Differential and Minimum Wage Fixing Criteria', *International Labour Review*, August 1970, p. 147; also ILO, *Minimum Wage Fixing and Economic Development*, Studies and Reports, New Series, 72, Geneva, 1969, pp. 43 ff.

[11] 'Unemployed Youth: an African Symposium', *International Labour Review*, March 1963, p. 194.

In Senegal the current and the two previous Five-Year Plans have tried by investment orientation and fiscal incentives to steer development away from the overcrowded Cap-Vert area round Dakar and to create most new employment opportunities in other parts of the country. This is another aspect of the policy of industrial decentralisation described in Chapter 3. It can be supported by advising labour exchanges, where such exist in small towns or rural areas, to make efforts to direct job-seekers to the new growth centres rather than to the capital city.

Unfortunately, however, experience indicates that the various corrective measures mentioned above, even taken in combination, do rather little to restrain the exodus toward the big cities. Governments wishing for noticeable results have been obliged to resort to more coercive action. In a number of African countries, already prior to independence, compulsory registration was required of workers in the more important urban agglomerations, a system which has been maintained since and extended to other countries. Labour cards, residence permits and other methods of control have been used for instance in Guinea and in the Central African Republic, but the practical implementation of these measures has proved extraordinarily difficult because of the natural mobility of the population and the shortage of police and other supervisory staff. Certainly, the population influx into the major cities continues at a rapid pace. A few governments have sought to imitate the systems operating in the socialist countries of Eastern Europe where no one is permitted to change place of residence or employment without an official permit and where the immigration into the cities is regulated so as not to exceed the rate of construction of dwellings. thus avoiding the multiplication of shanty towns.

In some developing countries the more ambitious policy has been adopted of trying to organise a reverse flow of manpower by settling groups of urban people on farms or in rural public works projects. Action of this kind belongs to the programmes of land settlement already discussed in Chapter 7 as a means of employment promotion in rural areas. Most of the recruits for such schemes are found among the existing farm population who can be expected to adapt better than city people to the tasks of opening up new lands. However, in some African countries the settlers have also included townsfolk, especially those recruited through the National Youth Services, Pioneer Corps, etc. In Mali the Civic Service working in rural areas was composed as to 25 per cent of people from the towns; in the Central African Republic the recruitment of young people eligible for military service was confined entirely to the towns; in Congo (Brazzaville) any young persons between the ages of eighteen and twenty-three who had no regular job were conscripted into temporary or permanent rural work. Recruits who have had education are frequently assigned to their villages of origin to act there as community leaders among people they know. Because of the expense of reimplantation programmes and because of the psychological and other difficulties in getting townspeople to adapt to the rural way of life, most of these schemes have been modest in scope; they cannot be said to have had a significant numerical influence on the rural exodus which in all developing countries seems destined to continue for the foreseeable future on a massive scale.

Emigration

While the regulation of internal migration has the objective of securing a better geographical distribution of the labour force in relation to food supplies and employment opportunities, the policies adopted regarding migration across national frontiers are influenced not merely by these factors but also by wider considerations of national interest. For this reason emigration, unlike internal migration, is no longer a spontaneous movement; virtually everywhere it is closely controlled by governments, and immigration even more so.

SCOPE AND EXTENT

During the nineteenth century a considerable volume of emigration occurred in the form of slave labour and later in the form of indentured labour from underdeveloped countries to the industrialising ones or from one underdeveloped country to another, the latter chiefly for work on mines and plantations. Also in the half-century up to 1914 there was a massive movement out of Europe to the New World. Thereafter the flow decreased as the industrial countries, beset by rising unemployment and other economic difficulties, began to close their doors.

Since the Second World War the character of international migration has radically changed. It is true that a few years after the war certain developing countries, particularly in Latin America, encouraged the immigration of settlers, but it was on a small scale, it encountered many difficulties and has almost ceased. Today hardly any developing country government pursues an *immigration* policy; even those which desire to increase national numbers prefer to achieve this by a multiplication of their own citizens. As regards *emigration* from developing countries, this is oriented mainly towards developed countries and depends on the extent to which the latter permit entry. The flow of migrants takes place mainly between countries which have, or had, economic, political or cultural ties: for instance, to Britain and to France from their former colonial territories, to the United States from Puerto Rico and Mexico. In addition there is an annual flow, albeit on a modest scale, of political refugees who are found new homes through the process of intergovernmental negotiations.

What has become much more significant during the past twenty years than at any previous time is the phenomenon of temporary migration. This is especially concentrated in a movement from the developing countries of the Mediterranean basin to the industrial regions of Europe. Temporary migration has of course long been familiar for the harvesting of fruit and other crops, but the foreign workers who come for jobs in manufacturing industry and construction stay for more than a few weeks;

indeed, some of them eventually change their nationality and settle permanently. However, the Governments of the receiving countries mostly permit this on only a very limited scale, since apart altogether from long-term employment considerations the social problem of assimilation of foreigners seems to be regarded as far more daunting today than it was at the beginning of the century. Hence the length of stay of temporary workers is strictly controlled. Their contracts may be prolonged, or renewed after a brief return to their home countries, but they are fixed-term contracts giving the authorities of the receiving countries the right to repatriate such workers at any time they may no longer be wanted.

The attitudes of the developing countries' governments towards emigration varies considerably. In so far as permanent emigration is concerned quite a number of governments give it official encouragement at least as a transitional palliative while the national labour force so greatly exceeds the number of jobs available. Such is the policy of the governments of Algeria, Morocco and Tunisia. In the Tunisian Four-Year Plan of 1965–8 it was stated that the emigration of part of the surplus manpower must be envisaged until full employment is achieved. In Latin America the countries which have emigration opportunities, such as Mexico, Puerto Rico and Jamaica either passively permit or actively encourage an outflow in order to relieve pressure on the national labour market. The Jamaican Five-Year Plan of 1963–8 envisaged an annual emigration of at least 10,000 persons.[12] In Colombia the trade unions proposed sending unskilled workers to Europe; indeed in many developing countries the unions favour emigration as a means of reducing unemployment.[13] In some Asian countries, notably India, emigration is also favoured officially, though in the Asian region there are few countries willing to receive. In Africa south of the Sahara a limited amount of international migration still occurs but only a minor part of it is regarded as permanent. In the Ivory Coast, for instance, almost half the workers in the modern private sector are foreigners.[14] On the other hand, in some developing countries emigration is either discouraged or formally forbidden.

Attitudes towards temporary emigration tend to be more favourable, that is in the rather limited number of countries where this opportunity presents itself. The argument that the country is losing irrevocably part of its population does not apply, while the advantages of temporary relief to unemployment plus the skills and money which can be acquired abroad are appreciated. Even so it is a movement which governments endeavour to regulate, in so far as they can.

12 Jamaica, *Five-Year Independence Plan*, 1963–8, pp. 53 and 72.

13 Eighth Conference of American States Members of the ILO, Ottawa, September 1966, Report II, *Manpower Planning and Employment Policy in Economic Development*, ILO, Geneva, 1966, p. 138.

14 L. Roussel, 'Employment Problems and Policies in the Ivory Coast', *op. cit.*, p. 508; see also, *World Population Situation*, United Nations Population Commission, Doc. E/CN. 9/231, 23 September 1969, para. 76; see further, W. D. Borrie, *Trends and Patterns in International Migration since 1945*, United Nations World Population Congress, Doc. WPC/WP/474, Belgrade, 1965.

QUANTITATIVE EFFECTS

The effects of emigration on the quantity of manpower in the sending country will differ according as the outflow is permanent or temporary in character. A striking example of the effects of permanent emigration is provided by Puerto Rico where departures (mainly to the United States) were on a very substantial scale during the years 1940–60. Emigration reached its peak in 1953 with an annual rate of 3·17 per cent of the population, surpassing the rate of natural increase (2·73 per cent). Indeed, the *net* natural increase after allowing for emigration, which before the war had been above 3 per cent, progressively declined until in the period 1950–60 it was only 0·6 per cent. This decline was also partly caused by a declining birth rate, but some two-thirds of the fall was attributed to emigration.[15] The emigrants were composed largely of persons in the age group fifteen to forty-four whose numbers in Puerto Rico actually declined by 34 per cent during the years 1940–60. Thus the effects were even greater on the active population than on the population as a whole. Also, largely in consequence of the emigration, the participation rate fell from 32 to 25 per cent during the same period. It has been calculated that without any emigration the labour force would have been 50 per cent larger.

Although emigration on a substantial scale, as in the Puerto Rican case, may reduce the labour force it does not automatically reduce *pro tanto* the volume of unemployment. For this to happen it is necessary that those among the emigrants who were employed prior to leaving can be replaced from the pool of unemployed, which may not occur easily if, as is likely, the unemployed lack the required skills. Under favourable circumstances such replacement can take place quite rapidly. This seems to have been the situation in Puerto Rico where during the 1940–60 period it is alleged that the proportion of the active population unemployed would have been twice as high as the 13 per cent actually recorded, in spite of the considerable industrialisation of the island which was going on.[16] Likewise in Jamaica the notable reduction in unemployment in the late nineteen-fifties was officially attributed in part to emigration. In Tunisia where in the mid-sixties the pool of unemployed and under-employed was estimated at some 200,000 persons and where the population was increasing at the rate of 31,000 per annum, emigration was said to be reducing by 10,000 per year the number of persons in search of work. In Algeria in 1970 with unemployment close to 1·4 million there were some 350,000 persons working abroad, mainly in France, representing a substantial alleviation to the employment problem.[17] To some extent offsetting these advantages the loss of manpower may have a damaging regional impact, as in the Kabylie of Algeria, where the massive departures

[15] S. L. Friedlander, *Labor Migration and Economic Growth: a Case Study of Puerto Rico*, The MIT Press, 1965, Table 3–1, p. 47.

[16] *Ibid.*, pp. 91–2; see also L. Reynolds and P. Gregory, *Wages, Productivity and Industrialisation in Puerto Rico*, 1965, p. 30.

[17] M. Parodi, *L'Offre et la Demande de Main-d'oeuvre Migrante Algérienne*, 1969–80, *Rapport Général*, ILO, Geneva, June 1970.

resulted in neglect of upkeep of erosion-control terracing, drainage ditches, etc.; in Greece similar departures caused a fall in the agricultural output in certain regions. Greece provides an example of a country with much lower demographic dynamism than that of the countries so far mentioned – a net reproduction rate of less than 1 per cent since the nineteen-fifties – where the departure of so many male workers in the younger age groups to the industrial countries of Europe appears to have had an adverse effect on economic development at home, industrialisation being retarded by a shortage of skilled labour and in some instances even of unskilled labour.[18] The advantages and disadvantages of emigration clearly need to be evaluated in the light of the domestic situation; the advantages are likely to be more conspicuous the greater the disparity between the growth in the labour force and the growth in employment opportunities within the country.

QUALITATIVE EFFECTS

It is important to examine not merely the quantitative but also the qualitative effects on the manpower resources of the country of emigration, and here again a distinction must be made between emigration which is permanent and that which is temporary. Considering first the incidence of permanent emigration, everything depends upon the characteristics of the emigrants with respect to education and training. In cases where the emigrants are predominantly unskilled workers, the Puerto Ricans for example, the outflow improves the average level of skills of those remaining behind. In Puerto Rico the ratio of unskilled to skilled workers fell from 2·77 to 1 in 1950 to 2·14 to 1 in 1960, a more rapid transformation than could have been effected during a similar period by investment in training facilities. From some other countries, however, e.g. Greece and other countries of the Mediterranean region, a rather high proportion of the emigrants appears to be skilled workers.[19] If this be true, it means that the developing country has incurred the expense of giving a young person education, training and experience, only to lose him when he has reached the most useful period of his life.

The loss may be even more serious in the case of persons who have enjoyed the benefit of secondary and perhaps some higher education, who then go abroad to complete their studies and who fail to return. This 'brain drain', though occurring also in the developed world in the direction of the countries in which salaries and working facilities are superior, does much greater damage to developing countries which can ill afford to lose the fruits of their educational investments and which have a chronic shortage of certain professional skills, e.g. civil engineers and doctors.

[18] OECD, *Manpower Policy and Problems in Greece*, Paris, 1965; see also 'La Grèce et le Marché Commun', *Revue du Marché Commun*, May 1966, p. 307, and see, P. Grandjeat, 'Les Migrations de Travailleurs en Europe', *Cahiers de l'Institut International d'Études Sociales*, Cahier 1, October–December 1966, p. 53.

[19] Care must be taken in interpreting the statistics. A considerable percentage of the would-be emigrants who have no qualifications whatsoever pass themselves off as skilled workers in order to be able to obtain work permits in the receiving countries.

From one Asian country between 1957 and 1963 some 7,400 students left the country and only 500 returned. In Latin America it is estimated that every year about 8 per cent of the engineers trained in Latin American institutions emigrate. A Pan-American Organisation survey showed that between 1960 and 1965 some 3,000 graduates from Latin American universities went to settle permanently in the United States. Examples could be multiplied.[20]

For the great majority of developing countries this 'brain drain' type of emigration is the one which they are experiencing. Only very few developed countries are still prepared to receive unskilled workers on a permanent basis in substantial quantities, and these are almost all the special cases of countries having a tie with former colonial territories. Thus, these cases apart, the effects of permanent emigration on the quality of the remaining labour force are generally damaging.

In the case of temporary emigration rather different considerations have to be taken into account. As noted earlier, this type of emigration comprises many situations, from the short-term fruit picker to the industrial worker who may spend several years in the foreign country. Broadly speaking, the advantages to the countries of the workers' origin can be judged by the extent to which the migrants have during their stay abroad acquired skills and/or been able to send or bring home remittances in cash or in kind. While deferring the latter element for a moment, the evidence as to acquisition of skills is mixed and ambiguous. In a general way, of course, the mere act of transferring from a non-industrial and rural to an industrial and urban way of life provides a certain training in accepting the work disciplines of the modern economy. But in respect to particular vocational skills the foreign worker does not learn much, at least in the industrial countries of Europe where most of this temporary migration occurs. A survey in the Federal Republic of Germany revealed that 41 per cent of the Turkish workers learned their job in a single day. It is the normal preference of employers and of national trade unions that the foreign workers be utilised mainly for the unskilled tasks. Moreover, in view of language difficulties and lack of financial resources, it takes some considerable time for the foreign worker to advance to the point of acquiring a formal qualification in a vocational training centre or some other institution; an international seminar of employers organised by OECD in Athens reckoned that a stay of five years would on average be necessary. It is instructive to note that only one-quarter of the Greek emigrants remain abroad for as long as five years, one-third returning home within a single year. However, in Tunisia the average length of absence is close to five years and in the case of Algeria longer. In France

---

[20] *Alliance for Progress – Weekly Newsletter*, 4, 42, 17 October 1966; see also, S. Kannapan, 'The Brain Drain and Developing Countries', *International Labour Review*, July 1968, pp. 1–26; also, G. R. Gonzalez, 'The Migration of Latin American High-level Manpower', *International Labour Review*, December 1968, pp. 551–9; and also, G. Watanabe, 'The Brain Drain from Developing to Developed Countries', *International Labour Review*, April 1969, pp. 401–33.

in 1964 6·2 per cent of the trainees at the vocational training centres were foreigners; however, among the Algerians in France less than 0·8 per cent were receiving formal training, though this figure also includes those Algerians who had settled more or less permanently. It is indicative that in France, as in Switzerland and the Federal Republic of Germany, the majority of foreign workers are engaged in road construction and repair, in unskilled work in the building industry and in other essentially unskilled occupations. How the degree of qualification varies with length of stay is shown by the data concerning France in table 11.3. This probably shows

Table 11.3 *Qualifications and Length of Stay of Algerian Workers in France: 1970*

Occupational level	Length of stay in France		
	less than 3 years	3–6 years	over 6 years
	%	%	%
Unskilled	61·6	50·6	43·2
Semi-skilled	27·6	38·0	43·6
Skilled	10·8	11·4	13·2
Total:	100·0	100·0	100·0

Source: Ministry of Interior survey. Situation at 3 April 1970.

a more favourable situation than would emerge if similar surveys were conducted in other European countries, because, as mentioned, many of the Algerians in France have become permanent residents and therefore have made greater efforts to acquire some qualifications.

Positive measures can be initiated to ensure that migrants do obtain benefits from their stay in the recipient countries. These measures are most usually set out formally in intergovernmental agreements: France has such agreements with Morocco, Mauritania, Portugal, Senegal and Yugoslavia; Greece has agreements with the Federal Republic of Germany and with other countries. The agreements stipulate the types of vocational training which the host country will make available and define the host government's contribution toward its cost. In some instances prevocational training is envisaged comprising language courses, elementary mathematics, the manipulation of simple tools and a general initiation into living conditions in the new country.[21] Most receiving countries' governments recognise the right of the migrant workers to equality of access to vocational training facilities in conformity with the provisions of the ILO Convention on Migrant Workers (Revised) 1949 (No. 97) and the Recommendation on Migrant Workers (Revised) 1949 (No. 86), though in certain instances differences may arise over the manner of implementation.

[21] For an account of the prevocational training centre at Marseilles see P. Drouet: 'La Préformation, Facteur de Développement du Tiers-Monde', *Economie et Humanisme*, Caluire, Rhône, No. 189, September 1969.

The vocational training may also take place before the migrant leaves his home country. Thus in Yugoslavia the Federal Labour Office organises language and apprenticeship courses for intending emigrants, part of the costs being defrayed by the receiving countries. Greece has a Centre for Vocational Training and Emigration which provides accelerated training for industrial workers and for domestic and hospital (female) workers. The costs which range from $370 to $1,550 per worker are met in part by the International Committee for European Migration.[22] Those courses are the most successful which are oriented to the specific situation in a particular country of destination.[23]

The kinds of training which are appropriate for migrants who intend to settle permanently in the receiving country are materially different from those required by those intending to return home in due course. For the latter the skills imparted need to be ones which can be utilised in the home country, rather than those belong to a sophisticated manufacturing process which it does not have. For example most of the Greek and Turkish workers in the Federal Republic of Germany are employed in one or other branch of heavy industry and would have little opportunity of continuing in the same activity upon their return home. Moreover, experience has shown that even when the migrant worker has acquired skills which he could use in his own country, his preference after returning is to enter some artisanal occupation or start in commerce by investing in a shop.[24] There would seem to be scope in the migrants' home countries for initiatives both by private firms and by government agencies to recruit returning migrants into the occupations for which they have acquired a skill rather than allowing their training and experience to go to waste. Some attempts of this sort are currently being made in Algeria. The potential benefits of temporary emigration will not be fully reaped unless more conscious efforts are made to render reintegration into the national labour force easy and financially attractive.

EMPLOYMENT EFFECTS OF REMITTANCES
AND REPATRIATED SAVINGS

It is difficult to form any precise idea of the volume of savings remitted by migrants to their home countries because an important proportion does not pass through official channels and does not appear in the statistics. Indeed, for Algeria it has been estimated that unofficial transfers accounted (in 1957) for half the total, and for Italy the proportion was put at about 30 per cent.[25] However, some rough estimates are available indicating the order of magnitude of these transfers at least for some countries of the Mediterranean region. In Algeria in the late nineteen-sixties these transfers

[22] OECD, *Manpower Policy and Problems in Greece*, Paris, 1965.
[23] 'La Politique de l'Immigration', *Revue Française du Travail*, No. 1, January–March 1966, pp. 323–4.
[24] 'Pour que l'Émigration de la Main-d'oeuvre Soit Rentable', *l'Usine Nouvelle*, Paris, May 1967, p. 304.
[25] ILO, *International Migrations, 1945–57*, Geneva, 1959, International Institute for Labour Studies, p. 49.

were estimated at around 1 billion dinars representing about one-third of the earnings of Algerians in France at that time and covering almost 30 per cent of Algeria's imports.[26] In Tunisia in 1971 the remittances from France were believed to reach 12·5 million dinars (Tunisian) and constituted one-quarter of Tunisia's total exports.[27] In the case of Turkey the figure jumped from $9 million in 1964 to $107 million in 1968, the latter representing 14 per cent of Turkey's imports in that year.[28] In Greece the remittances rose from $94 million in 1960 to $234 million in 1967 covering one-fifth of all imports. This evidence sufficiently emphasises the importance of remittances to those countries which enjoy a favourable geographical position in relation to the European labour market.

The most immediate consequence might be expected to be a major contribution to the investment resources of these countries, and in fact this is the view officially taken in Turkey.[29] However, in several countries this does not necessarily happen. On the contrary, it may be that the greater part of the remittances, in the case of Algeria almost the entirety, is devoted to current consumption needs. Although the initial impact of such an injection of additional purchasing power may be inflationary, the longer-run effect is to promote employment to produce the additional goods – in so far as they are goods which can be produced locally.

A distinction needs to be made between the remittances made by the worker to his family in the course of his sojourn abroad and the accumulated savings which he brings with him when he finally returns. While some part of the latter may be transferred in kind – a motor car, a television set, and so forth – a significant proportion will generally be a sum of capital most of which will be used for investment. The employment-creating effect of this investment may be weak or strong according to its character. Capital which is used to purchase land, and consequently bid up its price, contributes little or nothing; that which is used to build a larger or better house for the family does create employment if only temporarily; that which is devoted to starting a shop or a café, and this absorbs much of the transferred savings, may have a beneficial effect. The most decisive employment effect occurs when the savings are used in economic activities which create new and permanent jobs and in which the capital – labour ratio is low; unfortunately, the evidence suggests that few of the returning workers have know-how and financial resources sufficient for these types of enterprise. Recognising this situation some governments endeavour to provide incentives. A first step is to try to persuade the migrants not to leave their savings invested in the foreign country as so many of them tend to do (for Yugoslavia it was estimated that in the mid-sixties the amounts invested abroad were more than double

[26] ILO, *The Supply and Demand for Algerian Manpower, op. cit.*, pp. 136–7.

[27] Secrétariat d'Etat au Plan et aux Finances, *L'Emploi en Tunisie en 1961 et 1971*, July 1964, pp. 98–9.

[28] OECD, *Economic Studies, Turkey*, Paris, August 1969, Table 7.

[29] State Planning Organisation, *Second Five-Year Development Plan*, 1968–72, Turkey, p. 158.

the amount transferred in remittances).[30] To this end the Government of Turkey offers to buy the foreign currency of returning workers at a rate some 25 per cent above the official rate of exchange. Further, it makes loans available to them on terms more favourable than those of commercial banks which may be used for starting small-scale industrial enterprises, for home-building and other approved activities.[31] Evidently a considerable number of measures of this kind would need to be taken if the potential financial benefits of temporary emigration are to be fully exploited.

Certain general conclusions can be drawn from the evidence presented in this chapter. This first is that the opportunities for emigration, either temporary or permanent, on any considerable scale present themselves to only a minority of developing countries. Most have no outlets for disposing of part of their surplus manpower, nor are they likely to have in the foreseeable future, since the policies of the developed countries towards immigrants are tending to become more rather than less restrictive. The fortunate minority have been able to exploit either their former ties with certain metropolitan countries or their geographical propinquity to an expanding industrial labour market; but in both these cases it would appear that the flow of migrant labour may have reached its maximum. For the future one may envisage at best the maintenance of present numbers, while there could occur a sharp decline due not so much to any falling off in employment opportunities as to the social tensions experienced when the foreign element becomes large in a particular occupation or region. It would therefore be illusory to count on migration for making a greater contribution than at present to the developing countries' unemployment problem.

The second conclusion is that for lack of coherent government policies the potential benefits of the present migration are not being being fully realised. Departures on a permanent basis relieve unemployment and improve the quality of the remaining labour force only if there occurs some deliberate screening of the emigrants to ensure that the great majority are unskilled rather than skilled workers. For workers who go abroad temporarily their governments need to make arrangements which assure them access to suitable training facilities. To deal with their return, machinery is needed to facilitate their absorption into types of employment where their acquired skills can be utilised. Incentives are also required to encourage the repatriation of savings and their use in productive activities. In respect to students and other trained persons going abroad for further education, the authorities may find it justifiable to offer strong incentives to ensure their return. To the extent that such policies are pursued the net effects of either kind of migration can indeed be beneficial, especially to countries where population is still growing rapidly and where the generation of new employment is proceeding slowly.

[30] A. M. Rose, *Migrants in Europe, Problems of Acceptance and Adjustment*, Minneapolis, Univ. of Minnesota.   [31] P. Grandjeat, *op. cit.*, p. 60.

Chapter 12

Demographic Policies

Apart from the influence of permanent emigration, or immigration, the size of a country's labour force depends in the long run on the rate of growth of its population. To a lesser extent the labour force is also affected (as mentioned in Chapter 2) by changes in the age distribution of the population, and hence in the proportion which is of working age, but these changes are in turn largely the result of changes in birth and death rates.[1] Therefore the attitudes which governments adopt with respect to demographic policy can decisively affect the supply of labour, especially in the years ahead.

Recent Trends

Very striking are the differences in population growth rates as between developed and developing countries. At the time of writing the average for the developed group is a rate of just 1 per cent per annum whereas for the developing group the average is 2·7 per cent. Moreover, during the past twenty years the growth rate in the developed group has declined from 1·3 to 1·0 per cent and may even decline somewhat further. By contrast the average for the developing countries has increased during the same period from 2·4 to 2·7 per cent. For these countries it cannot yet be said with any degree of certainty whether the growth rate will increase still further or whether 2·7 per cent represents a peak from which a gradual decline may be expected to begin.

In a situation like that of the developing countries where death rates have been diminishing rapidly while birth rates have remained high, the effect is to increase the proportion of the population in the youngest age groups and, by the same token, reduce the proportion in the fifteen to sixty-five age group – i.e. those available for work. The proportion currently in this age group taking the developing countries as a whole is 40 per cent compared with 65 per cent in the developed. In one sense, the developing countries are rather fortunate in having this age group, the so-called 'active population', such a small proportion of the total at the stage in their development when the problem of employment presents such daunting difficulties. From another point of view, however, this unusual age distribution constitutes a burden inasmuch as the 40 per cent

---

[1] The size of the labour force is influenced too by the participation rate which is chiefly determined by social factors.

222

active have to support the 60 per cent inactive, a task made more arduous by the low average level of earnings.

The present situation cannot be projected into the future. As will be noted below, there are already some developing countries in which the birth rate is beginning to fall, the immediate result being to slow down the rate of growth of the youngest age group and, more slowly, to reduce the proportion of children in the total population. At the same time continuing improvements in developing countries' health services will keep more old people alive. The implications of these trends for the future evolution of the labour force and for employment policy will be examined in the last part of this chapter.

Meanwhile, attention must be directed to another aspect of demographic changes, namely their influence on incomes; and as has been repeatedly emphasised in this report the level and distribution of incomes constitutes an integral component of employment strategy. Other things being equal, a rapid rate of growth of population diminishes the growth of *per caput* income. For example, suppose that in a country a gross national product is increasing at a rate of 6 per cent per annum, which happens to be the target set by the United Nations for the Second Development Decade, then if population is expanding at say, 3·5 per cent as it is in several developing countries, *per caput* incomes will be increasing at an average of 2·5 per cent; whereas with the same rate of growth of GNP and a population growth rate of 1 per cent, the *per caput* income increase would be 5 per cent per annum. In other words a fall in the population growth rate from 3·5 per cent to 1 per cent could, without any other changes, double the rate of growth of incomes.

This theoretical picture has been drawn in terms of national averages, but the *distribution* of the national income is also affected. Because the most rapid increase in numbers is found in the lowest income groups where also unemployment tends to be concentrated, a high population growth rate redistributes *per caput* incomes to the disadvantage of the poor; in other words it exacerbates income differentials. And this occurs on a scale which is beyond the capacity of the developing countries' governments to correct.

It is argued in some quarters that other things do not remain equal and that a fast-growing population itself stimulates national product to a faster rate of growth. Particularly in those countries where natural resources are abundant in relation to the present level of population, larger numbers could, so it is said, bring about over-all development more rapidly. Where these favourable circumstances obtain, the argument may indeed have justification provided that the increasing numbers are in fact put to work either in opening up virgin lands or in other productive activities, and do not merely swell the ranks of the unemployed or underemployed. But in the many countries where such opportunities do not exist on any significant scale, the conclusion remains valid that the present rapid population growth rates augment the task of creating sufficient employment.

National Policies

Because the ration between natural resources and population and other local circumstances differ from country to country, it is natural to find a wide variety of policies being pursued in respect to population matters. A number of developing countries' governments have announced their intention to reduce the population growth rate to more moderate levels, and these include the governments of some of the most populous countries in the world, e.g. India, Indonesia, Pakistan and the People's Republic of China. This group covers about two-thirds of the population of the developing countries. There is a second group where governments adopt a neutral attitude, permitting private initiative to spread information regarding family planning but not themselves giving it specific encouragement. Finally, there are countries where family planning is discouraged or forbidden and where for religious, social or political reasons a much larger population is officially considered to be desirable.

This general pattern of policies represents an enormous evolution of attitudes over the past twenty years. The first official population control policies were formulated in the People's Republic of China in 1953, in India with the first Five-Year Plan of 1951–6, in Pakistan in 1954. At the international level the changes began to take place some ten years later. The International Labour Conference in 1964 adopted a Recommendation (No. 122) regarding employment policy which stated (paragraph 28) that countries 'should study the economic, social and demographic factors affecting population growth with a view to adopting economic and social policies that make for a better balance between the growth of employment opportunities and the growth of the labour force'. The following year (1965) the Population Commission of the United Nations went on record as favouring the provision of technical assistance on request in the field of population policy and the first expert mission was dispatched to India in response to a request by the Indian Government. In 1966 the United Nations General Assembly adopted a resolution, No. 2211 (XXI), inviting the specialised agencies of the United Nations 'to assist, when requested, in further developing and strengthening national and regional facilities for training, research, information and advisory services in the field of population.' In 1967 the United Nations Fund for Population Activities was established. In the same year the United States Agency for International Development (AID) which hitherto had merely assisted study and research programmes concerning the health of mothers and children switched its policy to permitting assistance, on request, in family planning and to financing the import of contraceptives or the equipment for their local production. Other donor countries, e.g. Sweden, had begun this policy earlier. Thus within the space of comparatively few years what amounts to a revolution has taken place in the attitude of public agencies, national and international, toward population control policies. To a considerable extent this change must be attributed to the persistent pressure of non-governmental organisations active in this subject field –

the family planning associations in numerous countries, the International Planned Parenthood Federation and other bodies.

Among the many family planning programmes in developing countries by far the most important, because of its numerical extent and the energy devoted to the campaign, is that in the People's Republic of China. When the 1953 census revealed a population of 583 million and the likelihood, if existing trends continued, of a total of 760 million by 1970 (the United Nations independent forecast was for 773 million), the Chinese Government determined to inaugurate a nationwide family planning programme which is operated through the network of health centres in towns and at factories and by the 'barefoot doctors' who tour the villages. All techniques of birth control are utilised: oral contraceptives (the most popular), IUDs, condoms (distributed free in some districts), vasectomy, sterilisation (chosen by almost 30 per cent of the staff of one Shanghai factory) and postponement of the date of marriage. Two visiting Japanese experts recently reported that 85–90 per cent of Chinese couples are practising some form of birth control.[2]

In India there are some 50,000 government family planning centres and at the end of 1969 nearly 8 million couples were estimated to be practising birth control. The Government's target is to reduce the birth rate to 25 per thousand (from over 40) and the growth rate to 1·5 per cent by 1978–9. The Indonesian Government's programme aims at 2,450 family planning clinics and 6 million acceptors by 1976. In Pakistan the Government's target is to reduce the birth rate, which was 49 per 1000 in 1965, to 33 per 1000 by 1975. Official family planning programmes are also being operated in Ceylon, Japan, Korea, Malaysia, Nepal, the Philippines, Singapore and Thailand. In the Near and Middle East the governments of Egypt, Turkey and Iran operate programmes.[3]

The African situation is different. Only six governments (Ghana, Kenya, Mauritius, Morocco, Nigeria and Tunisia) have adopted family planning programmes. In a number of countries the official view favours larger populations for reasons of national prestige and/or to achieve a more rapid exploitation of the countries' resources. In much of French-speaking Africa there are laws restricting the use of contraceptives. Elsewhere the control of population growth is inhibited by lack of health facilities and trained medical personnel.[4]

[2] *International Planned Parenthood News*, No. 218, June 1972.

[3] *Family Planning in Five Continents*, International Planned Parenthood Federation, London, July 1971: see also, G. Ohlin, *Population Control and Economic Development*, OECD, Development Centre Studies, Paris, 1967. 'La Régulation des Naissances en Inde', *Population*, November–December 1966, No. 6. also: Ministry of Health, Family Planning and Urban Development, *Progress of Family Planning Programmes in India*, New Delhi, November 1968; Pakistan Family Planning Council, *Report on the Working of Pakistan's Family Planning Programme for the month of November 1968*, Rawalpindi, January 1969; also, United Nations, *Measures, Policies and Programmes Affecting Fertility*.

[4] Concerning Tunisia see: A. Daly, 'First Experiences in Family Planning in Tunisia', *Africa*, 1966, No. 32; also J. Vallin, 'Planning Familial et Perspectives de Population en Tunisie', *Revue Tunisienne des Sciences Sociales*, No. 12, January 1968, pp. 71–88; also a series of articles in *op. cit.* No. 22, July 1970.

In Latin America family planning is presented primarily as a measure for family health and welfare rather than for population limitation. There are thirty-two private family planning associations and in twenty-eight countries the Government either operates a programme or supports private initiative, in several cases allowing the national clinics and health centres to be used by private organisations for the dissemination of advice and contraceptive materials. A number of public bodies have been set up to study and undertake research in family planning questions, e.g. in Chile, Peru and Venezuela; work is also undertaken in several universities. However, as in Africa, certain governments favour a rapid increase in population while some, for religious and social reasons, maintain their legislation prohibiting sterilisation, abortion and the sale of contraceptives.

In all regions of the developing world, and for that matter in developed countries too, attitudes towards population control policies are rapidly changing, so that a policy operative today may well be revised next year or the year after; and these revisions are virtually all in one direction, namely toward adopting the view that a reduction in the population growth rate is in the national interest in cases where it is still high, e.g. 2 per cent or more per annum. Hardly any countries are moving in the opposite direction, that is toward a tightening of restrictions on the use of contraceptives and on propaganda in favour of family planning.

Problems of Implementation

In those countries where the policy of family planning has already been accepted, one of the chief obstacles to the initiation of a nationwide programme is the expense. It has been calculated that a programme in which IUD's account for half the contraceptives used the total cost is about U.S. $1 dollar per participant. In India in the late nineteen-sixties something of the order of $380 million per annum was being spent on family planning programmes (75 cents per inhabitant) of which one-tenth was supplied by foreign aid. In Korea the programme was costing 45 cents per person;[5] in Pakistan much less – only 8 per cent of the Government's public health budget. While such expenditures, reckoned on a *per caput* basis, appear modest, they can attain very large amounts when the intention is to reach all females of child-bearing age.

Numerous attempts have been made to elaborate a cost-benefit analysis of family-planning programmes, setting off the costs in respect to the allocation and training of medical and para-medical personnel and the purchase and distribution of contraceptive devices against the economies achieved by families having to support a smaller number of children and by the State in its provision of education, health and other services. For instance, in one country the cost of each birth prevented was estimated at $5, while government expenditure on maternity services alone came to $6 for each child born. The total saving on each prevented birth was

5 Population Council, *Korea Monthly Report*, February 1969.

evaluated at \$250.[6] Other authors have arrived at rather different results because of the inevitably subjective nature of some of the computations, but all concur in concluding that whatever values are put on the individual factors the economic benefits far exceed the economic costs.

Another obstacle is the shortage of medical and para-medical staff, especially for reaching the rural areas where the great bulk of the population lives. In India in 1965 the number of suitably trained persons was 10,000 compared with a need for over 100,000. In some countries crash training programmes for para-medical personnel have been organised. In Korea, in order to interest regular medical practitioners in the programme the Government grants doctors a subsidy of \$1·50 for each IUD inserted. In some countries young doctors are required, in exchange for financial help with their studies, to spend the first two or three years after qualification serving a rural district where the shortages are most acute.

Another difficulty is to secure acceptance of the idea of family planning, especially in societies where a numerous family is still a source of pride and badge of prestige. Experience, at least in Asian countries, has been demonstrating that social attitudes are less of an obstacle than was formerly supposed. For example, the reduction achieved in infant mortality is now so great that ordinary people begin to see that it is no longer necessary to have many children in order to ensure the survival of one or two. Further, the generalisation of primary education and the enforcement of legislation forbidding child labour have the consequence that children no longer from an early age contribute to the family's income, but on the contrary have to be maintained at their parents' expense until they are adolescent. Being no more a source of profit they are no longer desired in such numbers. Where the campaign is well organised, acceptance grows rapidly.

Employment Effects

Even though a majority of developing countries have come to adopt population policies and even if most of the social obstacles to the dissemination of information regarding family planning can be overcome, it remains to ask whether the implementation of such policies has any appreciable impact on the problem of unemployment and under-employment. In examining the evidence two points of a general nature have to be borne in mind. First, a distinction must be made between the effects of these programmes on the rate of growth of population and the effects

[6] *International Conference on Family Planning Programmes*, Geneva, 1965, Univ. of Chicago Press, 1966, p. 365; see also, St Enke, 'The Economic Case for Birth Control', *Challenge*, May–June 1967; also P. Demeny in *Demography*, Vol. II, 1965, p. 222; and G. Ohlin, *op. cit.* pp. 122–7; and J. L. Simon, 'Family Planning Prospects in Less-developed Countries, and a Cost-Benefit Analysis of Various Alternatives', *The Economic Journal*, **80**, 317, March 1970, pp. 58–71.

on the size of the labour force, which is something different. Second, most of the programmes have been operating for comparatively few years which makes reliable statistical evidence hard to come by, since most developing countries only collect very limited data respecting births on an annual basis. Much more interesting indications will become available when the census data of 1980 can be compared with those of 1970, thus spanning an entire decade of these activities.

The country having the longest sustained campaign in family planning is the People's Republic of China and that country fortunately conducted a populations census in 1953 just before the campaign began and another one in 1970. The latter census revealed a total of 62 million fewer people than had been predicted and a growth rate over the seventeen years of 1·0 per cent per annum instead of the expected 1·7 per cent. Most of this reduction occurred in the latter part of the period when the family planning propaganda had begun to take effect. In one particular township of 23,000 inhabitants the birth rate is said to have fallen from 46 to 13·6 per thousand between 1963 and 1971.[7] Similarly, in certain individual districts of India where the campaign was strongly focused birth rate declines of from 3 to 2 per cent and of from 2·5 to 1·5 per cent have been recorded; but because the programme is still far from covering the whole country no significant results have yet been achieved at national level.

A few countries can, however, be cited where a significant fall in the crude birth rate (a yardstick with many imperfections) occurred during the nineteen-sixties; in Hong Kong from 36·0 to 21·8; in Puerto Rico from 32·3 to 25·1; in Singapore from 38·7 to 23·7; in the United Arab Republic from 43·1 to 38·2 (all figures are per thousand of the population and relate to the years 1960 and 1968). Some of these declines are certainly dramatic and are indicative of the swiftness of change which is possible, at least in small countries. In the larger countries where the organisational problems are formidable it is too early to draw any conclusions (except in the case of China) as to how effective a population control policy can be.

As was pointed out at the beginning of this chapter, the first effect of a decline in the growth rate brought about by a fall in the birth rate is upon the numbers of children in the youngest age groups. This already has beneficial consequences, for instance in moderating the need for ever larger educational budgets and the pressure on the available quantity of housing accommodation; but in itself it has no immediate effect on the size of the labour force. Assuming very schematically that children become 'available for work' at the age of fifteen (in practice a considerable number start work earlier), then the number of children born in, say, the year 1970 will be the number entering the labour force in the year 1985 – minus the deaths occurring in that age group in the interim. Hence any fall in the birth rate does not begin to affect the numbers in the labour force until some fifteen years later. This inevitable time-lag characterises the manner in which family planning policies influence the manpower

7 *Neue Zürcher Zeitung*, 9 October 1972.

surplus. However effective these policies may be, they cannot have any short-term impact on the numbers that are of working age. That does not mean they are irrelevant. As the man replied when asked why there should be any hurry to plant oak trees since they grow so slowly: 'it is precisely because they take so long to reach maturity that one must start them off as early as possible.'

A significant investment effect may also be noted. In a country where families are large because population is growing rapidly it is not possible for individuals to save much out of current income, but as families become smaller the volume of private savings can increase and, when translated into investment, will generate additional employment. Furthermore in the public sector, in conditions of rapid population growth a high proportion of government investment has to be devoted to education, health and other services for the young yet without being able to achieve the desired *per caput* standards, whereas at slower population growth rates not only can the standard of these services be more satisfactory but some funds can be oriented to encouragement of consumption goods industries.

There are many demographic questions which have not been touched on in these pages. There is, for example, the issue which is beginning to be debated as to what is the optimum population for a particular country, an issue which is acquiring a new dimension in the light of the present concern for environmental considerations. There is the issue of the relative political importance and strength of countries – those with larger populations having greater influence in world affairs – and therefore the danger of competitive proliferation of population analogous to the competitive proliferation of weapons. There is the longer-term issue of how many persons this planet can support at acceptable standards of living, whether this quantity has an upper limit and if so whether sooner or later the objective must be some intergovernmental agreement on zero population growth. On these matters much discussion lies ahead. The purpose here has been the narrower one of examining how demographic policies relate to the employment problem of developing countries. Even in respect to this more precise problem there are differences of opinion among social scientists and among governments. There are some who maintain that a reduction in unemployment and under-employment cannot be achieved by trying to diminish the size of the labour force and that, on the contrary, a rapidly increasing population provides the best stimulus to investment, to the exploitation of the nation's resources and to economic growth in general. Such views can be found predominant in a number of African and Latin American countries. But the majority of developing countries' governments, and of social scientists in their several disciplines, incline to the view that a more modest rate of population growth (without being able to lay down precisely how low a rate) would facilitate the process of matching the number of jobs with the numbers seeking work. They recognise that policies of population restraint have to be regarded as in the category of long-term influences; from the time they begin to take effect on the birth rate many years will elapse before the growth in the labour force begins to lessen; but the conquest of unemployment like the attainment of full economic development is a campaign which has to be fought over decades, perhaps even generations; and therefore employment strategies have to be formulated in a long- as well as in a short- and medium-term perspective.

Part Four

THE TASK AHEAD

Chapter 13

Goals and Strategies

What are called the developing countries comprise nearly 100 nation States containing within the group immense differences and contrasts in size, in population, in race, historical tradition, natural resources, pattern of society and form of government; yet one thing they have in common, they share a determination to achieve levels of human welfare compatible with the dignity of man. The task which they have set themselves is a tremendous one, nothing less than the radical transformation of the economic and social structure of their societies. Such a transformation cannot be achieved overnight, it will take time; but over the past two decades encouraging progress has been made, at least in certain respects. As noted at the beginning of this report an average annual growth rate in the 1960s of nearly 5 per cent per annum for the group as a whole compares very favourably with what today's industrial countries achieved at a similar stage in their development. Of course the peoples of the developing countries are not satisfied. An increase of 5 per cent on a *per caput* income of less than $100 does not buy much, which is why targets are being set higher – the United Nations has recommended 6 per cent for the Second Development Decade, and many countries hope to do better than that.

But the dissatisfaction refers not solely, or indeed mainly to the rate of economic growth. It stems from the accumulating evidence of the gross inequality of the distribution of the gains currently being made – a few people enjoying very high incomes facing a great mass living in extreme poverty, as can be seen from table 13.1.

Extreme poverty is generally, though not invariably, associated with unemployment, under-employment and/or types of work which yield an unacceptably low return in income. The earlier view that continuance of this poverty was a price which had to be paid for the accomplishment of economic growth is now giving place to a new approach which sees numerous possibilities of alleviating poverty without damaging the rate of increase of GNP; and the present book has examined some of these possibilities in detail.

This new approach sets alongside economic growth a group of social objectives as being entitled to equal importance in the concept of development strategy; and among these, as the Director-General of the ILO has recently said:

'employment should be an objective in its own right, in addition to that of increased national production and income, improved health and other

233

development goals. Since the attainment of higher levels of productive employment in the developing countries calls for difference paths and patterns of economic and social development from those followed hitherto, it would not be possible to attain this objective unless it were made a major separate goal of development strategy.'[1]

The significance of this approach was recognised in the ILO Employment Policy Convention and Recommendation of 1964 (No. 122) and employment goals feature prominently among the tasks included in the Strategy for the Second Development Decade. A more precise definition of these goals and of policy measures for attaining them has been spelt out in the ILO's special country reports on Colombia, Ceylon, Iran and Kenya which have been frequently referred to in previous pages.

Table 13.1 *Estimates of Income Distribution in Developing Countries (Percentage shares by income levels)*

Region	Poorest 20 per cent	Poorest 60 per cent	Richest 20 per cent	Richest 5 per cent
13 Latin American and Caribbean countries	4·3	23·5	57·1	32·8
15 African countries	5·6	22·1	62·6	34·8
8 Asian countries	5·3	28·1	53·1	25·5

N.B. Data refers to various years in the 1950s and 1960s. Regional averages are arithmetical means of countries covered.

Source: I. Adelman and C. T. Morris, 'An Anatomy of Income Distribution Patterns in Developing Nations', in U.S. Department of State Agency for International Development, *Development Digest*, Washington D.C., 9, 4, October 1971.

The employment problem in developing countries stems in one way or another from certain imbalances in the evolution of national development. There are likely to be, for instance, imbalances in rates of growth – between the growth of the labour force, the growth of the urban population, the expansion of educational facilities and the over-all growth of the economy. There is also likely to be found an imbalance between on the one hand people's aspirations and expectations for work and, on the other hand, the structure of incomes and opportunities available. Simply to provide more jobs within the existing framework of imbalances may make the problems worse, important though job-creation may be. But an attack on imbalances will in many cases imply or require the pursuit of a greater degree of

[1] ACC Functional Group on Employment Policy in the Second Development Decade, *Employment Policy in the Second Development Decade*, ILO, Geneva, 1973, paragraph 4, (Offset).

equity in the face of gross inequality in earnings, education, land holding, etc. Not that equity and economic growth should be set up and regarded as mutually incompatible objectives; the one is no substitute for the other and the area of conflict between them can be easily exaggerated. A reconciliation between the two was emphasised in the ILO Kenya employment mission report as being imperative and was summed up in the phrase: 'a strategy of redistribution from growth'. Without a larger national cake to divide, the act of redistribution would bring insignificant benefits; without some programmes for redistribution a larger national cake would hardly be worth striving for.

The analysis in the previous chapters has shown that three principal categories of unemployment and under-employment can be distinguished. First there is the low productivity and under-utilisation of the labour force in all sectors arising out of the inadequacy of the training and deployment of manpower, out of inefficiencies in the use of equipment and from lack of sufficient investment resources. Second, there is the unemployment of educated persons unable to obtain the kind of jobs which they consider their training would merit. Third, there is the low, poverty level incomes of the self-employed, whether on farms or in family industries, arising partly because their enterprises are generally over-manned and partly from lack of know-how to improve productivity.[2] An employment policy which encompasses these several aspects of the problem must of necessity be composed of a variety of programmes put into execution simultaneously.

As has been seen, such programmes have both social and economic components. They will include a better adaptation of the education and training curricula to the needs of the national labour market, the mobilisation of a larger volume of investment resources and their application to the creation of productive employment, a more efficient utilising of existing plant and equipment, and a major effort to increase the output of agriculture and of small-scale industries which together in most developing countries account for much more than half the population. In pursuing these policies job creation does not have to become an end in itself; it is rather a means to the achievement of a progressive reduction in poverty. But if the poverty is to be attached through employment promotion programmes which do not impair economic growth, such programmes have to be carefully chosen and, as has been seen in the preceding chapters, fully integrated into the national development strategies; they need to be consciously incorporated into each national plan. Since the techniques of strategy formulation are beginning to be better understood, it may be useful in this concluding chapter to give some broad indications of the procedures involved.

A convenient point of departure might be to set up a model of the evolution of the supply of and demand for manpower within the country for, say, a decade ahead. To take a hypothetical case, in a country with a population and labour force growing at 2½ per cent per annum[3] and having at present an occupational distribution of 60 per cent in agriculture, 15 per cent in industry and 25 per cent in the service sector, the economic growth rate target might be 6 per cent per annum or 3½ per cent *per caput*. Making allowance for a migration from agriculture, the non-agricultural labour force might be expected to grow at 4 per cent and the agricultural at 1·4 per cent per annum. By the end of the decade each 40 non-agricultural persons would have become 59 and each 60 farm persons 69. This would imply the creation of 9 additional jobs in agriculture for every 19 additional jobs in the other sectors, apart from any attempt to reduce the volume of unemployment. At this point and before going any further it might be desirable to pause and consider the rhythm of growth of the nation's labour force. At the end of the first decade the gain would be 28 per cent, but by the end of the second decade, assuming a continuation of the 2½ per cent growth rate, the total increase would be 64 per cent. If the view be taken that such an increase will be in the public interest and that within twenty years the required volume of additional employment can be provided, then no demographic action is needed; but if this expansion is deemed, in the circumstances of the country, too great then action would have to be taken *now* to restrict population growth if the restriction is to begin to take effect on the size of the labour force towards the end of the second decade (children born today entering the labour force fifteen years hence). Such a decision would involve initiating policies in respect to family planning and, in countries where this is an option, emigration.

Turning now to the income components of the model, and considering first the farm population, if this group which is expected to grow in numbers at 1·4 per cent is to enjoy the projected national average increase in *per caput* income of 3·5 per cent, it follows that the labour income derived from agriculture would have to increase at not less than 4·9 per cent per annum; and since in the process of agricultural modernisation the share of inputs other than labour is likely to increase it would be necessary for the value of gross agricultural output to grow at a rate in excess of 4·9 per cent, something nearer 5½ or 6 per cent. This immediately poses a dilemma. Hardly any country has been able to sustain over a period of ten years a rate of growth of agricultural output higher than 5 per cent, in fact few have got anywhere near that figure.[4] Unless therefore a sub-

---

[3] ILO projected annual rates of increase in the labour force from 1970 to 1980 in different parts of the developing world are as follows (in rounded figures):

Asia	1·9 per cent
Africa	2·2 per cent
Latin America	2·6 per cent
Caribbean	2·2 per cent

Our model is then based on a country rather near the top end of the spectrum so far as rates of increase in the labour force are concerned.

[4] In the aggregate, developing countries increased their agricultural production by an average of 2·7 per cent per annum in the 1960s. The target for the 1970s, taking account of the new possibilities opened up by the green revolution, is 4 per cent.

stantial acceleration of agricultural expansion can be accomplished, one of two things must happen: either the growth of *per caput* income in agriculture will fall below the national average or the rate of transfer of manpower out of farming must take place at a speed faster than that assumed above, in which case the model must be revised.

The policy options for modernising the agricultural sector were reviewed in Chapter 7. They comprised an intensification and diversification of production, a more egalitarian distribution of agricultural land through agrarian reform programmes and a package of other measures to expand irrigation and the supply of fertilisers, to bring credit and extension advice especially to the least advantaged farmers, to provide better roads and marketing and transport facilities. Undoubtedly some developing countries possess sufficiently favourable agricultural resources so that the energetic implementation of these programmes would in fact achieve a rapid expansion of production and a real improvement in the income position of the farm population. Others for a variety of reasons may find it unrealistic to set such ambitious expansion goals, but in that case the only remaining possibility of making a significant attack on agricultural poverty would be by accelerating the reduction in the farm labour force.

Before examining what this revision of the model might involve, it is necessary to envisage what would be happening in the non-agricultural sectors according to its original version. The first step is to determine how the projected increase of 4 per cent per annum, made up in part of natural increase and in part of exodus out of farming, might be distributed between manufacturing, construction and public works on the one hand and services, old and new, on the other. In the secondary sector (manufacturing, etc.) the recent experience of developing countries has been that a 2 per cent rate of increase in output has been associated with a 1 per cent rate of increase in employment; in other words for employment to expand by 4 per cent per annum output would have to expand by 8 per cent.[5] This is the target rate of expansion in manufacturing output in the 1970s for the developing world as a whole proclaimed in the International Development Strategy. However, since the recommendation is to stimulate the use of labour-intensive techniques in the years ahead, one might hope that this 8 per cent might yield a 5 per cent annual increase in industrial employment. Our hypothetical planners do not want the secondary and tertiary sectors both to expand their manpower at the same rate; the tertiary sector is already overmanned, there being roughly five persons in the tertiary for every three in the secondary. Supposing a target were set of an annual increase of 5 per cent in secondary sector

[5] Industrial production in the developing countries in the 1960s expanded by about 7·4 per cent a year on the average. This growth owed much to expansion in the mining sector, especially petroleum mining, in which output rose by 8·5 per cent a year. Growth in manufacturing production (not counting handicrafts and village-type industry) averaged a more modest 6·6 per cent a year. Manufacturing employment increased by a mere 3·5 per cent and its growth decelerated during the decade: in the second half it was barely equal to the rate at which the total labour force was expanding.

employment during the decade, this would imply an annual increase of over 3 per cent in tertiary occupations.

Such a rate of expansion must be reckoned quite ambitious, and yet it still fails to take three other desiderata into account. The first of these is the need to be prepared to absorb an agricultural exodus larger than that assumed in the model, partly because there might well be a shortfall on the agricultural output targets and partly because of the desirability anyway of making a start on reducing the gap in living standards between the farm population and the rest. The second reason for doubting the adequacy of the industrial output target is that it includes no plan for reducing the existing volume of unemployment; it provides merely for absorbing the natural increase in the labour force. To make an inroad on unemployment would require doing still better. Third, to rely on the service sector to absorb as many as 3 per cent more workers annually is to rely on a sector that already contains a great deal of low-productivity precarious 'pseudo-employment'.

This over-simplified arithmetical model of the basic elements of employment strategy represents, of course, only a beginning in the formulation of appropriate policies, but it is an essential first stage because it will reveal in each country what are the parameters of the national problem, what is possible and what is wishing thinking. Even at this stage in the exercise various internal contradictions will become manifest, obliging the planners to go back and adjust their model to achieve greater consistency and viability. Furthermore, remembering how such planning exercises consist in attempting to integrate the plans produced by sectors and by sub-sectors, there will probably have to occur a series of references back to these sectoral units until, by successive approximations, a reasonable national framework can be established.

It is at this point, when the orders of magnitude have become clear, that the formulation of implementation policies begins. And it is here where the utilisation of fairly sophisticated methods of programming may obviate certain breakdowns, at least by utilising some simple equivalent of critical path analysis, since it is usually the occurrence of unforeseen bottlenecks and constraints, which prejudices plan fulfilment. Some of these have already been discussed in the preceding chapters, but they deserve re-emphasis here in order to illustrate some of the aspects of policy formulation which have to be taken care of if employment promotion is to succeed.

A rate of growth of food production which was quite adequate so long as industrialisation proceeded slowly and most of the population remained living on farms or at least in the rural areas may become seriously insufficient if the movement away to the towns is accelerated; the reason being that such a transfer demands a rapid increase in the *proportion* of the food output which is marketed and this may be a change which the farmers are either psychologically unwilling to make or physically unable to accomplish for lack of transport or other facilities. Some countries have experienced food shortages in their cities even while production on the farms was increasing steadily. Programmes, including the requisite incentives, have to be framed to ensure that the food supplies are available where they are wanted. Such provision should be easier in future inasmuch as some countries have begun to reap the benefits of the Green Revolution while many can avail themselves of food aid.

A second constraint relates to the technical competence of the manpower available for employment. A planning model considers the growth of the labour force and its distribution between sectors in purely quantitative terms, whereas in practice the demand for labour, far from being general and undifferentiated, is composed of rather precise requirements for certain occupational skills – architects, surveyors, carpenters, electricians, motor mechanics, foremen, etc. – together with a complement of semi-skilled and unskilled workers. However, in most countries the existing training facilities are not only inadequate but have developed in haphazard fashion with the result that too many may be being prepared for one occupation and not enough for another. Training is an expensive process and this sort of waste is something which poor countries can ill afford. Yet little has been done to develop projections of manpower requirements by occupation and to match the training programmes to these requirements, though some governments are moving in this direction. Admittedly the forward programming of labour demand in qualitative terms is one of the more difficult aspects of planning even in advanced countries, but in their case it is unlikely that deficiency in some particular skill will occasion a serious bottleneck; in the developing countries by contrast very real dislocation of economic and social progress may occur unless the major shortages are foreseen and provided for in advance.

This leads to a related problem, namely the geographic distribution of the new employment being generated. Present trends, unless deliberately re-oriented, are bringing about an ever-increasing concentration of economic activity in the developing countries' major cities. Apart altogether from environmental considerations and the other aspects of social amenity, such massive concentrations of population prove extremely costly in respect to the provision of housing, water supplies, drainage, and other public services. It is therefore important to incorporate a spatial element in employment promotion which envisages creating jobs as far as possible in the districts where the people currently live.[6] This means deliberate allocation of public works programmes to rural areas and the devising of incentives to entrepreneurs to establish new plants in the small towns designated as growth centres; in other words, employment policies should be integrated into regional development policies. Such an orientation can be expected to achieve on average a much lower capital–output ration than would result from allowing the present centripetal tendencies to continue unchecked.

Another option which may have much to do with the success or failure of employment programmes is the choice of an appropriate technology.

[6] ILO, *op. cit.*, p. 12.

From the considerable discussion in Chapter 3 of the merits of more labour-intensive and of more capital-intensive technologies it emerged that where a choice exists it has to be made in the light of the particular industrial process and of the particular circumstances in which the plant in question will have to operate. If powerful arguments can be advanced for choosing a labour-intensive process, wherever the real costs of the operation permit, because this suits the employment-creation needs of the present, nevertheless the process or equipment chosen should be capable as far as possible of adaptation to less labour-intensive operating methods at a later stage of national development when supplies of capital become more adequate. To play its part in employment promotion technology has to be both appropriate and progressive – appropriate in the sense that it results in a fuller use of idle and under-employed manpower and raises the average productivity of the labour force, progressive in the sense that it evolves and becomes more sophisticated *pari passu* with the increasing sophistication and complexity of each nation's social and economic development.[7] In the farm sector, where most of the population will remain until many more non-agricultural job opportunities have been created, it is the spread of new technologies and of the facilities which will enable farmers to adopt them which will be the chief weapon in the attack on rural poverty.

This leads to a reminder of the influence which income distribution can have on the level of employment. Not only do the rich in developing countries devote a greater proportion of their expenditure to imported products than do the poor but also the labour content of the commodities which the rich purchase is generally lower. The Colombia employment report found that 'The basic goods which are widely purchased by those on low incomes – essentially food and rather simple manufactures like clothing and footwear – are precisely the goods which are (or can be) produced with techniques considerably more labour-intensive than those used in the production of the goods demanded by the rich. To produce the latter usually requires high capital-intensity'. Not only this, but doubts are now widely expressed regarding the old theory that inequality of incomes had a beneficial effect on the volume of savings and therefore, via investment, on the volume of employment. Some studies have shown a high propensity to save on the part of many self-employed persons and the tendency of some high-income groups to prefer conspicuous consumption to saving. But the complex interaction between income distribution and employment is a topic which deserves more detailed emprical study.

The income distribution issue arises not merely between the 'rich' and the 'poor' but also between different categories of workers where it raises extremely complex issues and is difficult to discuss briefly without giving occasion for misunderstandings. This question of wage levels and wages policy directly influences the amount of employment that can be offered. In a developing country in an early stage of economic development it is

[7] ILO, *Human Resources for Industrial Development, op. cit.,* Chapter 7, pp. 201–17.

typical to find several quite distinct labour markets existing side by side, so that the same work, for instance earth-moving by hand, may be paid at one rate in the village, another rate by the Public Works Department in the towns and yet another rate by the expatriate mining company. As the situation develops, trade unions come into existence, usually first among the best-paid workers who are likely to be the most articulate, but later spreading to other worker groups particularly those in the big cities. Quite naturally these unions have the objective of securing for their members the best possible wages and other conditions of work. At the same time, however, they already tend to be among the best paid workers in the country so that the more their leaders succeed in obtaining improvements the greater becomes the gap in living standards between them and the non-unionised labour, not to mention the urban unemployed and the rural workers in general. Nor is this the only difficulty. Local circumstances are such that in many instances the unions are able to secure wage increases unmatched by parallel increases in labour productivity, thus augmenting labour costs per unit of output. Where this occurs the employers are strongly stimulated to turn to labour-saving equipment and so-called capital-intensive techniques, which may be in direct opposition to the Government's policy of promoting labour-intensive technologies. There have been a number of cases, particularly in some of the newly independent developing countries, where a comparatively small section of the labour force has won massive improvements in living standards, while the remainder of the population continues to struggle near the margin of subsistence. Because the emergence of these inequalities can gravely impede the attack on unemployment and under-employment, it must be part of governments' policies to examine these issues with a view to deciding how far a policy of permitting a concentration of economic advantages should be modified in the direction of securing a wider spread of the benefits of development. This brings us back to the choice of how far the people should be strung out in their march towards affluence and how far some official interventions are desirable in order that the advance shall be accomplished in a somewhat more egalitarian manner. Thus wages policy is seen as a central component of the strategy of reducing poverty by the creation of employment, but if wage restraint is called for, so is restraint on the growth of other incomes.

As a tripartite ILO meeting of experts reported some years ago:

'If such industries are allowed to make larger profits than are necessary to induce them to operate in the country concerned, and especially if they take these profits out of the country, the trade unions will naturally try to secure for their members a bigger share in the profits of such industries by pressing for the highest wages they can get.

While unions may sometimes virtually be forced to adopt such an approach because of the indifference of governments and of certain wealthy companies to considerations of national welfare, this is not true in all countries. There are wealthy undertakings with a sense of responsibility

241

towards the countries in which they operate and governments which, without driving away foreign capital or enterprise, prevent excessive profits. When the wealth produced by large modern undertakings is widely shared there is less incentive and less justification for unions to try to obtain a specially privileged position for the workers employed by these undertakings.'[8]

Another delicate policy issue which has both direct and indirect bearing on employment promotion is that of population. In countries where a population planning policy has been adopted it has been noted that, because the first result of a successful campaign is a decline in the birth rate and in the numbers of children in the youngest age groups, this already has the beneficial effect of moderating the need for ever larger educational budgets for primary schooling and likewise the pressure on the available quantity of housing. Also, as the size of families begins to decline the scope for personal savings increases. More important can be the long-term effects. It was, for instance, shown in the Ceylon Employment Report that if a family planning campaign had been implemented at the same time as the malaria eradication campaign in the 1940s and had reached the present target birth rate of 25 per thousand in 1955, existing and past output trends would have been sufficient to reach full employment by the 1980s, i.e. just a generation after the family planning programme had come to full effect. Thus, both in the shorter and in the longer run a population policy can aid or hinder the implementation of an employment policy.

Because shortage of investment capital acts as a perennial constraint on the creation of more employment, much will depend upon the vigour with which investment resources can be mobilised, either by private sector incentives, or through forced savings achieved by fiscal and monetary policy, or through the appropriation of public funds. In this context will often arise the question of the role of foreign firms and whether or not their participation in the nation's development should be encouraged, a question which sometimes has to be dealt with less on its economic than on its political merits. There is also the question of the role of the State in operating enterprises: considering the matter exclusively from the employment angle it may be easier to insist on the use of labour-intensive technologies in publicly operated businesses than in those belonging to private enterprises, on the other hand experience suggests that the application of a wages policy is no easier in the former than in the latter. Behind all these considerations is the constraint imposed by the necessity of maintaining law and order; there can be cases where the introduction of, for example, certain fiscal measures required for employment-generating programmes, though in themselves eminently desirable, would arouse too much opposition in the existing climate of opinion and might even threaten

[8] Report of a meeting of Experts on Minimum Wage-Fixing and Related Problems, paragraphs 54 and 55, published in ILO *Minimum Wage-Fixing and Economic Development*, Geneva, 1968, pp. 156-7.

the security of the State. In such circumstances patience may be required while a clearer understanding is sought of what policies may be in the national interest.

Finally an expansion of Developing countries' exports can make an important contribution to their employment programmes. National authorities can provide a range of incentives including fiscal benefits to encourage production for export; they can also set up or strengthen marketing services both at home and in the countries where the goods may be sold. But a major part of the initiative has to come from the developed countries through policy changes designed to offer greater market access and to improve the competitive capacity of the developing exporters in world markets. In the difficult negotiations concerning the improvement of trade flows between developed countries the problems of improving trade flows from developing to developed countries are sometimes in danger of being given insufficient attention.

If considerable space in this concluding chapter has been allotted to the bottlenecks and constraints which hinder the adoption of employment creation programmes and to suggesting some of the ways in which these can be dealt with, it is because this book has been deliberately oriented towards a discussion of the practical aspects of employment policy rather than to matters of economic theory and broader philosophical considerations. Most people are today agreed that the creation of employment should figure as one of the central objectives of the Governments and peoples of developing countries. Once such a goal has been defined it is comparatively easy to each national case to formulate a model of the economic and other variables which have to be manipulated in order to prevent the emergence of dangerous imbalances. The model indicates the order of magnitude of the tasks to be performed, but it has to be translated into policies and implemented in programmes. Many of the causal relationships are still unclear, some of them economic others social in character. For many years ahead there will exist a continuing need for policy-oriented research and for advisory activities relating to the employment problem in its broadest sense. But while more facts, more information more analyses are needed, action programmes must also go forward. Indeed, the Governments of the developing countries already possess substantial room for manoeuvre in the choice of policies. A wide variety of weapons is available for use in the attack on poverty and the extremer forms of income inequality, weapons which do not demand the sacrifice of benefits already achieved. Neither need they prejudice any nation's economic progress, provided they be prudently selected. But one thing clearly emerges from this analysis of possible employment promotion programmes, namely that no one of them can accomplish very much if operated in isolation. They are programmes which support and complement one another, which are oriented to the needs of different segments of the population, which in concert should be able to maintain a balance between, for instance, rural and urban areas as well as between the pro-

243

vision of consumer goods and the construction of a modern infrastructure. They need to be conceived as a 'package' and, still more than that, as a package consciously integrated into the nations' overall development plans. If many governments were vigorously to pursue such employment policies, as a few have indeed begun to do, then the end of the Second Development Decade could witness some massive improvements in the welfare of the least advantaged people of the developing countries.

Author Index

Country Index

Subject Index